FOR Dummies

BESTSELLING
BOOK SERIES

NASCAR For Dummies®
2nd Edition

W9-BDH-690

What the Flags Mean

During every NASCAR race, a NASCAR official (called the flagman) sits above the start/finish line, waving different colored flags at the competitors as they zoom by in their race cars. He's signaling them to slow down, speed up, move over, get off the track, stop, or, best of all, that they've won. These are the various flags used:

- **Green flag:** The flagman waves this flag to start a race or to restart a race. Green means go, so when a driver sees this flag, he slams on the gas pedal and takes off.

- **Yellow flag:** A yellow flag means NASCAR officials have called a caution period because an accident or debris on the track makes driving conditions dangerous. When drivers see a yellow flag, they know they must slow down and drive cautiously around the track.

- **Red flag:** Drivers must stop on the track — wherever they are — when they see the flagman wave a red flag. It means it isn't safe for drivers to circle the track because of inclement weather or poor track conditions.

- **Black flag:** When the flagman waves a black flag at a driver, that driver must get off the track and go to the pits immediately. He did something wrong or his car isn't fit to be on the track.

- **Blue with diagonal yellow stripe:** This flag signifies to a driver that a faster, lead-lap car is about to pass him and he must yield to that car.

- **Green-white-checkered flag sequence**: If there is a caution during the final laps, this flag sequence announces that there will be a green-flag restart of a couple laps. A green flag signals the first lap of the restart, and the white flag signals the final lap that leads to the checkered flag. It was added in 2004 to help ensure a race doesn't end under caution.

- **White flag:** This flag means that the race leader has one lap to go in the race.

- **Checkered flag:** When the checkered flag waves, a driver has crossed the finish line.

The Main Series

The three main NASCAR series are as follows:

- **NASCAR NEXTEL Cup Series:** The NASCAR NEXTEL Cup Series is where you can find NASCAR's superstars, including Jeff Gordon, Jimmie Johnson, and Dale Earnhardt Jr. NASCAR NEXTEL Cup Series cars weigh 3,400 pounds, and their engines produce about 750 horsepower, meaning the cars can reach speeds approaching 200 mph at some tracks.

- **NASCAR Busch Series:** Many drivers from the NASCAR Busch Series move to the NASCAR NEXTEL Cup Series as they hone their driving skills. Some drivers, such as Ron Hornaday Jr. stay in this series because they prefer the competition. NASCAR Busch Series cars weigh 3,300 pounds and their engines produce about 550 horsepower, making the cars slightly slower than their NASCAR NEXTEL Cup Series counterparts.

- **NASCAR Craftsman Truck Series:** The Craftsman Truck Series is NASCAR's newest, inaugurated in 1995. It features souped-up pickup trucks with engines that produce about 710 horsepower. Trucks are capable of going about 190 mph on certain tracks. This series is similar to the NASCAR Busch Series, with many drivers hoping to advance to NASCAR NEXTEL Cup competition and others who are happy earning a living driving race trucks.

A Few NASCAR Records

Diehard NASCAR fans know their stats — here are a few to get you started:

- NASCAR's winningest drivers:
  - Richard Petty — 200
  - David Pearson — 105
  - Bobby Allison — 84
  - Darrell Waltrip — 84
  - Cale Yarborough — 83
- NASCAR's top pole winners:
  - Richard Petty — 126
  - David Pearson — 112
  - Cale Yarborough — 70
  - Darrell Waltrip — 59
  - Bobby Allison — 58
- Multiple NASCAR Cup Series Champions:
  - Richard Petty and Dale Earnhardt — 7
  - Jeff Gordon — 4
  - David Pearson, Lee Petty, Darrell Waltrip, and Cale Yarborough — 3
  - Buck Baker, Tim Flock, Ned Jarrett, Terry Labonte, Herb Thomas, and Joe Weatherly — 2
- Fastest lap of all time: Bill Elliott — 212.809 mph (pre-restrictor plate qualifying in 1987 at Talladega Superspeedway in Alabama)
- Driver to top 200 mph more than anyone else: Cale Yarborough — 15
- Most career race starts: Richard Petty — 1,177 (1958–1992)
- Most career second-place finishes: Richard Petty — 158
- Most consecutive top-five finishes: David Pearson — 18 (1968)
- Most years leading the circuit in wins: Richard Petty — 7
- Most consecutive years leading the circuit in wins: Jeff Gordon — 5 (1995–1999)
- Most money won in a season: Jeff Gordon $10,879,757 (2000)
- Most consecutive races started: Terry Labonte — 781 (1979–2003)
- Most wins during a season in the modern era (1972 to present): Richard Petty and Jeff Gordon — 13
- Most consecutive wins in the modern era: Cale Yarborough (1976); Darrell Waltrip (1981); Dale Earnhardt (1987); Harry Gant (1991); Bill Elliott (1992); Mark Martin (1993); Jeff Gordon (1998) — 4

Copyright © 2005 Wiley Publishing, Inc.
All rights reserved.
Item 7681-X.
For more information about Wiley Publishing, call 1-800-762-2974.

NASCAR® FOR DUMMIES® 2ND EDITION

by Mark Martin with Beth Tuschak

NASCAR NEXTEL Cup Series driver

WILEY

Wiley Publishing, Inc.

NASCAR® For Dummies®, 2nd Edition

Published by
Wiley Publishing, Inc.
111 River St.
Hoboken, NJ 07030-5774
www.wiley.com

Copyright © 2005 by Wiley Publishing, Inc., Indianapolis, Indiana

Published by Wiley Publishing, Inc., Indianapolis, Indiana

Published simultaneously in Canada

For general information on our other products and services, please contact our Customer Care Department within the U.S. at 800-762-2974, outside the U.S. at 317-572-3993, or fax 317-572-4002.

For technical support, please visit www.wiley.com/techsupport.

Wiley also publishes its books in a variety of electronic formats. Some content that appears in print may not be available in electronic books.

Library of Congress Control Number: 2004116497

ISBN: 0-7645-7681-X

Manufactured in the United States of America

10 9 8 7 6 5 4 3 2

2O/RS/QR/QV/IN

WILEY

About the Author

Mark Martin has been racing all his life . . . well, practically. Mark began his professional racing career in the 1970s in the American Speed Association, where he was a four-time ASA champion. He successfully made the transition into the NASCAR scene in 1981 and has been racking up series points ever since. Since 1988, he has won 33 races, fourth among active NASCAR NEXTEL Cup drivers. He is considered by many to be the greatest active NASCAR NEXTEL Cup Series driver without a championship. Martin's second-place finish in 2002 marked the fourth time he has finished second in the final NASCAR Cup Series point standings. Mark has finished in the top eight in 13 of the last 15 seasons. Mark also has a record four International Race of Champions (IROC) titles to his credit and is the winningest driver in the NASCAR Busch Series, with 45 wins. In 2004, he started his 600th career Cup race in Phoenix, the seventh longest streak in NASCAR history. Off the track, Martin owns Mark Martin Performance, a company that sells quarter-midget racing chassis like the one his son, Matt, races in. He also helped build a quarter-midget track in New Smyrna, Florida.

He lives in Florida with his wife, Arlene, and son, Matt.

Beth Tuschak is a freelance writer associated with NASCAR and has been invaluable in updating this second edition of *NASCAR For Dummies*. A syndicated columnist for NASCARMEDIA.com, she also writes freelance stories from her home in Concord, North Carolina.

About NASCAR

The National Association for Stock Car Auto Racing (NASCAR), organized in 1947 by Bill France, Sr., is America's premier motorsports and entertainment sanctioning body. NASCAR is guided by the third generation of the France family. Brian Z. France took the helm as Chairman of the Board and CEO in October 2003. Mr. France's father, Bill France, Jr., led NASCAR during a period of astounding growth since January 1972. NASCAR's best-known and most popular series is the NASCAR NEXTEL Cup Series. NEXTEL became the series' primary sponsor in 2004. Other top national series include the NASCAR Busch Series and the NASCAR Craftsman Truck Series. These marquee divisions are well-known to the millions of fans who attend these events and to the millions more who watch events on television. NASCAR also sanctions nine other regional touring series, as well as the NASCAR Weekly Racing Series.

New to 2004, the NASCAR NEXTEL Cup season features the Chase for the NASCAR NEXTEL Cup. In this new format, the top 10 drivers in points after the 26th race are assigned new point standings and compete for the championship in the last ten races of the season.

NASCAR has become a recognized leader in the entertainment industry, with NASCAR Online (www.nascar.com), NASCAR Café restaurants, NASCAR Speed Parks, and NASCAR Silicon Motor Speedway.

Publisher's Acknowledgments

We're proud of this book; please send us your comments through our Dummies online registration form located at www.dummies.com/register/.

Some of the people who helped bring this book to market include the following:

Acquisitions, Editorial, and Media Development

Project Editor: Laura B. Peterson

Acquisitions Editor: Kathy Cox

General Reviewer: Bob Zeller

Editorial Manager: Carmen Krikorian

Editorial Assistant: Courtney Allen, Nadine Bell

NASCAR Publishing: Jennifer White, Sr. Manager of Publishing; Herb Branham, Communications Manager; Catherine McNeill, Publishing Coordinator; Buz McKim, Coordinator of Communications

Photos: Cover, insert, and chapter photos: © 2004 NASCAR Photography/Sherryl Creekmore; Selected graphics provided by NASCAR®.

Cartoons: Rich Tennant, www.the5thwave.com

Composition

Project Coordinator: Adrienne Martinez

Layout and Graphics: Carl Byers, Andrea Dahl, Joyce Haughey, Barry Offringa, Lynsey Osborn, Heather Ryan, Brent Savage, Rashell Smith

Proofreaders: Leeann Harney, Joe Niesen, Carl Pierce, Dwight Ramsey, TECHBOOKS Production Services

Indexer: TECHBOOKS Production Services

Special Help: Clint Lahnen

Publishing and Editorial for Consumer Dummies

Diane Graves Steele, Vice President and Publisher, Consumer Dummies

Joyce Pepple, Acquisitions Director, Consumer Dummies

Kristin A. Cocks, Product Development Director, Consumer Dummies

Michael Spring, Vice President and Publisher, Travel

Brice Gosnell, Associate Publisher, Travel

Kelly Regan, Editorial Director, Travel

Publishing for Technology Dummies

Andy Cummings, Vice President and Publisher, Dummies Technology/General User

Composition Services

Gerry Fahey, Vice President of Production Services

Debbie Stailey, Director of Composition Services

Contents at a Glance

Table of Contents

Introduction

M ost of the time, people group NASCAR racing into one of two categories. It's a sport that's too simple because the cars just go around in circles. Or it's a sport that's too technical because it's centered on engines, aerodynamics, and the physics of going fast. This book, however, shows you that NASCAR racing is really both of these things: It's simple in some ways but complicated in others. That's what makes it so fun.

At first the simplicity draws you in. You find that out when you go to a race — even if you close your eyes. When you sit in the grandstands, you can hear the cars roar by. You can feel the tremendous power of the engines when the stands shake, your seat vibrates, and your guts rumble. Then you can smell the distinct odor of burned rubber that hovers above the racetrack. NASCAR racing is a total body experience; you don't even have to see the cars — much less understand the inner workings of race cars — to get a thrill from racing.

If that's true, though, why read this book? Even though sitting in the stands with your eyes closed is entertaining, sitting there with an insider's view of the sport, including the technical side, enriches your experience so much more. You know what's going on when NASCAR officials give a driver a 15-second penalty. You won't be lost when the cars line up single file for a restart — and you'll know what a restart is! And a day later, you'll be able to hang out at the water cooler and talk to your co-workers with authority about the race. My job is to share with you all that a fan needs to know about NASCAR racing. That way, you can enjoy the sport as much as I do.

About This Book

I learned how to drive when I was just five years old, even before I could reach the pedals of a car. My dad propped me up in his lap, gave me the wheel, and then smashed his foot on the gas. From then on, I was hooked. I started to drive a race car at 15, even before I had a driver's license, and I woke up thinking about racing and went to sleep dreaming about racing. And in my spare time, I worked on and raced cars. It's no wonder the sport is such a big part of my life.

Sometimes, though, it's difficult to explain why NASCAR racing is so addictive, particularly to people who've never driven a race car and competed bumper-to-bumper at breakneck speeds. It's not like basketball, baseball, football, or other sports you play during recess in grade school.

I decided that the best way to explain my love for NASCAR racing wasn't by sticking fans in a race car and making them drive laps around Daytona International Speedway. It was by writing this book. If you can't discover the beauty of this sport by doing — and riding down the highway going 80 mph in your Honda Accord doesn't count — you may as well discover it by reading.

If you're a novice to NASCAR, I help you with the basics of the sport — the differences between the NASCAR NEXTEL Cup Series and the NASCAR Busch Series — so you can build upon your NASCAR knowledge from there. If you're more advanced, I share the subtleties of the sport so that you can sound like an old pro. No matter what level of NASCAR knowledge you have, you can find something new in the pages of this book — I believe it's the most comprehensive book available: I talk about NASCAR's origin, sponsors, engines, race teams, race strategies, pit stops, racetracks, and all you need to know if you want to be the quintessential NASCAR fan — and that's just the beginning. My goal is for you to understand everything you see when you watch a race and be able to converse and debate intelligently with the most ardent, well-informed NASCAR fans.

I hope that, in reading this book, you'll understand why NASCAR racing is my passion. Maybe it'll become your passion, too.

Foolish Assumptions

Even though this is a *For Dummies* book, I don't assume that you're a fool. You're just trying to find out more about NASCAR racing so that you can enjoy the sport, as millions of people already do. Maybe you're a sports fan who's curious about racing. Maybe you're an avid race fan who wants to brush up on a few things. Maybe you're my mom who wants to read my book to boost my ego.

Maybe you just want the answers to some of these questions:

- ✔ Why does some guy stand above the track and wave all those flags? Is he telling the drivers something or part of an off-beat rhythmic gymnastics team?
- ✔ What is a restrictor-plate track and what's being restricted?
- ✔ Does it really matter where a driver qualifies for a race?

✔ Why do drivers have short tempers at short tracks?

✔ Are drivers athletes?

✔ Why are tires such a big deal during a race?

✔ Why doesn't a regular Chevrolet Monte Carlo at a local dealership look like the one Jeff Gordon drives?

✔ Who are the sponsors and why do race teams need them?

In this book, I answer these questions and more.

How This Book Is Organized

This book isn't just a few hundred pages of statistics and scintillating commentary. It's broken into six parts to be user-friendly. Each part deals with a major aspect of NASCAR racing and the parts are organized so you can find out more about the sport in a simple, painless manner. Each chapter within the part dissects a specific detail of the sport — such as qualifying, the racetracks, or different NASCAR series. Feel free to skip to the parts and chapters that interest you most.

Part 1: NASCAR 101

If you've never seen NASCAR racing or only glanced at a race once or twice while flipping through the channels on your TV, you're probably wondering what all the hubbub is about. Why is NASCAR racing the nation's fastest growing sport? What is the allure? Why do I see the drivers on different cereal boxes or soda bottles every time I go to the supermarket? Is there a NASCAR invasion no one told me about? In this part, I reveal the mystery behind the boom of NASCAR racing.

Part II: What Makes It Stock-Car Racing?

I drive a Ford Taurus and make it go nearly 200 mph at some racetracks. I'm sure a few NASCAR fans wonder why their Taurus can't do the same thing. In this part, I tell you not only why your Taurus can't go that fast — besides the fact that the speed limits don't allow it — but also why yours has four doors while my Taurus doesn't have any. This is perhaps the most technical part of the book, detailing the race cars, the race teams, and many of the rules. It gets down to the nitty-gritty, which can help even the most avid NASCAR fan feel just a little more like a pro when tuning into a race or going to the racetrack.

Part III: What Happens on (and off) the Track

Sometimes NASCAR drivers do strange things. They come in for pit stops and opt for just a splash-and-go. They draft behind other drivers on super-speedways with carburetor restrictor plates in their engines. They wear funny shoes. In this part, I decipher and explain racing itself, staying safe, and winning an event. No longer will you be perplexed when a driver talks about racing for championship points or doing the hat dance. The chapters in this part help you follow every word of racing jargon — and there's plenty of that to go around. NASCAR racing is its own world, and in this part, I invite you in and teach you about the native customs.

Part IV: Keeping Up with NASCAR Events

There's nothing worse than showing up at a NASCAR race in a hoop skirt and a bonnet. In this part, I tell you how to fit in at the racetrack by dressing like a NASCAR fan, talking like a NASCAR fan, watching a race like a NASCAR fan, and following NASCAR like a NASCAR fan.

Part V: The Part of Tens

If you don't have time to get drawn in by an entire chapter, the Part of Tens is perfect for you. In this part, you can find little morsels of information, packaged into neat, manageable (and short) chapters about NASCAR's all-time greatest drivers, the best NASCAR races, and future NASCAR stars. The lists aren't definitive so you can debate about it with your friends, but I picked my favorites.

Part VI: Appendixes

In NASCAR racing, people talk in NASCAR language — which isn't at all similar to the conversational French or obsolete Latin you studied in high school. It's a unique language used in racing circles and you can find a big chunk of it in Appendix A. They're all the racing terms you'll need to know.

The other appendixes list NASCAR statistics and key NASCAR milestones. It's trivia you should know if you're planning to be a contestant on *Jeopardy!* sometime soon.

Icons Used in This Book

To make things easier, I use icons — little pictures in the margins — to high-light important information: giving you advice, a warning, or knowledge in order to impress friends at dinner parties.

This icon points out information that helps you save time, money, and effort.

If you know these words, you won't seem like an accountant among a group of rock stars when you're in a conversation with die-hard NASCAR fans.

Take heed when you see this caution flag. Its goal is to save you from losing money, getting hurt, or exposing yourself to other dangers.

When you see one of these icons, you'll know you're about to read a story from my years of NASCAR racing experience.

This information is for the real geeky fans who want to know all the details, no matter how complex. Non-geeks can skip these icons.

Where to Go from Here

You know when you're reading a great book and you're dying to get to the last chapter because you can't stand the suspense? Well, in this book you can. It won't ruin the story for you — because there is no story. There isn't a beginning, middle, or end, so just flip to the last chapter and read it first if you want. Go ahead. Your high school English teacher isn't looking. Actually, you can turn to any chapter and read it. There's nothing to be ashamed of because that's the way I've designed the book. Every chapter is written to stand alone and provide information about NASCAR's nuances. The Table of Contents and the Index list what's in this potpourri of NASCAR racing, so choose where you want to begin your journey — then have fun!

Part I
NASCAR 101

The 5th Wave   By Rich Tennant

"As a valued sponsor, sure, you can ride along during Happy Hour, but you'll have to leave your drink at the bar."

In this part . . .

NASCAR racing is everywhere nowadays: Races are on TV, racetracks are in nearly every part of the country, and drivers have their pictures on cereal boxes and billboards. If you're new to NASCAR, you may be perplexed by this invasion, so in this part I reveal the mysteries of NASCAR racing and tell you why so many fans are flocking to the sport. I also answer all your questions about corporate involvement in the sport and why at times it seems as if NASCAR is one big, uninterrupted commercial for motor oil, beer, and laundry detergent.

I also describe each NASCAR series so that you can tell the difference between the NASCAR NEXTEL Cup Series, the NASCAR Busch Series, and the NASCAR Craftsman Truck Series. You also find out that the NASCAR Featherlite Modified Series isn't racing's version of a boxing division.

If your dream is to be more than just a fan of the sport, I can help you out in that department, too. This part gives you a few hints on how to become a race car driver or get a job on a NASCAR crew.

Chapter 1

NASCAR Racing:
The Best Sport Around

- -

- -

Most people don't know what it's like to dunk a basketball or hit a 100-mph fastball 500 feet for a home run, but almost everyone knows how to drive a car — and that familiarity is the appeal of NASCAR and stock-car racing. Whether they admit it or not, lots of people speed down the highway and daydream about winning the Daytona 500. That daydreamer could be a 17-year-old high school student who just got a driver's license, a 35-year-old orthodontist, or a 70-year-old retired teacher. Driving is nearly universal.

NASCAR's allure has grown in recent years because of its tremendous television exposure; the drivers' accessibility to their fans; and close, competitive racing. In 2003, nearly 7 million fans went to see the NASCAR Cup Series races, which is quadruple the attendance in 1980. And more than 280 million viewers tuned into NASCAR Cup Series events on television in 2003, making NASCAR one of the most popular sports to watch on TV, second only to the NFL.

Here are a few more stats that show how NASCAR has grown from an originally Southern-based sport to a truly national phenomenon:

- ✔ #1 sport in brand loyalty of fans
- ✔ #2 rated sport on television
- ✔ Over $2 billion in licensed sales
- ✔ 75 million fans

MARK SAYS

The first NASCAR race

In February 1948, two months after NASCAR was founded, more than 14,000 people showed up at a race course just south of Daytona Beach. The 150-mile event was held on a unique track that was half on the beach and half on the highway behind the sand, making it interesting for drivers and spectators alike, particularly when the tide came in and the beach narrowed. Red Byron, a driver from Anniston, Alabama, whose left leg was injured when his bomber was shot down in World War II, won that first NASCAR-sanctioned race, enhancing his reputation as one of NASCAR's greatest early drivers. It also made him the answer to a common NASCAR trivia question: "Who won the first NASCAR race?"

Red Byron also won NASCAR's first Strictly Stock championship. This series — the forerunner of today's NASCAR NEXTEL Cup Series,

debuted in 1949 and was limited to full-sized American production, or "stock" cars. The first Strictly Stock race was held in June 1949, and anyone with a car was eligible to race. And I mean anyone — people who had never raced before made the trip to the .75-mile dirt track in Charlotte, North Carolina, to see how they could do. All they needed was a car and a fair amount of guts.

The cars were plain vehicles like Buicks, Fords, and Lincolns, not like today's race cars, which are built from the ground up by multi-million-dollar teams and tuned specifically for racing. If drivers wanted to race back then, they could drive the family car right onto the track! Of course, if a driver crashed and destroyed his car, he could be stranded. Hitchhiking home was not out of the realm of possibility.

If you're one of the sport's new fans, this chapter gives you NASCAR in a nutshell, including enough details about its history, cars, drivers, teams, races, and statistics to make you sound like a veteran. If you're an old hand, you can brush up on what's new, as the sport is constantly evolving.

From Back Roads to the Big Time

A few decades ago, stock-car races weren't the professionally run events that they are now, even though many organizations — including the United Stock Car Racing Association, the Stock Car Auto Racing Society, and the National Championship Stock Car Circuit — sanctioned races. The schedule wasn't organized; instead, random races were held here and there, sprinkled throughout the southeastern United States wherever tracks were available (some were well-built, but most were pretty shoddy). Drivers didn't race in each event, so fans had no idea which of their favorites would show up until they got to the track. Worse, some race promoters were less than honest, running off with the ticket receipts and race purses, never to be seen again.

Bill France, Sr., a tall, dynamic stock-car driver and race promoter, thought this was an unprofessional way to run a sport and was determined to set a standard for drivers and track owners. He decided to devote his energy to establishing one preeminent stock-car racing sanctioning body — NASCAR (National Association for Stock Car Auto Racing) — that would oversee different series. A *racing series,* such as the NASCAR NEXTEL Cup Series, is similar to a baseball league, featuring a group of drivers who compete in a set number of events and follow rules determined by the sanctioning body. At the end of the season, the sanctioning body in charge of making the rules, running the events, and making sure competitors follow the rules, crowns a series champion. That's exactly what France, also known as "Big Bill," created with his brainchild — NASCAR. In the beginning, France had several goals:

✔ **Racetracks that were safe for the drivers, and track owners who repaired their facilities between races.** If a car crashed into or through a guard rail, it would have to be repaired by the track owner before the next race.

✔ **Rules that wouldn't change from week to week or race to race.** Before NASCAR was organized, different tracks had different rules, which drove drivers to distraction. Some even had quirky on-track rules, made up the morning of a race by a promoter seeking to make things more exciting. Because of these inconsistencies, drivers didn't know what to expect when they showed up at a racetrack. These days, rules still occasionally change but are often studied for a period of months before being implemented.

✔ **A set schedule allowing the same drivers to compete against one another each week.** This way, a single national champion recognized by all could be crowned at the end of the year.

✔ **A uniform point system to calculate which driver performed the best throughout the season.** Drivers would earn points according to how they finished in a race, with the winner receiving the most points and the last-place driver getting the least. With a points system like that, the series could crown a definitive champion instead of having many "national champions" crowned at different tracks or in different, smaller series. Having just one national champion made winning the title something special.

✔ **An insurance and benevolent fund:** This was meant to give the drivers something to fall back on in case they got hurt or couldn't compete due to injuries.

France's goals were realized and today NASCAR sanctions several racing series. The top one is the NASCAR NEXTEL Cup Series, and I spend most of the book talking about this series. I give you a quick rundown on the NASCAR Busch Series, the NASCAR Craftsman Truck Series, and several NASCAR touring series in Chapter 3.

What Is Stock Car Racing?

When different people think of auto racing, the same image of a race car doesn't necessarily pop into their heads. That's because many different types of race cars and hundreds of racing series, or racing leagues, exist throughout the world.

NASCAR stock cars are unique in that they look very much like what a suburbanite drives. But looks can be deceiving. Almost nothing is "stock" when it comes to NASCAR vehicles, whether they run in NASCAR NEXTEL Cup Series, NASCAR Busch Series, or NASCAR Craftsman Truck Series events. In addition to bodies (or chassis) reinforced with roll bars, multi-part driver restraint systems, and an escape hatch through the roof, NASCAR vehicles are among the fastest — and safest — on earth.

Three brands of cars compete in the NASCAR NEXTEL Cup Series — the Chevrolet Monte Carlo, the Ford Taurus, and the Dodge Intrepid. The manufacturers of these brands of cars see the sport as a great marketing tool, hence the saying, "Win on Sunday, sell on Monday."

Here's a quick rundown on the other types of racing vehicles (Figure 1-1 shows you some of the differences):

- **Open-wheel:** The cars that run in the Indianapolis 500, perhaps the most famous race in the world, are open-wheel cars. They're agile, lightweight racing cars with an open cockpit. Open-wheel cars also have no fenders, so they can't bump and bang as stock cars do or they would crash. The three different leagues that use open-wheel cars are

    - **Formula One:** The world's best-known open-wheel series.

    - **Indy Racing League (IRL):** Which competes exclusively on oval tracks in the United States and features the Indy 500 on its yearly schedule. The IRL plans to add road courses in the near future.

    - **Champ Cars (formerly CART):** This series races in various countries but mostly the United States on road courses and ovals.

- **Dragsters:** Speedsters that race a short distance in a short period of time. They race in pairs on a straight, flat quarter-mile strip of asphalt or concrete. The fastest ones can go from 0 to 100 mph in less than one second, topping out at speeds in excess of 320 mph. The premier dragsters are called *Top Fuel cars,* which are specialized cars that look more like rocket ships than anything else. They have long, tapered noses with two small front tires. The driver sits in an open cockpit about ten feet behind the wheels, with the engine behind him or her. Other dragsters are a little less exotic: *Funny cars* are highly modified, jazzed-up stock cars, while *Street Stock cars* look like passenger cars.

✔ **Sports cars:** Most are production (sports) cars with highly specialized engines, but the fastest are open-cockpit cars that sit close to the ground (like Ferraris). The cars are prototypes, which means they are built specifically for racing and aren't sold to the public.

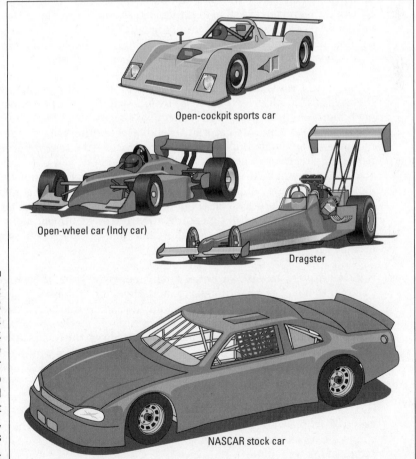

Open-cockpit sports car

Open-wheel car (Indy car)

Dragster

Figure 1-1: NASCAR stock cars look more like passenger cars than do open-wheel racers, most dragsters, or sports cars.

NASCAR stock car

The Racing Team

One of the best aspects of NASCAR is that its drivers are regular people — that is, until they get to the race track. As is the case with all competitive athletes, NASCAR drivers have their own personalities, which are often magnified when they get behind the wheel. The legendary Richard Petty, whose 200-victory record will probably never be topped (he raced up to 60 times a season) is one of the nicest guys in the garage area, always stopping to sign autographs while flashing his signature smile. But Petty didn't win seven NASCAR Cup championships by being the series' sweetheart during a race; he bumped and banged with the best of them.

Drivers like Tony Stewart and Robby Gordon prefer their on-track performance to talking, while the colorful Rusty Wallace has never been asked a question that he answered in less than 300 words. These days, the prototypical driver more closely resembles multiple NASCAR Cup Series champion Jeff Gordon and up-and-coming star Jimmie Johnson, who keep their tempers to themselves and remain composed in virtually any situation.

During a time when many athletes are out of touch with the fans who pay their bills, NASCAR drivers are seen by many of their supporters as the guy next door. And they are definitely the most accessible of highly hyped superstars. Although some are naturally friendlier and others are more reserved, many retain an innate humbleness, which comes from remembering the early days of their careers when they built and worked on their own cars. They also recognize that without fans, NASCAR wouldn't exist. Although in this modern era drivers are pulled in many directions, from testing their vehicles to making appearances on behalf of their sponsors, they remain fairly accessible. NASCAR drivers still sign autographs and make appearances at malls in the cities in which they race. (For more information on drivers' schedules and their fan clubs, see Chapter 15.)

NASCAR drivers are also known as family men, who bring their wives and children to many races — thanks to modern, comfortable motor homes replacing the need to stay in hotels. Many attend church services on the morning of a race and are very aware they are role models to kids and teens watching their every move. When people talk about the NASCAR family, they don't mean just the competitors. NASCAR fans tend to "adopt" a certain driver to root for, and he becomes a member of their extended family.

Although NASCAR's drivers are front and center when it comes to recognition and attention, they wouldn't be in the racing business were it not for the hundreds of people who run the sport, create the teams, work on the crews, sponsor cars and races, and bring the action to the nation via television, radio, and newspapers.

MARK SAYS

How I got started

Growing up in Batesville, Arkansas, I thought racing was the greatest thing in the world. My dad got me interested in it, and, considering racing is for people who love taking risks, it was no wonder he liked it so much. My dad was the wildest, fastest-running guy around, and he wanted me to be the same way.

My dad used to prop me up in his lap while he was in the driver's seat of the car and, without taking no for an answer, would make me take the steering wheel. Then he'd slam his foot on the accelerator and off we'd go. It scared me to death, but I was stuck steering that car sometimes at speeds over 80 mph on gravel roads

around our hometown. But the more we drove, the more I got used to it — and the more I fell in love with the sensation of going fast and taking the car to the edge.

I started racing cars when I was 15, even before I had a driver's license. That's when I discovered that everything about the sport of stock-car racing thrilled me. I became obsessed with the sounds and the speed — but mostly with the prospect of becoming a successful driver. For me, there was nothing better than driving a race car, especially because I was good at it. I won my first race in only my second start at a local track in Arkansas.

At the top of any individual race team is the owner, who pays the bills and calls the shots. Team owners also spend a vast amount of time searching for and pleasing sponsors, who spend millions of dollars for the right to put the name of their company across a car's hood. The team owner gets a great deal of help from his general manager and crew chief, who are in charge of everything from hiring employees to setting the testing schedule to being responsible for a car's performance on any given Sunday. Teams employ a large number of specialists who work at the race shop doing everything from painting the driver's cars to answering the telephone.

During the last ten years, it has become common practice for an owner to field more than one team, which is obviously more expensive but gives him or her more chances to share information between teams and have more opportunities to visit victory lane. (For more on team ownership, see Chapter 6.)

Winning a Race Takes Strategy

NASCAR racing is about much more than making rules and driving fast. In fact, becoming successful in NASCAR entails much more than the ability to wheel a race car at high speeds. By the time a race starts, a driver and his crew have put in many hours of work building and tweaking the vehicles so that they handle well for that particular track, whether an oval track, a road course, or a superspeedway. Once at the track, drivers hit the pavement for practice laps, trying to coax the most speed they can out of their cars in order to both qualify and race well. A *qualifying lap* determines where a driver will start a race; the one who is fastest over one lap gets to start from the front *pole position* and the second-fastest driver starts next to him on the *outside pole*.

When the race starts, the objective is to move to the front (if you started in the back) and hold onto the lead if you started up front. The most successful drivers are well-schooled in the art of passing the competition, either by having that day's fastest car or by hooking up with their rivals in a draft, as two or three cars end-to-end can push one another past a car stuck out on its own. (For more information on drafting and race strategy, turn to Chapter 9.) A good pit crew that can change four tires and fill two cans of gas in less than 14 seconds is also crucial to having a winning car. The first car off pit road, especially near the end of the race, often is the one that makes the hard left into victory lane.

Winning has become increasingly difficult as the sport has become more popular and more drivers enter races. That makes winning more special than it used to be. Don't get me wrong, it was special when I won my first NASCAR Cup race in 1989, but today, there isn't as much disparity in equipment between first- and last-place teams. This is fine with me because it makes winning more satisfying.

Rules keep the fans happy

Like other professional sports, NASCAR has a rule book. Unlike other professional sports, however, that rule book changes during the season — and can even change from week to week. For example, if a driver's team gets an edge over everybody else with the car's aerodynamics or in a particular part of the engine, NASCAR may change the rule regarding that area and the team's advantage disappears. While some rules changes sometime appear to help or hinder a certain manufacturer, there are those that affect drivers equally, such as the introduction in 2004 of the Chase for the NASCAR NEXTEL Cup, which opened the title race to the top-10 drivers in the standings (or those within 400 points of the leader) with 10 races remaining. While some rule changes are difficult to swallow at times, I appreciate how exciting the changes make the races for the fans. Without great racing, there would be no fans. And without fans, I wouldn't be living my dream and racing for a living. It's a necessary trade-off between the rules and success. And, unlike the rules changes before NASCAR was formed, at least we know our changes in advance. We also know there's a reason new rules — to keep the competition as thrilling and as even as possible.

Heading Out to the Track

Watching a NASCAR race is a total-body experience: the earth-shattering sound of a 790 horsepower engine roaring when a driver flips the ignition switch, the sight of 43 colorful cars flying around a track fender-to-fender as the grandstands shake, and the gritty smell of burned rubber mixed with gasoline. If watching races on television from your living room isn't enough of a rush for you, it's time to head out to the track. Here are several great races you may want to check out yourself (see Chapter 14 for more info on going to races):

✔ **The Daytona 500:** NASCAR's annual Super Bowl, which is held in February and signals the start of the season. Teams spend several weeks at Daytona International Speedway getting ready for the year's most hotly-contested event. Even past series champions say they don't consider their resumes complete unless they have won the Daytona 500.

✔ **The Brickyard 400:** Long the hallowed ground of the Indy 500 (open-wheel) race, NASCAR has had no trouble packing the Indianapolis Motor Speedway stands with more than 300,000 spectators each August. Jeff Gordon is the event's master, having won four Brickyard 400s since NASCAR's inaugural race there in 1994.

Mark Martin fans

It's hard to believe how many NASCAR fans buy racing paraphernalia to support their favorite drivers. Then again, as a driver, it's even harder to believe how many fans root for me. I drove for a long time before that sunk in, but I'll never forget the moment it did. In 1990, seven long years after my first NASCAR Cup race, I was driving at North Wilkesboro Speedway in North Carolina, battling Dale Earnhardt for the lead. At that point, Earnhardt had won three of his seven NASCAR Cup championships, and my goal was to keep him from winning his fourth title that year and to beat him in that race. It wasn't easy getting by Earnhardt, but when I finally passed him, the crowd went wild.

Usually a driver doesn't see the fans because he's concentrating so much on the race. On that day, though, I could see the crowd out of the corner of my eye as soon as I began the pass. They were standing up, hooting and hollering as I pulled next to Earnhardt. They only got louder as we raced side-by-side down the frontstretch, which is the straight section of racetrack between the first and last turns. (See Chapter 8 for more details on the layout of racetracks.) It created an even bigger stir when I passed Earnhardt for good and won the race. At that moment, standing in Victory Lane and seeing all those fans, I realized that the crowd was rooting for me and that I had a pretty big following. Even though Earnhardt won the championship that year and I was the runner-up, I still felt pretty good about that moment at North Wilkesboro. It was unforgettable.

✔ **Talladega Superspeedway events:** Both races at NASCAR's longest track (2.66 miles) are hot tickets. Even with the introduction of carburetor restrictor plates, which have kept average speeds under 180 mph, fans can't get enough of the high-speed action. (For more on restrictor plates, see Chapter 13.) Many races end with last-lap surprises at this Alabama track.

✔ **Bristol Motor Speedway events:** This short half-mile track brings out the beast in every driver, with close-quarters racing sending many drivers to the garage area long before a winner is declared. The bumping and banging is the bane of many teams, who spend weeks afterwards smoothing out the dings and dents in the car's superstructure.

Reaching the Big Time

Millions of fans dedicate a portion of their weekend to attending or watching NASCAR events, a far cry from the hundred or so who turned up in the sport's early days to witness the competition on small dirt or asphalt tracks. In addition to unparalleled action, NASCAR has grown in leaps and bounds thanks to two entities: Sponsors and media coverage. Without either, NASCAR most likely would still be a regional sport with limited opportunities to get a first-hand look at the action.

Signing up the major sponsors

In 1970, Robert Glenn Johnson, Jr., a legendary driver and car owner who made his name as a bootlegger before racing in NASCAR, took a trip to Winston-Salem, North Carolina, and changed the sport of stock-car racing forever. Johnson, who goes by Junior instead of his given name, went to the town to talk to R.J. Reynolds Tobacco Company (RJR) executives and convince them to sponsor his race team. The meeting resulted in much more than anyone imagined. Instead of sponsoring Johnson's race team, RJR ended up sponsoring the entire series.

But things are always changing and in 2003, NASCAR and Nextel announced a 10-year series sponsorship beginning in 2004. The wireless communications leader wanted to build on the opportunities associated with the 55-year-old sanctioning body, as well as the numerous ways Nextel's technology enhances the sport for fans, competitors, officials, media, sponsors, and tracks.

Nextel's investment in the NASCAR NEXTEL Cup Series goes beyond the race track, activating fan interactive opportunities as well as community and charity initiatives. The marketing pact between NASCAR and Nextel has proved to be a gold mine of opportunity. A FORTUNE 500 company, Nextel is a leading provider to fully-integrated wireless communications services and has built the largest guaranteed all-digital wireless network in the country.

MARK SAYS

Where are the women?

As you may guess, stock-car racing started out as a male-dominated sport, but change has come. Several women drivers and women team members have made it into NASCAR NEXTEL Cup Series, NASCAR Busch Series, and NASCAR Craftsman Truck Series. Janet Guthrie raced in NASCAR Cup series in the mid-1970s and competed in the 1977 Daytona 500, making her the only woman to compete in NASCAR's top series. She finished 12th. Patty Moise raced several seasons in the NASCAR Busch Series, and Shawna Robinson became the only woman to win a pole position for a NASCAR Busch Series race, but took a hiatus when she had difficulty securing a sponsor and then decided to have children. More recently, Tina Gordon has raced regularly in the NASCAR Busch Series, and Kelly Sutton is a regular NASCAR Craftsman Truck Series competitor.

Although not many women race, the ones who do aren't harassed or berated. Robinson has said that people treat her just as they do the men drivers — and she prefers it that way because she would rather distinguish herself as a good driver than as a good *female* driver.

Today there are many women in the garage area, working as journalists and public relations representatives. While the number of women working in the garage grew slowly over the years, the number of female fans has exploded. Today, nearly 40 percent of fans who attend races are women, which is a tremendous gain from 1975 when just 15 percent of attendees were women. This is all part of the overall growth of NASCAR.

The sponsors

It costs tens of millions of dollars to operate a NASCAR team, so team owners must get companies to sponsor their racing organizations to ease most of the financial burden. These companies use NASCAR as a vehicle (no pun intended) for their marketing campaigns, with their logos plastered on the cars and the drivers' uniforms. But it's a two-way street because NASCAR and its drivers also benefit. When NASCAR fans see an advertisement for Budweiser they think of Dale Earnhardt Jr., who is sponsored by that company. The same holds true for DuPont, which has reaped immeasurable benefits from its association with Jeff Gordon. Sponsors are integral in boosting NASCAR's popularity and in turn gaining financial rewards. If it weren't for sponsors, teams wouldn't have the financial wherewithal to travel across the country so fans can see them compete in person.

Catching races on the tube

When ESPN began broadcasting in 1979, it needed to fill 24 hours a day with sports. Broadcasting racing was an ideal way for them to fill hours. It was a perfect fit — a sports station looking for sports to televise and a sport that was looking to be televised much more extensively than it was. TV rights to races were less expensive then, costing the networks about $50,000 per event. After the two came together, some viewers stumbled upon racing, including NASCAR, because it was on so often. Existing fans couldn't get enough to begin with, and the more races that ESPN broadcast, the more they watched.

The modern era of NASCAR television broadcasting is considered to have begun in 1979, although it was a coincidence that was the same year as the birth of ESPN. In 1979, CBS aired its first live, flag-to-flag telecast of the Daytona 500, catapulting the sport into a new age. In 2004, FOX and cable partner FX broadcast events during the season's first half, while NBC and cable affiliate TNT combined to provide coverage of the second half. Now, nearly every major network and many cable stations can say they have broadcast a NASCAR race or have had some NASCAR coverage. That includes not only the major networks and ESPN but also specialty stations such as SPEED Channel.

Chapter 2

The Big Business of NASCAR

*I*f you think NASCAR is just a bunch of guys driving souped-up race cars, you're mistaken. It takes much more than someone working on his grand-dad's old Plymouth — no matter how powerful the engine — to race in NASCAR today. And the money invested and reaped is pretty hefty, too.

You can see NASCAR's growth everywhere. While you may have expected to find life-sized cutouts of four-time NASCAR Cup Series champion Jeff Gordon greeting you at a General Motors dealership, nowadays you bump into like-nesses of NASCAR drivers in places you may never expect: on TV, in toy stores, and even in supermarkets.

While NASCAR started as a primarily Southern-based sport, this is no longer true. Once the media began paying attention to the fierce competition and the incredible bonds between drivers and fans, the sport inevitably boomed. Today, with impressive race tracks opening across the country, as well as multi-million-dollar sponsorship packages, licensing deals, and television contracts, NASCAR is everywhere.

Sponsors Pay the Bills

NASCAR racing is more sponsor-oriented than any other sport in the world, with major companies sponsoring both major races, including the Pepsi 400 and Coca-Cola 600, and individual racing teams — which you're not likely to forget. Not only are the cars covered with decals of the companies that spon-sor race teams and provide race car parts, but the drivers' and racing team's uniforms are plastered with company names — on the chest, on the back, going down both sleeves and the sides of both legs.

A driver obviously isn't going to wear a sponsor logo when dressed in a tux, but when making official appearances at a car dealership or a mall, they wear hats and shirts with their sponsors' name on them. Hey, it's a break for their clothing budget because sponsors provide all those hundreds of shirts and hats free of charge.

Different levels of sponsorship exist, primary or associate, based on how much the company pays to the team. But no matter how much or how little the company spends, they all do it for the same reason: sponsoring a race team gives companies a fantastic marketing tool on race day — a rolling billboard. Many companies, including those in the *Fortune 500*, take advantage of that.

Companies also become associated with NASCAR through the title sponsorship of races. Coca-Cola, Pepsi, and Mountain Dew spend big bucks to have their company name listed as a primary event sponsor. When television announcers mention a race, they include the sponsoring company's name in their reports, such as the Chevy Monte Carlo 400 or the Golden Corral 500.

The primary sponsors are loaded

Primary sponsors are the bigwig companies that pay tens of millions of dollars to put their name on the car's hood, which is the best place to advertise because fans can see it so well. The average price tag for being a primary sponsor of a NASCAR NEXTEL Cup Series team is $8 million per season — but higher profile and more successful teams get much more, many times in excess of $10 million. Teams have to secure a good primary sponsor because the costs of equipment, travel, and personnel are just too expensive for a team owner to absorb by himself. Without a constant flow of cash, a team can't hire the best employees or get the best equipment — and in racing today, those factors are key to winning.

Viagra is my current sponsor, but I've had other primary sponsors in the past, including Valvoline, Folger's Coffee, Stroh's Beer, and Amzoil. You can find all sorts of companies involved in racing today — companies you'd never expect to be interested in stock-car racing at all: Kellogg's, Target, M&Ms, and The Home Depot. Even Betty Crocker sponsored a car for a while. The diversity of these sponsors shows how much the sport has moved away from the days when oil and gasoline companies were the most common types of sponsors.

Primary sponsors also often help determine a car's *paint scheme,* or the way a car is painted and decorated. The paint scheme usually stays much the same throughout a season, but sometimes sponsors change that look for certain races, perhaps to market a specific brand of their product or unveil something new. Team owner Joe Gibbs, who recently returned to coach the

Washington Redskins, changes NFL team names on his cars throughout the season, under an agreement with his primary sponsors and the NFL. When a special paint scheme is unveiled, fans tend to flock to stores to seek out souvenirs — many of which will become collectors' items.

Not only do primary sponsors get the most exposure on uniforms and cars, they also get more of a commitment from the driver in terms of sponsor appearances. When a driver makes an *appearance,* he shows up to sign posters, programs, and trading cards for fans or employees at supermarket grand openings, auto shows, conventions, car dealerships, fairgrounds, auto stores, or other venues. Sometimes, sponsors also ask drivers to give a speech or host a question-and-answer session for fans or employees. With sponsors' increasing involvement in the sport, public speaking and public relations are big parts of a driver's life. How many appearances a driver is required to make depends on the contract he or she signs at the beginning of the season, which lists how many appearances the driver is obliged to provide. (See Chapter 7 for more information on a driver's sponsor obligations.)

You'll have better luck meeting a driver at an appearance than at the race track. Most of the time when races come to a town, drivers make local appearances, so keep an eye on the newspaper for those dates and places. You also can find out where they'll be during the week by checking with their race shops (see Chapter 15 for the addresses).

Associate sponsors: The price is right

Companies that can't afford to spend millions of dollars still get a chance to sponsor a race team. *Associates* pay less money and, in turn, don't get as much exposure on the car or the uniform as the primary sponsors do. But the company's logo is still plastered on the car, usually on the side — and on every diecast collector's car, in photos, and also on TV when the car is shown during races. Most teams have dozens of associate sponsors, their decals creating a colorful mosaic on the side of the car. The associates also get to use the driver in TV commercials or print ads and get the driver for a few appearances each season.

The various levels of associate sponsorships and costs vary depending on the team and the size of the company's decal on the car. In the NASCAR NEXTEL Cup Series, associate sponsorships can cost up to $5 million, with sponsorship of the higher-profile teams costing more. The highest level of associate sponsorship is *major associate,* which is the level just below a primary sponsor but above a regular associate. Sometimes, it's almost like having two primary sponsors, but one just happens to pay less and demand less than the other. (See the color photo near the center of this book for examples of sponsorship logos.)

Contingency programs: Stick with these guys to make some money

GARAGE TALK

Another way for companies to have their names linked with NASCAR is through the *contingency program*. Contingency awards are earned throughout the season by drivers whose cars display a company's decal. Some of the best-known contingency programs are the Bud Pole Award, which rewards a driver with $5,000 for winning the pole position. The Wix Lap Leader program rewards the driver who leads the most laps in each race with $5,000. (For a list of contingency awards, see Chapter 12.) Teams must display contingency program stickers on their cars or uniforms in order to be eligible for the bonus. Contingency programs are a way for race car parts suppliers and other companies to advertise with and gain recognition for all the teams they work with, rather than dishing out money to just one team.

From T-shirts to motor oil: NASCAR fans support their drivers

Sponsors know what they're doing. There's a reason why races are named the Sylvania 300 and not "That 300-lap race at New Hampshire International Speedway." There's a reason why Charlotte Motor Speedway was renamed Lowe's [Home Improvement Warehouse] Motor Speedway. And there's a reason drivers thank their "Ford DeWalt" team when they have a great day at the racetrack. It's because many NASCAR fans live and die by every word spoken by their favorite driver, every sponsor's logo shown on their favorite driver's car, and every paint scheme or uniform change. NASCAR fans are loyal — a recent study revealed 76 percent of them use NASCAR sponsors' products.

You can see evidence of how loyal NASCAR fans are without even going to a race. Just drive down the highway and look at bumper stickers. Some people just display the car number of their favorite driver; others show the car number of their least-favorite driver with a big, thick line through it. The same loyalty goes for the car manufacturers involved in the sport — some fans don't necessarily prefer any one driver, but root exclusively for Ford drivers. Not surprisingly, those fans usually have a bunch of Fords parked in their driveways — and vow never to own a General Motors car in their lifetime. Car companies couldn't be happier about fans like that, particularly because those companies initially became involved in racing to market and sell more of their vehicles.

NASCAR fans are even more supportive at the races. You can see my fans from a mile away, wearing Mark Martin T-shirts, Mark Martin hats, Mark Martin jackets, and even Mark Martin sneakers. It would be a tough task to find a fan in the grandstands wearing a plain, old shirt with no logos on it — except for the guys who get sunburned because they don't wear any shirts at all!

Keeping up appearances

A rookie driver who hasn't proven himself yet really doesn't have much control over which company will sponsor his team. In most cases, that driver is so eager for a sponsor that he'll take anyone. In my early years as a driver, I was thrilled to get a call from any company at all. Now, though, I can be choosy because of my success in the sport. I've been lucky to have Viagra as a primary sponsor.

When I was racing on the short tracks of Arkansas, I never thought I'd see people wearing T-shirts with my face on them or wearing hats with my name on them. But now it's really cool because it shows how many people support me at the racetrack and cheer for me when I drive by. Because I wear an ear piece while in the car (for the in-car radio), as well as a tight helmet, and have to contend with the roar of the engine, I can't hear fans cheering when I'm driving. But seeing fans wearing my name on their clothes lets me know that I have people behind me.

NASCAR fan loyalty goes way beyond filling wardrobes with logo-covered T-shirts. NASCAR fans are extremely faithful to the companies who sponsor their favorite driver. That's where a big chunk of the big business and big bucks come in. Not only do NASCAR fans support their driver by rooting for him, they also support him by buying his sponsors' goods. So, it's a good guess that Petty fans still use STP oil treatment, even though it no longer sponsors Petty Racing, because STP was the team's primary sponsor for so many years. And that makes NASCAR appealing to companies who want an interesting and effective marketing tool.

Licenses Aren't Just for Driving Anymore

With fans buying up all that NASCAR merchandise, it's not surprising some people would do anything to sell stuff to fans and get in on the action. But making that money isn't simple. Just like you need a license to drive on the highway, you need a license to sell merchandise bearing the NASCAR name or drivers' names. Otherwise, you can be fined or arrested. Getting licensed is a serious deal. Unless you want the cops chasing after you, taking all your merchandise, and giving you a big, fat ticket — get licensed if you're interested in selling NASCAR paraphernalia.

Licensing gives people the authority to sell particular goods with a particular name, logo, or likeness on it. Now there's a good reason why that's necessary, at least as far as I see things: It's embarrassing to have my name or picture on something ridiculously ugly, poorly made, or extremely inappropriate. Souvenirs are part of the image, so a driver doesn't want to be part of something that's too hokey or that's a cheap rip-off. Considering all the souvenir items floating around out there, drivers have lots of opportunities to be part of cheesy, junky stuff — so somebody had better be watching out for their interests. There's also a business aspect to insisting everyone sells licensed merchandise. Drivers make royalties off the licensed goods vendors sell — either a percentage of the selling price or just a flat fee.

When buying NASCAR souvenirs, make sure to look for the official NASCAR hologram sticker. If it has this sticker, along with the official NASCAR logo, it's guaranteed to be quality stuff and not some shoddy souvenir that will fall apart the moment you put it on or bring it home. The imitation may be cheaper than a licensed item, but don't be fooled — the low price may mean low quality. Buying souvenirs from a driver's souvenir trailer, which is located outside the track during races, is a sure way to be safe because it sells only licensed merchandise.

You can find nearly every souvenir imaginable relating to NASCAR, including some everyday items — and some really strange things:

- **Clothing:** The most obvious souvenirs are T-shirts, jackets, hats, and button-down shirts. Some less obvious (for NASCAR fans who like a complete look) are socks, a water bottle, or a seat cushion with a driver's name and car number on them. Fans are proud of the drivers they cheer for and often show up at events outfitted head-to-toe with merchandise that identifies them as a driver's number-one supporter.

- **Jewelry:** With NASCAR's growing popularity among women, NASCAR jewelry has taken off in sales. Souvenir stands and retail outlets stock almost anything you can imagine, including necklaces, bracelets, rings, or anklets.

- **Home decorating:** NASCAR fans don't have to go far to fix up their homes with a NASCAR motif. Some licensees sell just about anything for the home, and a lot of that stuff has my name on it, too. You can find Mark Martin wallpaper, Mark Martin quilts, Mark Martin sheets, Mark Martin chairs, Mark Martin dishes, and even Mark Martin carpeting. You can even purchase NASCAR crystal platters and silverware for entertaining purposes. I'm not saying that buying all this stuff will make your house stylish, but it will definitely get a point across to your guests — that you're a NASCAR fan through and through.

- **Office supplies:** Looking for NASCAR scissors or a Mark Martin ruler? Don't fret, you can find them, along with stationery, pens, pencils, telephones, and nearly everything else you'll need to get your work done fast enough to take a couple days off for a NASCAR race.

- **Games:** The toy business is also involved in stock-car racing. NASCAR video games are a big deal and a huge seller in stores. You can also find board and card games relating to the sport — they're less high-tech but just as much fun.

- **Books:** Publishing has become more visible in the NASCAR business in recent years. The NASCAR Library Collection was introduced in early 2004, helping differentiate authentic NASCAR licensed books, like the one you're reading, from others in the marketplace.

- **Diecast cars:** Perhaps the best-selling NASCAR souvenirs over the years have been diecast cars, made up with the current year's paint scheme on them and a driver's name above the door, just like on real stock cars. These babies aren't just your run-of-the-mill toy cars, though. They have working hoods, detailed cockpits, tiny engines, and functioning wheels. Many fans see them as collector's items — and their price usually reflects that. They come in several sizes (1:64 scale to 1:24 scale), and sometimes their price tags are hefty. Some cars, particularly older ones with a hard-to-find paint scheme, are priced in the hundreds of dollars. For serious collectors, some are made of 24-karat gold and platinum.

My fans had a perfect chance at buying the quintessential Mark Martin souvenir through the Neiman Marcus catalog. The store had one of my race cars for sale, all painted up with a working race engine under the hood. I guess it was for die-hard fans only because it cost $125,000 and wasn't even legal to drive on the street! In fact, the headlights were only decals, as with all NASCAR cars, so driving it home from the store at night would have been challenging. But I bet the trip would have been quicker than usual.

Smile, You're on NASCAR Camera!

There's one tell-tale sign that NASCAR is popular in the United States: its races are on TV. Every NASCAR NEXTEL Cup Series, NASCAR Busch Series, and NASCAR Craftsman Truck Series race is broadcast on television. (See Chapter 3 for the lowdown on the differences among the NASCAR NEXTEL Cup Series, NASCAR Busch Series, and NASCAR Craftsman Truck Series.) Qualifying rounds and even some practices are also televised. That's amazing, considering the first NASCAR race broadcast live, flag-to-flag was only 26 years ago. That race, the 1979 Daytona 500 on CBS, brought racing action into America's living rooms for an afternoon. Now racing is more than just a once-in-a-while show on TV. You can find it virtually every day because the racing season lasts from February through late November, the longest season of any professional sport. And one cable network, the Speed Channel, is exclusively devoted to motor racing, with NASCAR competition making up much of its coverage.

If you're curious about racing but not ready to devote yourself to it, you can catch a peek of the sport before you dive into it as a fan. Turning on your TV is the first step. It won't be long until you stumble upon a *racing show,* in which races, qualifyings, and practices are dissected, and everyone from the driver to the car owner to the guy that puts gas in the car is interviewed. You can find out more about racing than you ever wanted to know if you watch those shows long enough.

Knock-down, drag-out NASCAR coverage

The first NASCAR race broadcast on live TV certainly made racing seem exciting to non-NASCAR fans who tuned in. It also made racing seem lawless. While Richard Petty won that 1979 Daytona 500, the most thrills came from drivers off the track. Bobby Allison and his brother Donnie Allison got into a scuffle with Cale Yarborough, with the TV cameras rolling as America got its first taste of NASCAR. Although this incident doesn't fit with the squeaky-clean image that many NASCAR drivers have now, it shows how emotional the sport can get. It also reveals that, just like any other pro sport, competitors can't help but lose their tempers at times.

You can find NASCAR race broadcasts on the major broadcast networks and cable. The networks are beginning to delve into the sport more and more because TV ratings have grown each year since NASCAR races began showing up on TV. (For a listing of NASCAR's television and radio partners, see Chapter 15.)

TV has become such a big deal in racing these days that broadcasters are quite innovative in the way they bring the sport to viewers. Developments include in-car cameras as well as cameras underneath the chassis. From inside the car, viewers can see the driver turn the wheel and shift. From outside, viewers can see a car ahead of or behind the driver — and also see whether there is any contact between the two cars. When a driver crashes, the camera picks up plenty more action — like a wall coming straight at it or another car smacking into the rear bumper and then flying off into another car to cause mayhem on the track. In really hard crashes, the camera can take only so much. Upon impact, the camera breaks and the transmission goes black. Not all cars have these cameras for every race, but the shots from those cameras give great insight into what is going on during a race — a real feel for what's going on.

Shying away from cameras

When I began racing, I didn't want to talk that much — much less look into a camera for the entire world to see. All I wanted to do was drive race cars and win races, and I was pretty shy about everything else. I figured that if I wanted to be famous and on TV, I wouldn't be much of a racer.

As my career progressed, however, I figured out that being on TV was a great way to market myself, so I forced myself to get used to it. I was interviewed a lot when I ran on short tracks in the Midwest, mostly on local radio stations or on local television stations, so I had a lot of practice before graduating to NASCAR NEXTEL Cup Series racing. Now, I don't even think about being nervous because I'm on TV. I just think about winning races, as all top-level drivers do. Compared to that, the TV part is easy.

In the spotlight, under pressure

While sponsors drool about how much TV coverage of the sport has grown (more TV means more footage of cars on the track, all zooming around with big corporate logos stuck onto them), for drivers that exposure heightens the pressure to lead races because the cameras get plenty of shots of the car out front.

TV coverage also puts a lot of pressure on drivers to speak well and behave in front of the camera. Every time drivers climb out of cars, camera lenses are watching, and reporters with microphones are asking questions. After an on-track incident, drivers have to explain why and how it happened. The moment you come out of the infield care center, which is where you are taken after every crash even if you're not hurt at all, the cameras and microphones are waiting. And at the end of the race, no matter how frustrated or angry or hot or sweaty or thirsty or tired you may be, reporters are there waiting for you to talk to them the instant you crawl out of your car.

Pro football, baseball, and hockey players at least get to cool off for a while in the locker room before the cameras and microphones come running. But for NASCAR drivers, that immediate media blitz has become a way of life.

Chapter 3

Understanding the Different NASCAR Series

*N*ASCAR racing is more than just one group of drivers traveling all over the United States to race. NASCAR has many different series, featuring drivers from different places and with different levels of talent. From its smaller series to its biggest series, NASCAR racing has a series for every driver. And for every fan, too.

NASCAR NEXTEL Cup Series: Where the Superstars Are

NASCAR's highest-profile series is the NASCAR NEXTEL Cup Series, a racing league akin to the top leagues of other sports. The best hitters play in Major League Baseball, the best quarterbacks play in the National Football League, and the best stock-car drivers race in the NASCAR NEXTEL Cup Series. It features the most recognized drivers in stock-car racing, including ones you've probably seen on TV in some way or another — whether driving in a race, selling souvenirs on a 24-hour shopping network, or smiling into the camera during a commercial. Some of the most popular NASCAR NEXTEL Cup Series drivers today include the following:

- ✔ **Jeff Gordon** began NASCAR Cup Series racing in 1993 and quickly earned the nickname "Wonder Boy" because he was only 21. He legitimized that nickname when he won his first NASCAR Cup Series title in 1995 at 24, becoming the youngest champion in NASCAR's modern era, which dates back to 1972. Gordon followed that title with back-to-back championships in 1997 and 1998, and a fourth in 2001. En route he broke records, won races, and frustrated his older and more experienced competitors. Gordon has since grown out of his Wonder Boy nickname and into a more mature role. He's NASCAR's unofficial spokesman, especially to new fans who may not be familiar with the sport and who may not be from the southern United States. Gordon's no good ol' boy — he grew up in California before moving to Indiana when he was 13.

- ✔ **Jimmie Johnson,** a California golden boy straight from Hollywood casting, finished as NASCAR Cup runner-up to champion Matt Kenseth in 2003, and then powered straight back to the top the following season. Consistency has been a Johnson trademark throughout his NASCAR career, which began with winning the pole position for his first Daytona 500 in 2002. A teammate of Jeff Gordon in the Rick Hendrick Chevrolet stable, Johnson is on track to become a champion at the sport's highest level.

- ✔ **Dale Earnhardt Jr.,** the son of seven-time NASCAR Cup Series champion Dale Earnhardt, came into the sport already a fan favorite, then backed up his family name by winning NASCAR Busch Series championships in 1998 and 1999. Jumping up to the NASCAR top series ranks in 2000, Earnhardt Jr. made steady gains each year, finishing third in the 2003 standings while also being voted the series' Most Popular Driver. Junior's immense popularity is obvious by the sea of red and white hats and T-shirts in the grandstands on any given weekend.

- ✔ **Tony Stewart** is perhaps the last link between NASCAR's new breed and the barnstorming racers of past decades. NASCAR's Raybestos Rookie of the Year in 1999, Stewart has finished in the top-10 every year since his first season, and in 2002 he was crowned NASCAR Cup Series champion. Prior to jumping to NASCAR competition, Stewart was an outstanding open-wheel racer, winning the 1997 Indy Racing League title. He continues to race in the Indianapolis 500 (an open-wheel race — see Chapter 1 for an explanation of the different types of racing) in May before jetting back to North Carolina the same day for the Coca-Cola 600 during the evening at Lowe's Motor Speedway. Stewart is also known for his generosity; he's a celebrity who doesn't forget the "little guy," such as gate guards, mechanics, and local short-track racers.

- ✔ **Dale Jarrett,** son of two-time NASCAR Cup Series champion Ned Jarrett, grew up watching his dad win races. Following Dale's first Daytona 500 victory in 1993, Ned said his son had more racing talent than he had ever possessed. Over the past few years, Jarrett has won more than 30 NASCAR races and has been a consistent contender for the championship. He won the NASCAR Cup Series championship in 1999, driving the No. 88 Ford for Robert Yates Racing, to make him and his father only the second father-son duo to win championships in NASCAR Cup Series history, joining Lee and Richard Petty.

✔ **Terry Labonte,** a two-time NASCAR Cup Series champion from Texas, is called "Mr. Consistency" by his peers because he has been so good for so long and because his seasons usually aren't filled with too many highs and lows. For example, in both years he won the championship (1984 and 1996), he won only two races, but was always racing near the front of the pack. People also call him "The Ice Man" because of his even temper both on and off the track. Labonte's younger brother, Bobby, was the 2000 NASCAR Cup Series champion.

✔ **Rusty Wallace,** the 1989 NASCAR Cup Series champion, grew up in St. Louis and learned how to drive on tracks in the Midwest before moving up to the NASCAR Cup Series. He's known as one of the most knowledgeable drivers when preparing a car to race — a reputation he earned by building and working on his own race cars before coming to NASCAR. He still works on his cars today, helping his crew get it just right. Wallace intends to retire from driving following the 2005 NASCAR NEXTEL Cup Series season.

My goal always was to make it to NASCAR NEXTEL Cup Series racing, which I believe is the hardest and most recognized racing series in the world. If you race open-wheel cars (see Chapter 1), you dream about making it to Formula One someday. But if you race stock cars, you think about the NASCAR NEXTEL Cup Series day and night: it gets the most live TV coverage, pays the most money, and earns the most fame for its drivers.

Going overseas

Even though NASCAR racing is based in the United States, it has held several exhibition races outside the country. Drivers raced in Japan once a year from 1996 to 1998 — twice on a road course in Suzuka and once on a newly built oval track in Motegi. It was quite a culture shock for NASCAR drivers and their teams to travel about 8,000 miles from home and arrive in a place where they didn't understand the language, customs, or food and drink. You've got to remember: *sushi,* which is raw fish, and *sake,* which is a beverage made from fermented rice, aren't exactly part of the menu when racers travel to events in Talladega, Alabama, or Darlington, South Carolina. When I went to Japan in 1997, however, I didn't think about the food or surroundings as much as I thought about the race. I won the pole at the road course in Suzuka and finished second in the race, right behind Mike Skinner.

Not only does NASCAR NEXTEL Cup Series racing feature some of the best and most colorful drivers in motorsports, but it also has some of the closest finishes. Many times, cars race bumper-to-bumper and side-by-side during an event — mostly because NASCAR monitors its rules so closely that no car or car manufacturer has an unfair edge over the competition. Even after a 500-mile race, it's not uncommon for drivers to cross the finish line within less than one second of each other. Even in *qualifying,* where drivers complete only one or two laps at full speed in order to earn a spot in the race, the fastest and the slowest cars are often separated by a fraction of a second.

NASCAR NEXTEL Cup Series races are held at tracks across the United States — from Daytona Beach, Florida, to suburban Los Angeles and Loudon, New Hampshire. Races are held nearly every weekend of the year, too. The NASCAR NEXTEL Cup Series had 36 races in 2004, making its schedule one of the most — if not the most — grueling in all of professional sports. But don't think that drivers work only 36 days out of the year. A race weekend entails at least two, and most often three, days of work (qualifying, practice, and the race), as well as one day of travel. See Chapter 7 for a day-by-day account of a driver's life.

Even so, drivers and crew members don't mind the rigorous schedule that much, particularly because they realize how fortunate they are to have made it to the top level of stock-car racing. While some drivers were able to get a job in the NASCAR NEXTEL Cup Series early in their racing careers, most drivers spend years trying to get there. Those drivers dedicated their lives to their goal of making it to NASCAR NEXTEL Cup Series competition, spending a lot of time away from their families while competing in the various series that travel throughout the country.

NASCAR Busch Series: One Route to the NASCAR NEXTEL Cup Series

A lot of drivers, including me, ended up in NASCAR NEXTEL Cup Series via the NASCAR Busch Series — a place where drivers can train themselves by getting experience, making mistakes, and learning from those errors. NASCAR Busch Series races are usually held on Saturdays, while NASCAR NEXTEL Cup Series races are most often on Sundays. But that's not the only difference.

NASCAR Busch Series racers drive stock cars and follow the same on-track rules (see Chapter 5) as in the NASCAR NEXTEL Cup Series, but the cars have a couple fundamental differences. Here are some unique aspects of each car:

   ✔ **Size:** Although both NASCAR NEXTEL Cup Series and NASCAR Busch Series cars are nearly the same height (51 inches and 50.5 inches, respectively), the wheelbase (the distance between the front and rear axles) is slightly different. On a NASCAR NEXTEL Cup Series car, the wheelbase is 110 inches, while on a NASCAR Busch Series racer, it's 105 inches. NASCAR NEXTEL Cup Series cars have an advantage here: their longer wheelbase gives them more stability.

- **Horsepower:** The biggest difference between the two cars is how powerful their engines are. NASCAR NEXTEL Cup cars have significantly more oomph to them, producing about 790 horsepower. *Horsepower* is a unit of measurement representing how much power an engine generates. The more horsepower, the faster the car. NASCAR Busch Series engines generate around 660 horsepower. Which means NASCAR NEXTEL Cup Series cars should be faster than Busch cars, correct? Yes — and no. One hundred pounds lighter than NASCAR NEXTEL Cup cars, NASCAR Busch Series racers do reach speeds that are nearly as fast. Though they have smaller engines, NASCASR Busch Series racers don't have to lug around as much weight as a NASCAR NEXTEL Cup Series car.

- **Compression ratio:** All three major series in NASCAR racing now use the same *compression ratio* (12 to 1), which is the volume inside a cylinder compared to the volume it compresses to when the piston is fully extended. The higher the ratio, the less space the mixture of fuel and air is shoved into, so the greater the potential for energy. (For more details on the technical aspects of stock cars, see Chapter 4.)

The NASCAR Busch Series — not bush league

Even though the NASCAR Busch Series, which evolved from the NASCAR Late Model Sportsman Series, is considered a stepping stone for the NASCAR NEXTEL Cup Series, many drivers bristle at that image. Some, like two-time NASCAR Busch Series champion Randy LaJoie, love racing in that series and have made a career out of it, saying it has the same intense competition as the NASCAR NEXTEL Cup Series and isn't just a stepping stone. LaJoie especially likes the fact that, even though he doesn't get paid as much as NASCAR NEXTEL Cup Series drivers do, he doesn't have to deal with nearly as much pressure.

The NASCAR Busch Series began in 1982 and has grown from races at small, unknown tracks to competitions at large, well-known facilities and includes nearly as many races as the NASCAR NEXTEL Cup Series does. Many races are companion events to NASCAR NEXTEL Cup races and are held on Saturday of a race weekend at a particular track. That gives NASCAR NEXTEL Cup drivers a chance to drive, as I do, in both races in one weekend. And even though NASCAR Busch Series drivers themselves are quite popular with fans, having NASCAR NEXTEL Cup drivers in the race lures even more people to the racetrack. But even without those well-known drivers competing, NASCAR Busch Series races have become popular events in their own right.

The NASCAR Busch Series was a valuable training ground for me, and I haven't turned my back on those races now, even though I have been successful in the NASCAR NEXTEL Cup Series for more than a decade. I still compete in a limited number of NASCAR Busch Series races every year, mostly because I love to race — and win. In fact, I've won more NASCAR Busch races than anyone in history, 45 times as of 2004. Because the cars are different, some technical information on how to set them up isn't the same. But overall, running in a NASCAR Busch Series race prior to NASCAR NEXTEL Cup competition gives me hints of how my NEXTEL Cup car will handle on a particular track.

Although winning a NASCAR Busch Series race on Saturday gives me more confidence for Sunday's NASCAR NEXTEL Cup Series events, racing twice in one weekend is tough. I hardly have any time to stop and take a breath. I get to the garage early to check out the Saturday car and talk to my Saturday crew chief, then hop over to my NASCAR NEXTEL Cup Series car. Then I have to juggle NASCAR Busch Series practice with NASCAR NEXTEL Cup Series practice and then qualify for both races. Sometimes I'm so busy with that and signing autographs on my way from one garage to the other that I forget to eat!

NASCAR Craftsman Truck Series: Pickups with Racing Stripes

In 1994, NASCAR decided to branch out and create another major racing series. But they didn't opt for just another stock-car series, which may have been too similar to the NASCAR NEXTEL Cup Series or the NASCAR Busch Series. Instead, they chose something completely different. And quite creative. They started racing pickup trucks.

NASCAR bigwigs sensed the series would catch on because an overwhelming majority of truck owners are interested in some type of motorsports. The truck manufacturers were into the idea, and plenty of talented drivers were looking for jobs, so why not?

In 1995, the NASCAR Craftsman Truck Series was created with Mike Skinner taking the first championship. The series has also worked as a breeding ground — many truck series drivers have advanced to the NASCAR Busch Series and NASCAR NEXTEL Cup Series ranks, although Skinner, after climbing the ladder, returned to the NASCAR Craftsman Truck Series.

Even though NASCAR Craftsman Truck Series vehicles don't look or feel much like NASCAR NEXTEL Cup cars, good drivers can handle both vehicles pretty well. To me, a vehicle is a vehicle and a race is a race. If a driver is skillful enough to be able to control a vehicle, he can succeed in any series and in any vehicle.

The following are some differences between passenger trucks (such as a Ford F-150, Chevrolet Silverado, Dodge Ram, and Toyota Tundra) and their NASCAR Craftsman Truck Series counterparts (see Figure 3-1):

- **Horsepower:** A passenger truck has 160 horsepower. Compare that to the race truck, which has about 650.

- **Length:** Passenger trucks are an average 194.5 inches long, while a race truck is 206 inches long.

- **Width:** Passenger trucks are an average of 76.8 inches wide. A race truck is 75 inches.

- **Height:** Passenger trucks are an average of 70 inches high, race trucks an average of 59 inches — shorter and much closer to the ground than their passenger truck counterparts.

- **Weight:** A passenger truck weighs an average of 3,829 pounds. A race truck is 3,400 pounds, just like a NASCAR NEXTEL Cup car. Because the race trucks don't have to be sturdy to haul things like fill dirt or your neighbor's couch, their bodies are much lighter and as streamlined as possible.

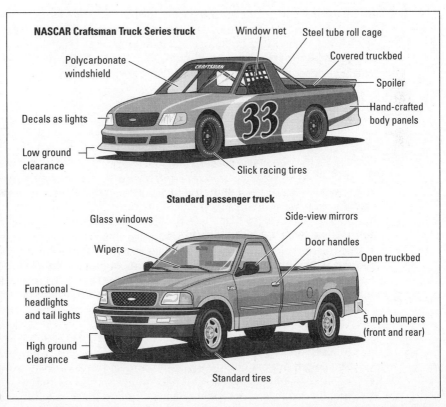

Figure 3-1: Race trucks certainly aren't for bringing hay bales to the farm. They are finely tuned racing machines, just like their NASCAR NEXTEL Cup Series cousins.

- ✔ **Wheelbase:** A passenger truck's front and rear wheels are 117.5 inches apart. On a race truck, that measurement is 112 inches.

- ✔ **Engine:** A passenger truck's engine is a 4.3 liter, V6 with fuel injection. A race truck has an 8-cylinder engine with a carburetor.

- ✔ **Compression ratio:** A passenger truck's compression ratio is 9 to 1. A race truck's ratio is 12 to 1. (For more information on compression ratio in racing vehicles, see explanation earlier in this section.)

NASCAR Touring Division: Where Stars Get Their Start

Most stock-car drivers begin racing at a track near their home, where the need for traveling money isn't an issue. Once a driver conquers his home-track championship, however, he often advances to one of NASCAR's *touring divisions,* which travel to different racetracks within the same region during their seasons. Touring division competition is where drivers step up on the financial ladder and start signing up well-heeled sponsors to help finance their efforts, in hopes of reaching the top NASCAR series. Racing at this level is much more expensive than running at a home track, where crew members work for free and often are chosen from among a driver's friends. It is less expensive, however, than racing in the NASCAR NEXTEL Cup Series, NASCAR Busch Series, or NASCAR Craftsman Truck Series.

Home and touring division tracks are generally less than a mile in length, compared with the much larger speedways in use by the premier series. The touring division, for example, doesn't race at the 2.66-mile Talladega Superspeedway in Alabama. However, the short-track skills a driver hones during touring division competition can benefit him greatly when he reaches NASCAR NEXTEL Cup Series or NASCAR Busch Series competition and races at tracks such as the half-mile Bristol Motor Speedway in Tennessee. When a driver jumps from the touring division to one of NASCAR's premier divisions, he is also able to earn a living as a professional racer. The following are brief descriptions of NASCAR's different touring series:

- ✔ **NASCAR Dodge Weekly Series:** Running at more than 70 short tracks across the country on a weekly basis, this series is the foundation of NASCAR. An early training ground for drivers, crew members, and officials, the NASCAR Dodge Weekly Series also creates hometown heroes for the fans. A wide variety of race cars are found in this series, including Late Model stock cars, Modifieds, Street Stocks, Trucks, Dirt Late Models, and Sportsman cars. Dodge has sponsored the series since 2002, with drivers competing at their home track for local prizes, as well as for a regional and national championship. Participating tracks are divided into geographic regions, offering teams and drivers at each facility a chance to compete against weekly stars from area tracks without leaving their home track. The NASCAR Dodge Weekly Series has been the starting point for many of today's top drivers, including Dale Earnhardt Jr., Jeff and Ward Burton, Kurt Busch, Kevin Harvick, Bobby Labonte, Jamie McMurray, Elliott Sadler, and Greg Biffle.

✔ **NASCAR AutoZone Elite Division:** Four separate series using identical cars comprise this division, which is designed to serve as a local driver's first step towards NASCAR's three national series. The Midwest Series, Northwest Series, Southeast Series, and Southwest Series compete on short tracks, superspeedways, and road courses, providing opportunities for teams and drivers to sharpen their skills and work toward their career goals. AutoZone, the nation's leading auto parts retailer, joined as the title sponsor of this division in 2004. The NASCAR AutoZone Elite Division features 2,900-pound race cars using metal or fiberglass bodies, powered by 350 to 358 cubic-inch engines. Midwest Series events are held throughout Illinois, Minnesota, Wisconsin, and as far west as Colorado. The Northwest Series, stretching across Washington, Idaho, and Montana, gave rise to 2002 NASCAR Busch Series champion Greg Biffle. The Southeast Series covers Kentucky, Tennessee, Alabama, South Carolina, and Virginia, with 2003 NASCAR NEXTEL Cup champion Matt Kenseth getting his start here. The Southwest Series covers Arizona and California and ventures into Colorado for select races. Kurt Busch, Kevin Harvick, and Ron Hornaday, Jr., are some of this series' most famous alumni.

✔ **NASCAR Busch North Series and West Series:** In 2003, changes to the weight, engine rules, tires, wheelbase, and other areas were implemented to bring these two series under one rule book. These cars are powered by 350 to 358 cubic-inch V-8 engines with a maximum compression ratio of 12 to 1. The cars have a 105-inch wheelbase, weigh 3,100 pounds, and run on Goodyear bias-ply tires. The Busch North Series, which entered its 18th season in 2004, runs at tracks in Maine, New Hampshire, Vermont, Massachusetts, Connecticut, New York, Pennsylvania, New Jersey, and Delaware. The Busch West Series, which entered its 51st season in 2004, competes in Washington, Oregon, California, Nevada, Utah, and Arizona.

✔ **NASCAR Featherlite Modified Series:** When NASCAR began more than 50 years ago, teams were permitted to "modify" their stock cars for better performance. The 1950s and 1960s-style coupes sprouted innovative suspension systems and better engines and soon, the cars looked and drove like nothing else in NASCAR. That tradition of innovation continued throughout the 1970s and 1980s, culminating in today's NASCAR Featherlite Modified Series. As the only open-wheeled division of NASCAR, the cars in this popular series are unique in many ways. Featherlite Modified cars weigh 2,610 pounds and have a wheelbase of 107 inches. Hoosier bias-ply tires are used to grip the track under the power provided by "small block" 350 to 360 cubic-inch engines. The Featherlite Modified Series competes throughout Maine, New Hampshire, Massachusetts, Connecticut, New York, Pennsylvania, and New Jersey on tracks ranging in size from a quarter-mile to the 1.058-mile oval at New Hampshire International Speedway.

So, You Want to Drive a Race Car?

Suppose you're sitting at home one day on the couch watching a NASCAR race, and you decide that NASCAR racing is for you. You want to be a rich and famous driver and you want to do it now. What's the first step?

Although you can buy yourself a NASCAR NEXTEL Cup Series car if you have enough money and you can find a team willing to sell, that doesn't mean you can sign up for the Daytona 500. NASCAR issues its own racing licenses; in order to qualify, a competitor has to meet a long list of specifications, including having previous racing experience. You also have to have a lot of cash — or the ability to get a lot of cash from sponsors, friends, or a rich uncle. Racing isn't cheap. Running a good car at a local track can cost $40,000 per season, and an engine can cost another $20,000. You also need more money to maintain the car; buy tires, oil, and gas; and fix the car when you dent it. And believe me, you *will* wreck it — because every driver, no matter how talented he or she may be, runs into obstacles every once in awhile. Some more often than others.

Pre-stock car (not prehistoric) vehicles

If you don't have enough money to buy a full-fledged stock car, you can race more inexpensively with a go-kart. Go-karts are similar to the ones you see on tracks adjacent to miniature golf courses. They are tiny vehicles — tiny in relation to stock cars, that is — with engines attached to the back. But starting out in go-karts doesn't mean you're starting out in racing kindergarten. Certain go-karts can reach up to 100 mph, and they even race on a course at Daytona International Speedway, using part of its high-banked track. Also, you have to sharpen the same driving skills to drive a go-kart that you do for a NASCAR NEXTEL Cup Series car or a NASCAR Busch Series car. Ricky Rudd showed the virtues of go-karts when he went straight from them to NASCAR NEXTEL Cup racing. Go-karts are a viable option — and a great place to get started — if you're itching to race.

You can also find all sorts of programs for kids who want to start young. Midget cars are one of them. *Midgets* are specialized open-wheel race cars that are small, fast, lightweight, and have no fenders. They graduate in size, going from quarter midgets to three-quarter midgets to midgets, the largest cars in the class. Quarter midgets are the cars kids squeeze into for some fun. Jeff Gordon started out in midget cars, so you must be able to learn a thing or two there.

My son, Matt, started racing quarter midgets several years ago, and watching him race is one of the most exciting things in my life. It's been fun to teach him all about the engine, the racing, and the competition — but it's up to him to figure out how to win. He's already done that by winning the championships in his division, showing that he has some racing talent in his genes. Even though he's young and is involved in the sport mainly to have fun, he's developing valuable skills when driving and controlling a car. Who knows — those skills may help him win a NASCAR NEXTEL Cup Series championship someday!

You've got a car — now what?

If you've scrounged up enough money to buy a stock car and want to begin your training, what should you do next? Taking a trip to your local short track is a start. There, you can pick up an application for a NASCAR license. Your car owner and your pit crew (everyone directly involved in your race team at the track) need to get a license, too. (See Chapter 6 for the lowdown on your racing team members.) After you receive your NASCAR license (sent to you or to the track), you're ready to race.

Memorize the rules and get a crew

With your NASCAR license, you also receive a rule book for the series in which you plan to compete. In that book, you can find a rule for every aspect of racing — especially for all the details and measurements of your car — so you should plan to tweak your car for at least a week or two before setting a date for your first race. In the meantime, gather up people for your pit crew because you'll need those people — at least two of them — on race day. Your pit crew will be in charge of your car, tires, and fuel, and will talk to you on the radio during the race. So when choosing a pit crew, choose carefully. Your 70-pound kid brother may not be the best choice.

Moving up and out

As you become successful on your local short track, you can move up to a touring series, which travels from track to track — and sometimes all over the nation. To be eligible for a touring series, you have to first get a license for that particular series, just as you do when you first start racing at your local track.

The better the series, the harder it is to get there

When you want to try your hand at the NASCAR Craftsman Truck Series, the NASCAR Busch Series, or NASCAR NEXTEL Cup Series racing, NASCAR officials get more involved in the licensing process. They do this mostly because they don't want some unskilled guy off the street getting in a truck or a car and taking out the whole field because he doesn't know how to drive. Before you get on the track in NASCAR's top series, you have to fill out a résumé and an application and then send it to NASCAR for review. Officials license you to race in those series when they determine that you're good enough, judging by your résumé and records in other series. Your car owner, race team, and everyone who participates on your team also has to obtain a license — the only difference is that they don't have to submit a résumé. After you're approved, you have to pay an annual fee for your license.

Working on a Crew

It's much easier to become a member of a race team than it is to become a driver, mainly because each car has only one driver but dozens of team members. Some team employees who work at the shop during the week also travel to an event and serve as race-day crew members, changing tires or putting in gas. In recent years, however, the majority of race-day crew members are specialists who don't work at the shop, while other team members, such as engineers, fabricators, and painters, don't travel on weekends. In this increasingly specialized field, one way to start working for a team is sweeping the shop floor — not a very glamorous job but an avenue that can be followed by someone wishing to eventually expand his duties.

You can't really become a NASCAR mechanic if you can't fix a car. Some people learn all about cars after getting their initial jobs at race shops. They show interest and learn from experts, all without getting caught under people's feet. I've got to warn you, though, that it may take you a long time to get promoted from sweeper to mechanic or from sweeper to fabricator (the ones who build the outside, or body, of the car) if you're learning along the way. If you already have a working knowledge of cars, you'll be promoted much faster.

Another way to sharpen your car skills is to go to a vocational school and take classes on how to fix engines or work on bodies. Some schools offer a specific curriculum that focuses on teaching students how to build and repair NASCAR-type cars. In fact, NASCAR has its own such school, the NASCAR Technical Institute, which it operates in partnership with Universal Technical Institute, a vocational school with locations across the country. The NASCAR Technical Institute opened on July 1, 2002, in Mooresville, North Carolina, just north of Charlotte, which is known as "Race City U.S.A." because of the many NASCAR shops located there. In the future, NASCAR plans to open technical institutes in other cities.

Pit crews aren't the pits

If you don't want to work on the car all week at the shop but want to help out during pit stops on race day, there are opportunities for you in NASCAR racing. (See Chapter 10 for more details on making pit stops.) You may have a tough time getting a job on a pit crew if you don't know somebody on the team, though, so be prepared to schmooze or make friends fast. Also, pit stops have become such a big factor in racing that you have to try out for the pit crew before you get the job. You'd better lift some weights and practice changing tires before you show up at a race team's door.

The easiest way to get on a crew is to be willing to do anything, including sweeping floors, to get your foot in the door. If you're an efficient, enthusiastic floor sweeper, people will notice you and you'll get promoted before you know it. It's true what they say: floor sweeper today, crew chief tomorrow. Well, maybe it takes longer than that, but that strategy has definitely worked in the past. Some people I know, including my former crew chiefs Robin Pemberton and Steve Hmiel, wanted to be on a race team when they were young and were brave enough to make a bold move. They just packed up, left their hometowns, and headed for Charlotte, North Carolina, where most of the NASCAR NEXTEL Cup race shops are, hoping to get a job (any job!) with a team. Obviously, it worked out for Robin and Steve, but others have gone that route successfully, too.

Going Fast without Going Broke

If setting up a racing operation is out of your budget, there are other ways to experience the thrill of driving a NASCAR-regulation car at above-average speeds. Many racing schools teach the fundamentals of on-track maneuvering, such as safely learning to run down straightaways and through corners as well as how to pass. These include the *Richard Petty Driving Experience,* which travels the country and allows you to either ride along with a professional or get behind the wheel yourself, and the *Fast Track Driving School,* which operates out of Lowe's Motor Speedway in Concord, North Carolina. Students divide their time between classroom instruction and actually driving on the speedway.

Part II
What Makes It
Stock Car Racing?

The 5th Wave   By Rich Tennant

©RICHTENNANT

WART·X
WART REMOVER

"It looks like your basic family sedan, but several of the body panels are made out of gingerbread."

In this part . . .

*N*ASCAR stock cars have no doors, no speedometer, and no stereo with a sub-woofer. If these facts bewilder you, dive into this part. Tucked into nearly every paragraph, you can find information about NASCAR race cars and how they differ from passenger cars. In the end, you realize why it's impractical and impossible to enter your four-door Ford Taurus in the Daytona 500, even though a herd of Ford Tauruses will be racing.

Even if you're fluent in several languages, understanding the talk of NASCAR-talk may still be difficult. Sway bar? Carburetor restrictor plate? Engine dynamometer? These phrases are commonly used in NASCAR racing, but not at your bingo parlor or hair salon. You can't even find most of them in your dictionary. But never fear, I define those words and plenty more in this part.

In addition to helping you understand the basic components of a stock car, this part fills you in on the rules and inspections of NASCAR racing. You meet all the people who have to follow those rules, including the important members of race teams. You also find out that I do other things besides drive a race car on Sundays!

Chapter 4

What Makes Them Stock Cars?

*N*ASCAR racing has changed since its early days of passenger cars with numbers painted or taped on the sides — the cars raced were often the family car you drove to the track. Races featured cars that fans could go out and buy off the showroom floor of the local dealership the same day they saw them race. Manufacturers wanted their cars to win so they could benefit from a unique type of advertising — as the saying went, "Win on Sunday, sell on Monday."

Today, however, the cars are anything but "stock." They are custom built from the ground up. The only thing vaguely stock about them is the general shape of the body. Teams have engineered ways to make the cars' bodies more aerodynamic, devised methods of producing more horsepower while keeping the engine sturdy, and, with much help and guidance from NASCAR, have devised new safety features to further protect the drivers. After all these innovations, describing the differences between a passenger car and a stock-car racer is like describing the differences between miniature golf and the PGA tour.

In this chapter, I discuss the major differences between passenger cars and NASCAR NEXTEL Cup Series cars, giving you an overview of what you see on the track every weekend.

What Cars Will I See Racing?

Three car models now make up the entries in the NASCAR NEXTEL Cup Series:

- Chevrolet Monte Carlo
- Ford Taurus
- Dodge Intrepid

The manufacturers all have a staff of engineers working in their racing divisions — located in or near Detroit — in order to make their brand more competitive on the track. They work on developing better aerodynamics, engines, and engine parts, and also work with their respective race teams to try to get an advantage over the other car makes. But, as I talk about in Chapter 5, NASCAR officials try to keep that from happening because their goal is for every car to have an equal chance of winning so that fans aren't bored by the same car and the same driver winning each race.

The race car versions of the Dodge Intrepid, Ford Taurus, and Chevrolet Monte Carlo look quite similar to each other, so it's not easy to tell one car from another if you're not familiar with racing. So manufacturers slap the name of the car on every vehicle. For example, the Chevrolets have a big decal with the words "Monte Carlo" on the nose of the car, Fords splash a big "Taurus" in the same spot, and the Dodges have an "Intrepid" decal where everybody can see it. When in doubt, check the front of the car to know which model is which.

Manufacturer loyalty

While some fans cheer for a particular driver or team, others have an allegiance to a specific car manufacturer. For example, if your grandfather drove a Chevy his whole life and your dad drove a Chevy his entire life, you may be persuaded to root for Chevys on race day. It's that kind of loyalty that car manufacturers love — and it's that kind of loyalty that keeps them in racing.

What Is "Stock" about a Stock Car?

Not much of a NASCAR NEXTEL Cup Series car is similar to a passenger car. Stock cars are built for speed and safety, not to take the kids to soccer practice, so they don't have cup holders or vanity mirrors, and none have an automatic transmission. Performance, not comfort or convenience, is what counts — which explains why stock cars last an average of three years, unlike passenger cars, which are manufactured for longevity.

The following are some things that you may be used to seeing on a passenger car but won't find on a NASCAR NEXTEL Cup Series car:

- **Doors:** That's why drivers climb through the window opening to get in.

- **Windows:** There's just a window-shaped opening covered with safety netting to prevent the driver's head and arms from going outside the car during a crash. On the passenger's side, teams install a plastic window that doesn't roll down, but only for tracks 1½ miles or longer. On tracks shorter than that, there's nothing covering the window opening.

- **A glass windshield:** In race cars, the windshield is in three sections instead of just one and it's made of Lexan, which is hard, shatterproof plastic.

- **Back seats or passenger seats:** There's just one seat — the driver's seat.

- **Brake lights or headlights:** The lights you see on the race car aren't real — they're just decals.

- **Speedometer**

- **Gas gauge**

- **Storage space in the trunk**

- **Stereo system or speakers**

- **An air conditioning or heating system**

- **Automatic transmission**

- **Anti-lock brakes**

- **Cruise control**

- **A key ignition:** Drivers just flip a switch to get the car going.

- **Air bags**

- **Locks**

- **Glove compartment**

- **A horn**

The body

The body of a NASCAR NEXTEL Cup Series car is only partly stock. The hood, the *rear deck lid* (or trunk lid, as it's normally called), the roof, the front grille, and the bumper panels are similar to the ones on passenger cars because they're obtained from the manufacturer, although they're modified a bit per NASCAR's specifications (see Figure 4-1). Car builders make the rest of stock-car bodies from scratch. The few factory-made parts on NASCAR NEXTEL Cup Series cars, however, make them recognizable as cousins of the Intrepids, Tauruses, and Monte Carlos that you see driving down the highway. It also helps that teams place decals of headlights on the cars to make them look similar to passenger cars.

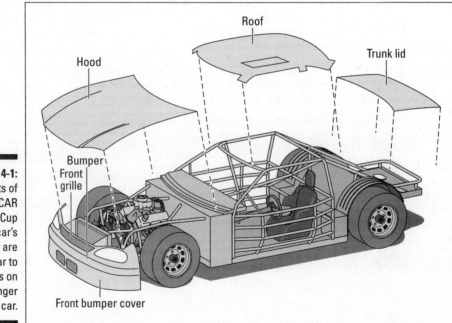

Figure 4-1: Few parts of a NASCAR NEXTEL Cup Series car's body are similar to the ones on a passenger car.

Aerodynamic features

NASCAR NEXTEL Cup Series cars each have a *rear spoiler,* which is a metal blade that runs the width of the car atop the back of its trunk (see Figure 4-2). The spoiler makes the car more aerodynamic by regulating the air as it flows over the car. It also provides stability to the back end of the vehicle. (Flip to Chapter 13 to read more on aerodynamics.) The spoiler collects air as it flows over the vehicle, and the air forces the back end into the ground, making it more stable. You may see passenger cars with spoilers on them, but most of the time they're for looks, not for aerodynamics. Spoilers need to be big enough and mounted at the right angle to help control airflow, and passenger cars generally never go fast enough for aerodynamics, or a spoiler, to make a significant difference.

Some fancier sports cars or snazzier passenger cars may have an air dam that's attached to the front bumper and goes nearly to the ground. Every NASCAR NEXTEL Cup Series car has one, though, because it plays an important role in aerodynamics (refer to Figure 4-2). An *air dam* blocks air as it hits the front of a car, keeping most of it from flowing under the vehicle, which would reduce speed. The closer an air dam is to the ground, the easier a car can cut through the air. The air dam also helps keep the front stable.

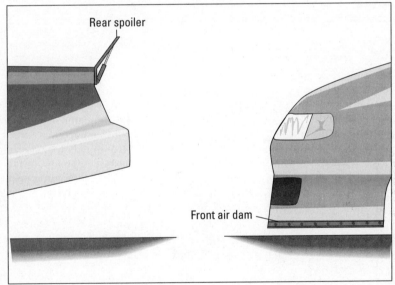

Figure 4-2: A spoiler helps provide stability to the back end of a stock car, while a front air dam regulates the amount of air that flows beneath a car.

Rear spoiler

Front air dam

The engine

A NASCAR NEXTEL Cup Series car uses an 8-cylinder engine (see Figure 4-3), just as the most powerful, sportiest passenger cars do. Here are similarities between a NASCAR V8 race engine and a typical V8 passenger car engine:

- The number of cylinders
- The location of the spark plugs
- The number of intake ports
- The number of exhaust ports

Show cars

If you want to see a race car up close, you don't necessarily have to go to the racetrack. From time to time, you can see one at your local mall or grocery store. Teams have *show cars* that travel around the country so fans can get a taste of NASCAR without having to pay for race tickets. While the cars are just for show, they are real race cars that were taken out of commission for being too old, suffering irreparable damage, or because they just weren't suited to the driver.

The car has everything that a real race car has, including a working engine so the show-car driver can demonstrate to fans how loud a NASCAR NEXTEL Cup car gets. The *show-car driver,* whose job is to drive the show car all over the country, brings the car to stores, fairs, and driver appearances. It doesn't cost anything to check it out, so if you're curious about race cars, these appearances are perfect opportunities to see one in person and get a good look at it.

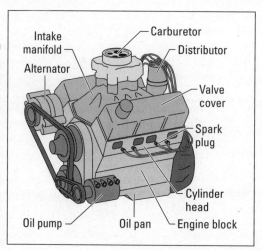

Figure 4-3: NASCAR NEXTEL Cup Series engines are much more powerful than the engines that power a passenger car.

The manufacturers provide teams with engine blocks that have an engine displacement between 350 and 358 cubic inches — cubic inches are one way to measure the size of the engine. A run-of-the-mill passenger car engine has an average of 150 to 200 cubic inches. In racing, the bigger the engine, the more horsepower it will produce.

The manufacturers also outfit the teams with certain performance parts built to withstand 500-mile races, high speeds, and other stresses. After teams get these parts, they start tweaking them to their liking — and that's why not every engine produces the same amount of horsepower. Most produce about 750 horsepower, much more than a passenger car, which averages about 200. The *rpm,* or revolutions per minute, can approach 8,900 in a race engine, which would blow your passenger car's engine to smithereens because its engine can't rev over 5,000 rpm for long. (RPM describes how many times the crankshaft turns. The *crankshaft,* which rotates the drive shaft that provides power to the wheels, is itself rotated by the up and down action of the eight pistons.) With all that wear on a NASCAR NEXTEL Cup engine, teams have to replace many of its parts after every race, including the pistons, valves, and springs — basically anything that may have been worn even slightly. That way, the team helps prevent the engine from breaking during the following event. It takes about two days of work to freshen up a used engine, even if nothing needs to be repaired, because team members must replace many parts and meticulously comb over the engine for potential wear or defects.

Carburetors

Unlike passenger cars that were switched to fuel-injected engines that get better fuel mileage and have fewer emissions that harm the environment, NASCAR stock cars still use carburetors. A *carburetor* mixes air and fuel that pass into the engine's cylinders for combustion, while in a *fuel-injected engine,* an electric pulse triggers the release of a specific amount of fuel, which is then sprayed into each cylinder for combustion. To put it simply, NASCAR teams can get more horsepower from an engine with a carburetor (shown in Figure 4-4) than with fuel injection.

Figure 4-4:
Race cars have carburetors, not fuel injection as passenger cars do, although the drive trains on the two cars are similar.

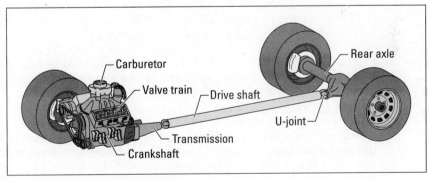

While teams can fiddle with the engines to enhance their performance, they can't do just anything that pops into their heads. NASCAR sets certain parameters for the equipment and makes sure teams follow the rules by policing engines during inspections (see Chapter 5 for more on rules). NASCAR officials have to approve all parts before teams use them to ensure that no one has an unfair advantage. NASCAR's goal is to make races as close and exciting as possible, so no one with an engine made of spaceship parts gets to use it.

Built for strength and speed

In racing, people make their living building high-performance engines that produce a lot of horsepower but can also withstand the grueling conditions of a long race. If that engine builder is a good one, he's bound to make a nice salary because good engines are vital to winning races.

An engine builder in NASCAR racing reinforces parts of the engine, such as the sections around the crankshaft (refer to Figure 4-4) by adding material to the bearing, which is a metal part that protects the crankshaft and the connecting rods from overheating and friction — to help prevent the engine from breaking down during a race. Only steel crankshafts are allowed, although most have been lightened and balanced for increased horsepower. Teams use other reinforced parts in a race engine — in fact, most parts are reinforced — including extra-strength valves, camshafts, connecting rods, and valve springs.

It takes an engine builder about seven working days to obtain parts, tweak those parts, and put together an entire engine. The cost of that completed engine is about $80,000. Some teams build their own engines, while others buy them from outside companies. Sometimes, teams even lease engines if they're trying to qualify for an important race or racing in a marquee event, such as the Daytona 500. The price of a leased engine isn't pocket change, though. It can range anywhere from $10,000 to $40,000 or even more — and you have to give the engine back when you're done.

Engine builders and engine tuners, who work on the engine after it's built to make it produce more horsepower, have turned high-tech along with everything else in NASCAR racing. They use special machines called *engine dynamometers,* commonly known as "dynos," which test an engine's performance and measure its horsepower. During these tests, team members may run an engine for several hours, mimicking a 500-mile race, just to see how the engine will hold up or wear under race conditions and how much horsepower it will produce over the course of a race. The information from the dynos is collected and relayed by computers for team members to analyze the data. If the team finds problems, the engine builder or tuner can make repairs before the car hits the track.

Teams also use machines called *chassis dynamometers* to measure the amount of power translated from the wheels to the ground (see Figure 4-5). It's different from an engine dynamometer, which only tests the engine when it's not in the race car. The entire race car gets hooked up and anchored down to this large gizmo that in many cases looks like a regular old, open car trailer. But two rotating drums spaced the same width apart as the rear wheels of the race car are built into the floor of the trailer, and the car's rear tires are positioned on top of these drums. When the engine is fired up and power is applied to the rear wheels, they begin turning, and the drums begin turning as well. Of course, because the rear wheels are turning the drums, the car stays in place. The measurements from the rotation of the drums allow teams and NASCAR officials to analyze the performance of the cars.

Figure 4-5:
A chassis dyna-mometer measures the power that transfers from the wheels to the ground.

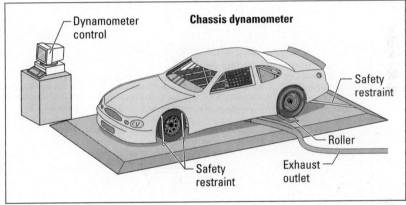

Teams don't build just one engine for a race and then hope it holds out for the duration of race weekend. Well-funded teams can have three engines just for qualifying — a primary, a backup, and a backup to the backup. If a race engine goes bad between qualifying and the start of a race, teams can make a substitution but must start from the rear of the field, regardless of their qualifying effort. Once the race starts, teams can fix individual parts but can't re-install entire engines.

Suspension

Perfecting the *suspension* — or the parts that affect the handling of a race car — is one of the most complex aspects of racing. The gist of making the suspension just right is figuring out how much force to put on each corner of the car. That determines how the car rides, how easily the driver is able to control the car, and how fast he can go through the turns. A car that has good balance among all four wheels handles better, allowing the driver to hit the brakes later going into the turns and mash the gas that much sooner coming out of the turns, which of course means he will go faster.

The suspension in passenger cars has springs and shocks that provide a smooth and comfortable ride at low speeds over a period of years, with few or no adjustments necessary. In race cars, however, a team makes constant changes to the suspension to improve the car's performance. The key is getting the right combination. NASCAR NEXTEL Cup Series cars have independent suspension on the front only, meaning the front wheels act and react separately from one another, while the back ones react the same to every bump, turn, or dip — see Figure 4-6 for a complete look. The adjustable parts of the suspension, as well as other elements that can affect the performance of the suspension, are some of the most important parts of a car's *setup,* which is how the car is prepared to drive on the track with optimum handling and speed. Here's a suspension primer:

- **Air pressure:** Changing the air pressure in the tires is the change most teams use as their first option to try to improve the setup of a car during a race. That's because they can change the air pressure in the new tires *before* the pit stop, so they don't lose any time making adjustments on pit road, which can add seconds to a pit stop, often causing a driver to lose positions. If the car needs more drastic changes because it still isn't riding to a driver's liking, teams can put different amounts of air pressure in each of the tires, change the pressure of only one tire, or change a combination of tires. The amount of air pressure put in or taken out depends on where the driver has problems in the turn (at the entrance, in the center, or exiting the turn).

- **Camber:** Before the race, teams monitor tire wear and tire temperatures to see how the tire is performing on the track. If the tires are wearing out too much on one side, or are too hot on one side, teams will change the *camber* of the tires — changing the angle of the tire so it touches less or more of the racing surface. Camber is measured in degrees from vertical. In addition, camber is adjusted on the front tires to assure they have a uniform temperature.

- **Shock absorbers:** *Shock absorbers* are cylinders attached to the car's wheel that make the car ride more smoothly over bumps. They take care of the tire and control how fast the wheel moves up and down. The key is to figure out the optimum combination of a smooth ride and fast wheel speed. To do that, most teams hire specialized "shock engineers" whose sole job is to build and test shocks and devise ways to make them work better so their car goes faster.

Teams even hook up the shock to a *shock dynamometer* (see Figure 4-6), which pumps the shock up and down as if it were in a real car. The computer prints out results of the test, which show how much force is used when the shock compresses and extends. That's how a team figures out the right shocks and how to adjust them for optimum performance during qualifying or a race.

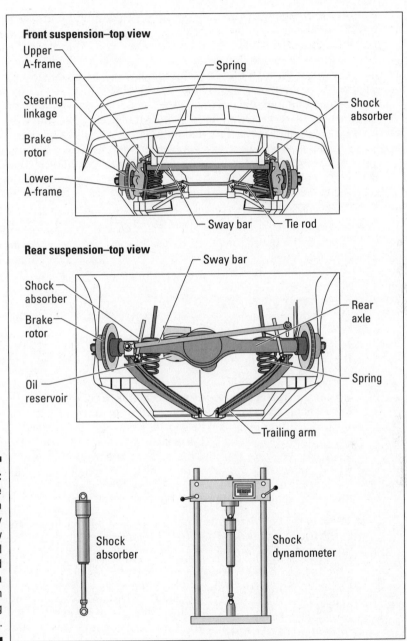

Figure 4-6:
The
suspension
plays a key
role in how
the car will
handle and
how fast a
driver can
drive during
a race.

At superspeedways, shock technology went a bit far in recent years. Teams began to adjust the shocks so that they would depress once the car got on the track but would never rebound. This made the car lower to the ground and improved the aerodynamics, allowing the lower-slung car to cut through the air easier and faster. The problem is that the ride was too bumpy and nearly uncontrollable for drivers — a particular danger at superspeedways. Drivers said the ride was so jarring, it felt like the fillings were going to come out of their teeth. But they were, and are, willing to endure just about any discomfort if it means another couple of horsepower or a couple of hundredths of a second off the stop watch. However, NASCAR decided to use a uniform shock for those racetracks. Teams pick up four shocks with equal specifications on qualifying day and race day at the superspeedways — Daytona International Speedway and Talladega Superspeedway.

✔ **Springs:** Teams have a closetful of springs. The tension on each spring, which is the *spring rate,* determines how smooth the ride will be and how much weight is put on each tire. Some springs compress more easily than others. The key is to get the right spring with the optimum spring rate in the proper corner of the car. What makes it even more difficult is that you can put different springs in all four wheels. Teams can't change springs during a race, but they can insert a rubber block (cleverly called a "rubber") between two coils of the spring to increase the tension or take it out to decrease tension. That makes the handling of the car looser or tighter, depending on which spring (and which wheel) the rubber goes into.

If a car's suspension is *loose,* the rear tires don't provide enough traction, making the rear of the car fishtail when a driver goes through a turn. The driver feels as if he's losing control of the car and about to spin out. This is also called *oversteer.* A *tight* suspension is the opposite: when a driver goes through the corners, the front of the car doesn't turn well because the front tires are losing traction before the rear tires are. When a car is tight, it also means it's *pushing* — and if a driver isn't careful, he'll end up zooming right into the wall.

✔ **Track bar:** The *track bar* is a part of the rear suspension that's attached to the frame on one side and to the rear axle on the other. It keeps the tires centered within the car. Without the track bar, the frame of the car would sway from side to side, making the car unstable and difficult to drive. Teams can raise or lower the track bar by inserting a wrench into a hole located above the right rear tire, and this adjustment makes the car easier to control at high speeds. The track bar is also called a Panhard bar.

✔ **Sway bar:** Most race cars have two sway bars — one in the front and one in the rear — which alter the amount a car rolls to one side or the other through the turns. The front sway bar, which is always used — although the rear sway bar isn't used at some tracks — is attached to the frame and the lower control arms of the suspension. During practice, teams change sway bars to change how much weight is transferring to the springs on each corner of the car. Teams can't make adjustments to the sway bar during a race, so they're stuck with what they put in before the event. At times, though, teams will disconnect the rear sway bar — which is connected to the frame and the rear-end housing — and remove it all together.

✔ **Wedge:** *Putting wedge in* means putting more weight onto a wheel by compressing the spring. Teams can put wedge into the rear wheels during a race by inserting a long socket wrench into a hole above the tires. *Putting a half round of wedge in* means they are turning the wrench in a half circle — and placing that much more pressure on the spring. *Taking two rounds of wedge out* means turning the wrench twice counter-clockwise and loosening the spring. A round of wedge is also called a *round of bite.*

Other differences

Here are some other features that make a NASCAR stock car different from a passenger car:

✔ The steering wheel is detachable, making it easier for the driver to enter and exit the car (see Figure 4-7).

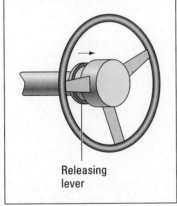

Figure 4-7:
The steering wheel detaches for an easy entrance and exit.

Releasing lever

✔ The car has *roof flaps* (rectangular pieces of metal) that pop up when the car travels backwards. When a car spins at a superspeedway, the aerodynamics change in a potentially dangerous way. The air is not being displaced by the front air dam, but is now rushing under the sides of the car and over the top in a way that causes a car to fly up into the air for a second or two. The roof flap, when it pops open, disrupts the airflow pattern over the roof so all four wheels of the car stay on the ground. See Chapter 11 for more on roof flaps. The roof also has an escape hatch, which allows the driver to pop through the roof of the car if the driver's side window doesn't allow an exit. The roof hatch, introduced in 2003, is not a mandatory installation.

✔ The gas tank — called a fuel cell — is located below the trunk and is farther to the rear than in passenger cars (see Figure 4-8). It's made of steel with an internal rubber bladder that's much stronger and more durable than a passenger car's gas tank.

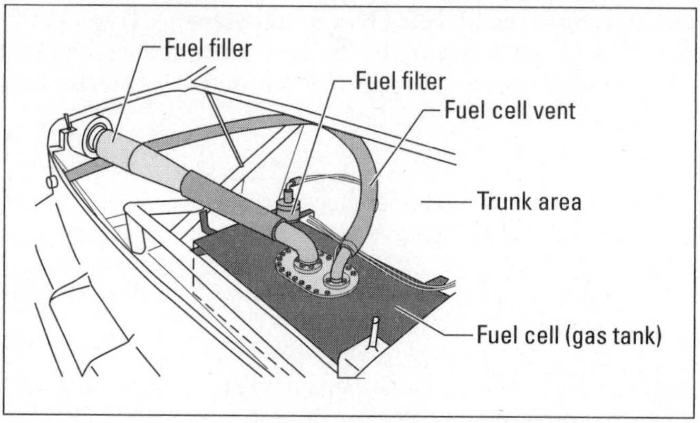

Figure 4-8:
NASCAR NEXTEL Cup Series cars have a 22-gallon gas tank.

Fuel filler
Fuel filter
Fuel cell vent
Trunk area
Fuel cell (gas tank)

✔ The trunk and the hood are fastened down with several steel pins, which allows for quick and easy access but secure attachment as well. Also, steel safety cables are attached between the frame and both the hood and trunk lid to keep them from flying off in an accident.

✔ An internal *roll cage,* made of tubular steel (see Figure 4-9), is a basic and primary safety feature that protects drivers during crashes.

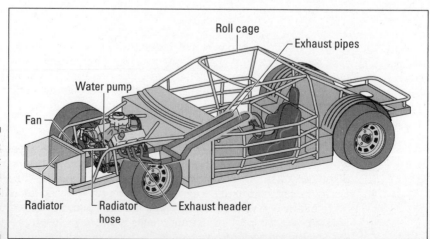

Figure 4-9:
The exhaust system exits the right side of the car.

Roll cage
Exhaust pipes
Water pump
Fan
Radiator
Radiator hose
Exhaust header

✔ The exhaust doesn't exit from pipes at the rear of the car. It exits on the right side of the car, opposite the driver, near the rear tires (see Figure 4-9). The exhaust used to exit on the left side of the car, underneath the driver's seat, but this made the car unbearably hot.

What's Inside?

If you peer inside a NASCAR NEXTEL Cup Series car, you won't find luxurious, finely upholstered leather seats, a radio, or a clock. It's as austere as possible, made for utility and function, not style or convenience. Figure 4-10 gives you a peek inside.

The gauges on the dashboard are a perfect example. You won't find a speedometer to see how fast you're going or an odometer to see how far you've traveled. All cars, however, have a *tachometer* that measures the number of revolutions per minute — or *rpm* — of the engine. It indicates how hard the engine is working.

The gauges in a NASCAR NEXTEL Cup Series car vary from car to car, depending on what the driver is used to, but some of the gauges — in addition to the tachometer — include the following:

✔ Oil temperature

✔ Water temperature

✔ Oil pressure

✔ Volt gauge to monitor the battery and electrical system

✔ Fuel pressure gauge

Next to those gauges you find a few switches, which always include an ignition switch. That's why drivers don't need a key to start their cars. They just flip the switch and the engine roars. There also is a second ignition switch that controls a second ignition box. Sometimes in a race, you see a car drop way back for no apparent reason and just as suddenly recover and start moving toward the front again. That's an indication that the car may have stalled because of ignition failure and that the driver has switched to the back-up ignition to remedy the problem.

Next to the ignition switches are switches that turn on the driver's cooling system, which sends air into the driver's helmet and suit. Also, you may find a brake fan that blows air on the front brakes to keep them cool and working properly. (Cars used at short tracks have rear brakes only, so the extra fans are in the rear in those cars.) A car may also have a rear end fan which to keep the grease cool so the rear-end gear doesn't burn up.

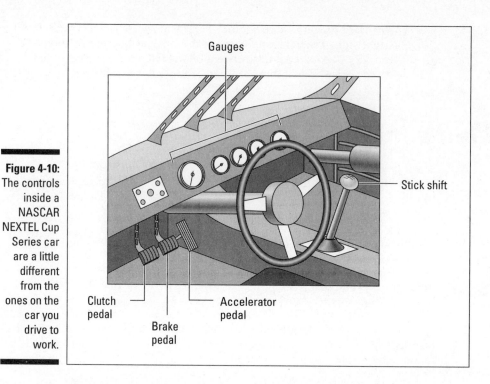

Gauges

Stick shift

Clutch
pedal

Brake
pedal

Accelerator
pedal

If you look at the pedals on the floor of the driver's seat, you notice a brake pedal, a gas pedal, and a clutch pedal. In a passenger car, everyday drivers use their right foot to control the gas and brake pedals and their left foot to control the clutch. In racing, it doesn't necessarily work that way. Most drivers use their right to hit the gas and their left to hit the brake and the clutch. Those who use this two-foot method, including me, believe it is a faster and more efficient way to get on and off the gas and brake.

Take a Seat

A stock car has only one seat, and that's for the driver. And it certainly isn't very comfortable to sit in — see Figure 4-11. The seats are made of aluminum or titanium, covered with padding, and custom-fitted to a driver's body. Even through a driver may spend four hours in that seat during a race, it can't be too comfortable because that would mean it isn't safe enough. The seats must be snug so there's no room to move around, which keeps a driver safer in case of an accident. To protect a driver's ribs, two extensions jut from each side, so that drivers have to wiggle into their seats instead of just sliding in.

The seat also has extensions to protect a driver's legs, head, and neck. Head and neck restraints also are mandatory. And no, the seat doesn't recline so the driver can relax when a caution flag slows traffic.

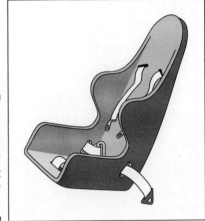

Figure 4-11:
Racing seats are made for safety, not so much for comfort.

Treadless Tires

NASCAR uses high-performance Goodyear tires that don't look much like the ones you use on your family car. And they certainly cost much more than what you'd pay for the ones on your family car. (What do teams pay for these upscale beauties? Roughly $350 to $400 per tire.) NASCAR tires are wider than passenger-car tires — the part that actually touches the ground is about 11 inches wide (see Figure 4-12). They are treadless so that the cars get as much traction as possible — the more rubber that touches the racing surface, the better.

Goodyear employees come to every race and prepare the tires for the teams, including balancing and mounting each tire onto its wheel. Each team has its own set of wheels at each race, sometimes color-coordinated with the car's paint scheme, which a separate company transports to and from each racetrack. Having a separate company deal with the wheels makes it easier for teams because it frees up room on their haulers (see Chapter 6 for more on the race team members) for other equipment. It also allows the Goodyear *tirebusters,* who mount and balance the tires, to start mounting tires even before the teams unload their equipment. On a typical race weekend, NASCAR teams use between 9 and 14 sets of tires, depending on the length of the track. At four tires per set, with 43 cars on the track, that means the NASCAR NEXTEL Cup

Series use up more than 1,000 tires in a single race, and sometimes more than 2,000. By comparison, an average set of street car tires is replaced approximately every three years. Goodyear uses 18 different tire codes to cover the needs of NASCAR NEXTEL Cup Series teams, providing tires with softer or harder compounds to match the tire-wear tendencies of each speedway.

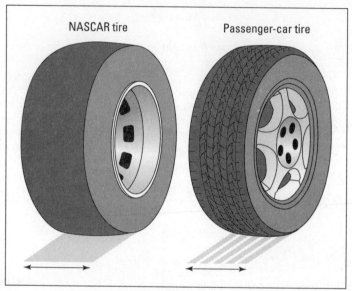

NASCAR tire   Passenger-car tire

Figure 4-12: NASCAR race tires are wider than passenger-car tires and have no tread.

Time Out for Technology

NASCAR NEXTEL Cup Series cars are supposed to be simple, not high-tech. They aren't outfitted with on-board sensors the way Formula One cars are (see Chapter 1 for more on other types of race cars). NASCAR officials make sure cars stay that way by checking the car before every race for computerized items, including the following outlawed instruments:

- On-board computers
- Recording devices
- Electronic memory chips
- Traction control devices
- Digital gauges

In certain cases, though, cars are outfitted with sensors — called *telemetry* — at the request of the network broadcasting the race. The sensors are placed throughout the car to monitor the rpm (revolutions per minute), mph (miles per hour), when and how often the brake and gas pedals are pressed, and which gear the driver selected (with the stick shift). Some networks broadcast that information during the race to show in graphic detail the performance characteristics of a certain car. This telemetry is usually used in conjunction with in-car camera shots broadcast from that car.

Every team has an electronic transmitter called a *transponder* on its car during a race. The transponder, shown in Figure 4-13, is a transmitter that teams affix to the bottom of their car — on the right side of the box that protects the fuel cell — to monitor lap times around a track. Every time the transponder hits a certain point on the track, it records the lap time on a remote computer. Teams huddle around a computer during qualifying to see lap times pop up and who is qualifying where. Also, during a race, those times register on a computer in the pits, so that teams can figure out how fast their car is going relative to the other cars on the track.

Figure 4-13:
The transponder is attached to the bottom of the car and helps time how long the car takes to complete a lap on a racetrack.

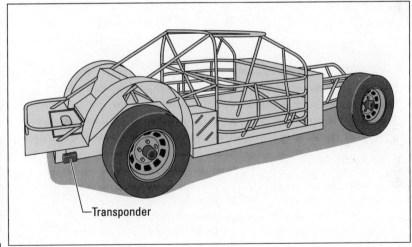

Transponder

Chapter 5

The Rules of the Road

*W*hen sitting in the grandstands at a NASCAR race for the first time, you may have trouble making sense of what the heck is going on. With your binoculars, you can probably see a lot of activity in the garage area, and with your own eyes, you can see what's happening out on the track — but you may not have any idea what to make of it. Don't fret. This chapter gives you the lowdown so you don't feel so lost.

Living by the Rule Book

At the beginning of each year, NASCAR officials hand out rule books to every driver, crew member, car owner, and anyone else with a NASCAR license. They don't give tests on the material, but they do have a clever, effective way to find out whether the racing teams know and follow the rules: NASCAR officials inspect each car several times during a race weekend, checking to see that teams follow the regulations. Inspecting the cars isn't an easy task, considering there are so many regulations to abide by — and so many that teams try to get around them.

A rule for everything

The rule book is crammed with pages of specifications, mandates, and "suggestions." These rules give teams details of how to do almost everything they need to compete, including how to build a car to NASCAR specifications, what safety measures to implement, and how to fill out paperwork such as entry blanks for races.

Some of the other rules deal with the following issues:

- ✔ **Engine:** A team can't have just any engine in their car. It has to be a certain size and must be set up in a certain way, so cancel your call to those NASA engineers for their rocket science advice.

- ✔ **Body:** Even though NASCAR car bodies are hand-crafted in a race shop, NASCAR still enforces rules on the basic shape of each vehicle. That means a team can't have a Ford Taurus body that looks like one of those rocket-type cars on *The Jetsons*.

- ✔ **Tires:** NASCAR tries to contain costs for car owners, so it has specific rules about how many sets of tires a team can use for qualifying and practice.

- ✔ **Gas tank:** Many times, races may come down to which team gets better fuel mileage (meaning which team can make it farther on a single tank of gas), so NASCAR makes sure to check that the *fuel cell* — the fancy word for gas tank — isn't bigger than it's supposed to be.

- ✔ **Testing policies:** Teams are permitted five two-day private car tests and four single-day tests each season at tracks that run NASCAR NEXTEL Cup Series events. Rookies are permitted seven two-day tests and five single-day tests. New teams or those not among the top-45 in the previous season's owner points receive one two-day test and one single-day test until they attempt to qualify for an event. Each time they attempt to qualify, these teams receive another two-day test package. Teams are free to test at tracks that do not run NASCAR NEXTEL Cup Series events, and those tests do not count against their allotment.

- ✔ **Pit stops:** When a car comes in for tires or fuel during the race, the team's pit crew jumps over the pit wall to service the vehicle. But that group can't just do whatever it wants. NASCAR specifies how many people can go "over the wall" to work on a car during a race and has certain rules for how the team should conduct the stop. For more on pit stops and the rules that govern them, see Chapter 10.

While NASCAR has many guidelines for building and preparing a race car for competition, it doesn't have specific rules that govern how drivers race against each other. However, NASCAR does reserve the right to penalize drivers for *rough driving,* such as bumping into the back of another car to pass it or causing another car to crash when an accident could have been avoided.

Drivers have unspoken rules among themselves called *gentlemen's agreements* about how aggressive you should be on the track. Not everybody follows those rules; it depends on the driver. Some are known to race like bullies, knocking cars out of the way to pass them.

NASCAR's rule book is packed with so many regulations regarding the race car that you'd be hard pressed to come up with something that it doesn't have a regulation for. Every crew member has a NASCAR rule book for the series they're involved in, and many of them spend a lot of time figuring ways to get around the rules. I get into that more in the "Being Creative with the Rules" section later in this chapter.

Covering the rules at the drivers' meeting

NASCAR teams and drivers really don't have to sit down with the rule book and study it from cover to cover. They have a pretty good idea of what's inside from starting out on local tracks and making their way through the ranks. If any specific rule changes are made for on-track activity — such as making a pit stop in a very small *pit stall* (the area a driver must pull into so that the crew can service the car) or starting the race on a restart at a particular point on the track — NASCAR officials review those changes during the drivers' meeting. That meeting is normally held two hours before the event, and it's the one time during a race weekend when all the drivers and crew chiefs are in the same place at the same time.

Even the drivers' meetings have rules. Drivers and their crew chiefs must attend the meeting — and be on time — or they're penalized. If a driver or his crew chief misses the meeting, the driver automatically starts the race from the last-place spot, no matter where he qualified. This can be embarrassing for a driver who qualified third but overslept, missed the meeting, and had to start the race in last place. His team gets upset because all the work it put in to qualify up front goes to waste. The sponsors aren't too happy about the driver falling back to last place in the field either. Companies don't pay hundreds of thousands — sometimes millions — of dollars to see their cars start last.

Even though drivers know the rules, they occasionally may ask questions at the drivers' meeting in order to clarify an issue. For example, if a driver isn't sure where to start accelerating when the green flag falls (signaling the start or restart of the race), he asks a NASCAR official to go over that point. Or sometimes a driver uses the drivers' meeting as a chance to speak up about something that has been bothering him. If practice before the race was particularly out of control, a driver may warn his fellow competitors that the race isn't necessarily won by who goes the fastest — it's won by who goes the fastest without getting into an accident. NASCAR officials warn the competitors, too. Often at the drivers' meeting, NASCAR officials tell the drivers, "You can't finish first unless you finish."

Many times, the drivers' meeting is held in an empty bay in the garage area, where chairs are set up for the drivers and crew chiefs. Sometimes, when there is enough room, fans are allowed to watch — but only from outside of roped-off areas. If you have a garage pass, get to the area early because many fans show up to see the proceedings. This is a great time to take a peek at your favorite drivers and snap their pictures while they relax and interact with other drivers. Don't make noise, though, because NASCAR officials can throw you out of the meeting area. You don't want to storm the drivers and crew chiefs for autographs as they leave the meeting either. That's one way to upset them, particularly because they don't have that much time to prepare for the race. They're trying to focus on the competition, not on the T-shirt you want them to autograph.

Passing Those Picky Inspections

Long before drivers go to drivers' meetings or teams put the final touches on their cars, NASCAR officials have to approve their cars to race. Throughout race weekend, NASCAR officials inspect cars to see whether teams are abiding by the rules. If the cars pass inspection, officials give teams permission for their cars to go on the track by placing a small sticker on the windshield. If they don't, teams must work on the cars until officials deem them ready to race.

A race weekend in the NASCAR NEXTEL Cup Series, the NASCAR Busch Series, and the NASCAR Craftsman Truck Series usually begins on Fridays — and inspections begin not long after the garage opens that morning. Teams arrive at the garage early and start preparing their cars for NASCAR inspectors to examine. If the car doesn't pass inspection the first time through, team members know right away that the weekend won't be an easy one.

In this section, I give you the ins and outs of the entire inspection process.

Surviving the initial inspection

The initial inspection begins the morning the track opens, when each car is put on four stands without its tires. Throughout the weekend, inspectors do a quick check of the following:

- ✔ **Body:** Even though NASCAR NEXTEL Cup Series racing involves only Fords, Chevrolets, and Dodges, there's a lot of room for tweaking. So officials must make sure that each of the cars conforms to a certain shape. No missiles or bullet trains allowed. They inspect the shapes of the various makes by using more than a dozen *templates* (see Figure 5-1), which are form-fitting aluminum sheets placed on various parts of the car body, such as the doors or the hood and roofline. If there's a significant gap between the car body and the template, the inspectors won't approve the car to go onto the track until the fabricators reshape the body to make it fit.

- ✔ **Safety belts and nets:** An inspector takes a quick look around the inside to make sure all the safety features are in order, especially the seatbelts and the window net. The seatbelts strap the driver in with five adjoining belts, while the window net is a piece of mesh fastened to the inside of the window to keep the driver's head or arms from coming out of the window during an accident. To make sure these items work, the inspector checks whether they're made of the correct material, that they're properly attached to the car, and that their locking mechanisms are functioning.

✔ **Roll bars:** If a driver rolls his car over, the roll bars are designed to protect the roof from caving in and crushing him. Roll bars now extend down the sides of the cars and help protect drivers in collisions with other cars. An inspector checks these bars with a special instrument to make sure the diameter and thickness of the steel tubing is correct.

✔ **Fuel cell (or gas tank):** Officials check the fuel cell to make sure it holds the correct amount of fuel (22 gallons) and that it has a foam rubber interior to prevent it from breaking open and spilling gasoline. The inspector also takes a look at the *check-valve,* which prevents fuel spills if the car turns over.

✔ **Engine volume and compression ratio:** Even though the engine is checked more thoroughly in subsequent inspections, officials like to give it a once-over during the initial inspection. They check to see whether the engine is the right size and whether the compression ratio is correct. Bigger engines (with more volume) produce more horsepower. Higher compression ratios produce more power, too.

✔ **Metal check:** To ensure teams aren't cheating by substituting a lighter material, such as titanium, for steel (to make their car lighter and faster), inspectors go over the main parts of the car with a magnet. If the magnet doesn't stick, they've caught a team trying to break the rules.

Figure 5-1: Templates are form-fitting aluminum measuring devices that each car must fit before it goes on the track.

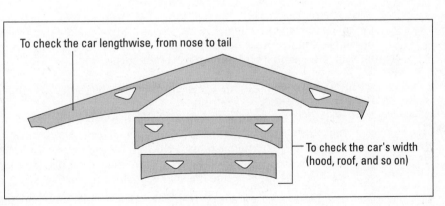

To check the car lengthwise, from nose to tail

To check the car's width (hood, roof, and so on)

If officials catch teams cheating or see something they don't like in this initial inspection, they can ask teams to fix or replace the part or parts in question. If NASCAR gives them an initial okay, the team's next step is to head for a more thorough inspection.

Heading to the inspection line

Even though a team may have gotten through the initial inspection, inspections aren't done for the day. Before qualifying, teams must take their car through a technical inspection line where several officials look at their car. Cars go through *tech,* which is NASCAR lingo for technical inspection, at the following times:

- ✔ Before the first practice of the race weekend.
- ✔ Before qualifying.
- ✔ After qualifying if they win the pole.
- ✔ Just before the race, which is why you may see a line of cars snaking through the garage the morning of race day, with crew members shepherding their cars through the line.

In the inspection line, officials conduct a more thorough check of the cars. If a car fails just one part of the multi-step inspection, the team has to roll the car back to the garage and fix the item in question. Then the team must roll the car through the inspection line again, whether it cuts into practice time or not. When the team gets to the front of the line, officials don't only check the item that didn't pass the initial inspection — they inspect every part of the car all over again. That's just to make sure the team didn't fiddle with anything when they went back to the garage area. If the car passes the inspection, officials put a sticker on the car's windshield indicating it can go out on the track.

For some teams, inspections continue after the race ends. Certain cars, including the winner's, must be inspected one more time before teams pack up and go home. Check out the "Even when a car wins, it's not over" section later in this chapter for more on post-race inspections.

In the NASCAR NEXTEL Cup Series, inspection officials review the following:

- ✔ **Weight:** Crew members push their car through the inspection line with the car's engine off. In order to be weighed, the car must go through inspection *wet,* which means filled with fuel, oil, and water. Without the driver, NASCAR NEXTEL Cup Series cars must weigh at least 3,400 pounds, with at least 1,600 pounds of that weight on the right side.
- ✔ **Height:** As the car rolls on the scales, it also rolls under an arch of metal with a pin attached to its center. That pin reaches down to the car's roof, measuring the roof height of the vehicle. NASCAR NEXTEL Cup Series cars must be a minimum of 51 inches.
- ✔ **Ground clearance:** Teams always want their cars to be as low to the ground as possible (without scraping the ground, of course) so that their cars can cut through the air easily. But NASCAR wants to make sure those cars aren't too low. Officials measure the ground clearance

at various points on the vehicle, ensuring teams aren't trying to get their cars to squat lower than the rules allow in order to get an unfair advantage.

✓ **Compression ratio and engine displacement:** Inspectors use instruments to ensure the compression ratio is 12:1. With higher ratios, engines produce more power. Inspectors also do a check for the overall engine displacement, which reveals the volume of the engine. NASCAR NEXTEL Cup Series engines must be a maximum of 358 cubic inches. Any bigger, and those engines would generate more horsepower. Inspectors also check one of the engine's eight cylinders — a different cylinder every time — each week to keep teams on their toes and make sure no one is cheating.

✓ **Safety:** As with the initial check, NASCAR officials examine the inside of the car, looking for sharp edges on which a driver could injure himself. They also check the safety belts and window nets for wear and tear.

✓ **Rear spoiler:** The *rear spoiler* is a piece of metal that runs the width of the car and is attached to the car's trunk. It plays a big role in determining how air flows over the car and how much downforce is created, which affects speed and handling (see Chapter 13). Officials check the height of the spoiler, from the top of the spoiler to where it meets the top of the trunk and also check the angle of the spoiler to ensure it meets NASCAR standards. NASCAR also uses the spoiler to help regulate the performance of the three car makes and keep them as even as possible. For instance, if the Fords are underperforming compared to the Dodges and Chevys, NASCAR may try to even the gap by increasing the size of the Ford spoiler or by reducing the size of the Chevy and Dodge spoilers, which increases or reduces downforce, allowing a car to go fractionally faster or slower.

✓ **Templates:** Each brand of car or truck has a set of *templates* — individual pieces of metal that conform to the body of a car — that ensure the car fits NASCAR specifications (see Figure 5-2). Each piece conforms to the car in different places — including the nose, the length of the body, and the width of the body — making it a metal blueprint for the shape of a car's exterior. In NASCAR's NEXTEL Cup Series, my Ford Taurus has at least 18 of those templates.

When drivers are fast, officials say "not so fast"

Think a team is off the hook just because their car passed through tech before it went on the track for practice? Not yet. NASCAR officials want to make sure teams aren't cheating, so they make cars go through tech inspection several other times during a race weekend, including just before qualifying (see Chapter 8 for more on qualifying). Afterward, they have to take their place in line on pit road to wait for qualifying to begin — so no chance to go back to the garage and tweak a little bit.

Figure 5-2:
NASCAR inspectors fit templates to a car during inspections.

Copyright Sherryl Creekmore/NASCAR

The top five qualifiers go through inspection again, where officials check height, weight, and the car's body. Even then, the car of the pole winner, who had the fastest qualifying lap, isn't finished with inspection. Prior to the race, pole-winning team members must *tear down* or take apart the car's engine while officials watch. When they have the engine in pieces, officials check everything over again to make sure that the engine is the right size and that all the parts conform to NASCAR rules.

Even though NASCAR officials do a great job inspecting cars, teams standing in line waiting for inspection also police each other. If something on a car looks funny, other teams are often the first to protest, and NASCAR doesn't mind. Other racers are NASCAR's second defense against rule breakers, and the intensity of the competition between the teams helps keep racing fair.

Special tests for special tracks

NASCAR officials use an especially thorough process to inspect cars at Daytona International Speedway and Talladega Superspeedway, the sport's biggest tracks. (Turn to Chapter 13 to get a more detailed look at those two tracks.) Officials conduct special tests at those tracks to ensure driver and fan safety because of the high speeds — upwards of 190 mph — that cars run there.

At Daytona and Talladega, where carburetor restrictor plates are required to reduce horsepower and slow cars down, an official handles the restrictor plates at all times. (See Chapter 13 for more on restrictor plates.) Teams receive their restrictor plates when they go through inspection, but they can't just grab one and slap it on their car's carburetor; it's a carefully regulated process. A team member reaches over a barrier to choose a plate randomly; then an official lifts the plate over his head for everyone to see. After that, the official places the restrictor plate on a pole that measures the diameter of the opening, ensuring it's the same size as every one else's restrictor plate. Finally, he places the plate on the car's engine — see Figure 5-3. Then the engine is sealed with an official NASCAR seal to make sure none of the teams tamper with the engine after it passes inspection.

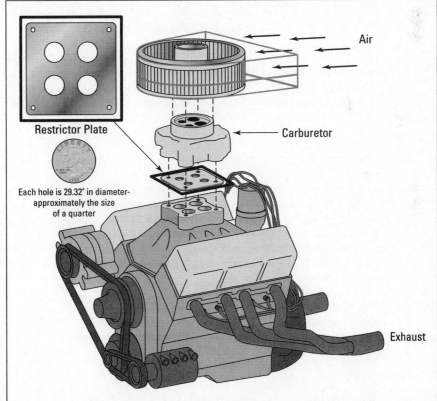

Restrictor Plate

Each hole is 29.32" in diameter-
approximately the size
of a quarter

Air

Carburetor

Exhaust

Figure 5-3:
Carburetor
restrictor
plates
restrict air
flowing into
a car's
carburetor,
reducing
horsepower
and speed.

NASCAR officials take the inspection process at superspeedways further than at other tracks. They often X-ray parts of a car's engine after the races, nearly eliminating the chance of a team getting away with even the smallest infraction. If there are holes in the carburetor, even ones the naked eye can't see, more air leaks into the engine — and the car goes faster, defeating the purpose of the restrictor plates. NASCAR ensures that no holes exist.

Even when a car wins, it's not over

Even after the cars cross the finish line and the winner drives into Victory Lane, the inspection process isn't over. In fact, the hardest part is yet to come. After a driver wins a race, officials follow his car into Victory Lane and watch over it — just to make sure his team doesn't tamper with it while he poses for pictures or sprays champagne over the crowd. After the driver and his team are done whooping it up, the team rolls the car to the gas pumps to fill the fuel cell. The other cars that finished in the top five have already filled up their fuel cells. Then the top five cars go through inspection again, during which NASCAR officials weigh them — which is why they need to fill their gas tanks — and place templates on the bodies for the last time.

The battery of inspections continues: The top two or three cars — depending on how many NASCAR officials choose — head for an empty garage to be inspected again. Another car, chosen randomly, also gets the privilege of joining them. (The first driver who falls out of the race because of an accident or mechanical failure picks a number out of a hat — whichever car finishes in that place becomes the random car to be torn down.) Having a random car torn down is the way NASCAR officials can police cars that consistently finish out of the top five.

Unlike other inspections during the weekend, post-race inspections can take several hours because the teams have to do a thorough tear-down, taking apart the engine, the suspension, the power train, and whatever else officials want to check out. Officials check not only for obviously illegal parts, but also for parts not approved by NASCAR (which may have been modified in hidden places) and illegal additives used in the fuel. Those things may appear legal at first glance.

Here's a quick post-race inspection list:

- Engine: size, compression and so on
- Ignition
- Rear-end gear
- Fuel tank
- Body

- ✔ Power train
- ✔ Fuel (fuel additives)

While teams are happy to win a race, they aren't so thrilled about their post-celebration work at tear-downs. At that point, they've had a long day, often beginning before dawn, and want to go home. When NASCAR officials finally give a team the okay, they place all the car's engine parts into a box to be shipped back in the team truck. The team must put the engine back together at another time, which isn't a big deal because teams use different cars at different tracks anyway. Each team has a fleet of about 12 cars at their shop, each built specifically for a different type of racetrack — some for super-speedways, some for high-banked tracks, some for road courses — all covered in Chapter 13. (Flip to Chapter 4 to find out more about engines and what teams do to prepare them for a race.)

Being Creative with the Rules

NASCAR racing has become so competitive — with so much money at stake — that teams do everything possible to get an edge on the competition. Getting around the rules has lots of names — *interpreting the rules, reading between the lines, using the gray area,* or *being creative.*

Take the templates as an example. Back when templates first came out, there were only two or three of them. So even though teams had to build their car to fit those two or three templates, they did whatever they wanted on every other part of their cars. Now, even though more than a dozen templates exist for each car, teams do the same thing. That's why NASCAR officials keep adding more and more templates — because teams keep trying to get around the rules.

Here are some of the ways teams try to skirt the rules:

- ✔ **Body:** Teams can get an aerodynamic advantage by putting all sorts of nearly indistinguishable bumps and ruts into a car's body.

- ✔ **Tires:** NASCAR officials don't routinely check teams' tires, so some have tried to use that to their advantage. Teams have soaked or chemically treated the tires to make them softer to get a better grip on the track — which does make the car faster, but only for short runs because the soaked or altered tires aren't very durable. If NASCAR officials think a team may be treating tires, they confiscate them for careful inspection, which in the past has even included shipping the tires off for a detailed chemical analysis by an independent laboratory.

- ✔ **Engine:** Teams try to lower the *motor mounts,* where the motor sits in relation to the body of the car, so that the car has a lower center of gravity and handles better.

✔ **Roof flaps or other parts:** To lighten the car, teams constantly try to figure out how to make parts out of lighter material — which is illegal in certain cases where parts must be made out of NASCAR-mandated materials, such as steel. Still, teams are constantly substituting those materials for lighter ones when they install roof flaps, drive shafts, wheel hubs, suspension components, or even nuts or bolts on the engine. They can also drill holes in these parts, another way to make the car lighter. Teams transfer the weight they save to a spot lower on the car to improve handling.

While figuring out ways to bend rules can be quite a creative process, if a team is caught cheating, NASCAR is pretty tough on it. If officials discover something illegal on your car after qualifying but before the race, they make the crew fix or replace the part, and later slap the team with a big fine or put the crew chief on probation, or both. *Being on probation* means that if a team member is caught doing anything illegal again, he can be temporarily or permanently kicked out of the garage. If NASCAR officials discover an illegal part on a car after the race, then they usually fine the driver or take points away from him. NASCAR inspections have become so thorough that the amount of cheating going in NASCAR garages is a fraction of what it was 20 or 30 years ago.

Watching the Flagman

After all the inspections, cars are ready to get out on the track. From that point on, keep your eye on the flagman, who is perched above the racetrack at the start/finish line in a crow's nest of sorts (see Figure 5-4).

Figure 5-4:
The flagman waves the yellow flag signaling a caution.

If you're not sure what all those flags he's waving around are, here's the lowdown:

- ✔ **Green:** To keep things simple, green means go. The flagman waves the green flag to signal the start of the race. During the pace laps, which are run at a slower pace so that cars can warm up their engines and tires, a pace car with flashing yellow lights on its roof leads the field. Just before the race starts, the pace car peels off onto pit road as the flagman waves the green flag. Then, they're off!

- ✔ **Yellow:** The yellow flag, or *caution flag,* comes out when drivers need to slow down because the track is unsafe. This happens in the event of an accident, rain, or when debris or oil is on the track. When the yellow flag is waved, drivers can't race or pass each other. The position of each car in the field is frozen at the moment when the yellow flag flew. Until late 2003, drivers were allowed to "race back to the yellow" because the caution period didn't formally begin until the leader crossed the start-finish line. Often, a driver with a big lead would slow his car on the way to the line to allow lapped cars to make up a lap. To compensate for the elimination of this tactic, NASCAR instituted a new rule that allows the first car one lap down to pass the pace car and make up his lost lap. This rule immediately became known as the "Lucky Dog Rule."

Some fans don't appreciate paying to attend a NASCAR race, only to see it end under a caution flag — which is completely understandable. For me, though, ending under a caution flag is just fine. As for late-race restarts, if I were assured no accidents would happen on the final lap and that every driver would use his head, I wouldn't mind it. After all, the fans are the reason that NASCAR is so popular, and I'm all for giving them a good race.

Drivers don't always feel the same way when a caution comes out. Sometimes, they are happy about it because they need a pit stop for gas or fresh tires, or because the car in the lead is a mile ahead of everyone and cars are bunched back up for a restart after a caution, bringing everyone closer to the leader. Sometimes, though, a driver hates to see a caution flag — especially when he's leading by a mile or when his car drives better after long runs at full speed.

- ✔ **Green-White-Checkered Sequence:** In an attempt to finish races under green-flag conditions, NASCAR in 2004 introduced the green-white-checkered flag sequence. This is used when a yellow flag flies with just a few laps remaining and the race would otherwise have finished under caution. The new procedure consists of a restart of two laps — the green flag for the first lap of the restart and the white flag signaling the final lap leading to the checkered flag. Used only during the last two scheduled laps of a race, the new format does not guarantee a green-flag finish, as only one restart under the green-white-checkered format will be attempted. If a caution comes out during that period, the race is finished. This procedure eliminates the need for a red flag in the final laps to immediately stop the race in an attempt to finish under green-flag conditions. One offshoot of the new rule is that crew chiefs have to recalculate gas mileage, as under regular racing conditions most cars have the exact amount of fuel needed to finish the race as regularly scheduled. With events possibly being extended by two laps, a crew chief has to decide whether to stop late in the race for a splash of gas or gamble that it will finish on the designated lap.

✔ **Red:** If there's too much oil or fluid covering the track surface, it's raining so much that drivers can't see the track, or a damaged wall or fence makes the track unsafe or impossible for cars to continue to circle the track under caution, a red flag comes out. When a red flag waves, cars must stop in line behind the pace car at the spot on the track where the pace car comes to a stop. During red flags for rain, however, they park in their pit stalls. Depending on how long a race is under the red flag, drivers may sit in their cars, get out and talk with one another, or — during a long rain delay — head for their trailers parked in the infield.

✔ **Black:** A black flag signals to a driver that he must get off the track and go to his pits. This happens when something is wrong with his car, such as oil leaking or smoke billowing from the exhaust, which may create a dangerous situation for other cars on the track. The black flag can also come out when a driver breaks the rules, like when he jumps the start.

When a driver is black-flagged, he knows it. Not only does the flagman wave that ominous, dark flag at him, but his car number is also displayed at the start/finish line so drivers know exactly who's in trouble. A driver can't really ignore getting black flagged, either, and just stay out on the track to race, because at some point, officials get peeved and the flagman breaks out a black flag with a white "X" on it, indicating the driver won't be scored any longer. In that case, a driver should give up and head to the pits.

✔ **Blue with diagonal yellow stripe:** When a driver sees this flag, it signifies that faster, lead-lap cars are about to pass him and he has to yield to those cars. A flagman usually waves this flag at a driver who is one lap down and is significantly slower than the cars racing for the win.

✔ **White:** This flag signals that the driver in the lead is on his final lap.

✔ **Checkered:** When a flagman waves the checkered flag, the winner is crossing the finish line.

Chapter 6

Working Together: The Race Team

*Y*ou may not think of stock-car racing as a team sport. Racing certainly seems like an individual sport because the driver gets most of the attention. While a driver is arguably the most important part of a race team, he isn't the only reason a team wins or loses. Dozens of people work on a race team and contribute to the performance of a car every weekend. From the owner to the crew chief, the engine builder, and the guy who orders parts, everyone on a team has to work well — together — in order for the team to succeed (see Figure 6-1).

Figure 6-1:
Working well as a team is essential to winning any NASCAR NEXTEL Cup Series race.

Copyright Sherryl Creekmore/NASCAR

Consider the driver racing's version of a quarterback. Even a good quarterback can't accomplish much if his team lets him get sacked.

The Owner Is the Boss

In NASCAR NEXTEL Cup Series racing, just as in any sport, the players — in this case, the drivers — get most of the credit. But drivers wouldn't have jobs if somebody didn't employ them. The person who employs NASCAR drivers is the team owner.

Characteristics of a good owner

The *owner* has the final say in hiring everyone who works on the team, from the driver to the crew chief to everyone who prepares the cars for racing. The owner spends money on cars and parts, which are quite pricey. For example, tires cost nearly $400 apiece. But a far larger expense is all the cash the owner shells out for payroll — which isn't cheap, considering how competitive the sport is and how valuable talented employees are. With all those bills to pay and paychecks to sign, an owner has to be a shrewd and savvy businessperson. The owner has to do one thing first: secure a sponsor.

The owner approaches large corporations and asks for anywhere from $4 to $10 million to sponsor a race team for the season. The owner has to convince the companies that paying that kind of money will lead to exposure, and ultimately, better sales for their product. To get sponsors, the owner needs to understand the business world beyond the business of running a race team. But he or she also needs to know racing. An owner has to be able to recognize driving talent on the racetrack, and much like a team owner or a coach in other sports, needs to be able to create an environment in which that talent can flourish.

Car numbers are the owners' domain

Car numbers are assigned by NASCAR to team owners. Although drivers change teams, the car number they previously drove remains the domain of the team owner, as long as the owner remains active. For example, when Bill Elliott began driving a reduced schedule in 2004, his replacement, Kasey Kahne, became the driver of the No. 9 Dodge and Elliott drove the new No. 98 Dodge.

Good team owners don't come around often

My car owner, Jack Roush, is in my opinion the best team owner in racing. I also consider him my surrogate father, since my father, Julian, died in a plane crash in August 1998. Jack has looked out for me since we teamed up in 1988 on his new NASCAR Cup Series race team, and we've been together ever since, through the good times (winning races and nearly winning the NASCAR Cup championship) and the bad times (going winless throughout the entire 1996 season). It's not an exaggeration to say that I wouldn't have been as successful if it weren't for Jack Roush.

The best relationships between owners and drivers are the ones with give and take, and lots of trust. You can see that trust in the top driver-owner relationships, including the one between Jack Roush and me and between Rick Hendrick and Jeff Gordon. Without mutual trust, Jack and I would have had less success.

Jack and I get along well right now because we're both proud of the team we've built and the success we've had in recent years. Also, Jack and I have similar approaches to dealing with the team and the race car. He's one of the most hands-on owners in NASCAR NEXTEL Cup racing, overseeing everything for each of his race teams, from the engine program to the body shop to the processes at the racetrack. And I'm one of the more hands-on drivers in the series, working with the crew chief, car chief, and engine specialist to understand exactly how the car is working and precisely what can be done to make it go faster. Some owners and drivers sit back and let the team figure things out, which definitely isn't our style. Jack and I are similar in the way we do things — and we both care about making our team as good as possible.

Most NASCAR owners are men, just as most drivers and team members are, but several women own teams. Georgetta Roush, the mother of Jack Roush, my team owner, owns one of Roush Racing's five teams, but she isn't involved in the day-to-day operations of the team, as is the case for many female team owners.

Some NASCAR NEXTEL Cup Series team owners have become as famous and as popular as their drivers, and some fans have a stronger allegiance to a team owner than they do to a driver. So, they'll cheer for any car, for example, that Robert Yates owns — no matter who's behind the wheel.

The following are a few of the more famous — perhaps even legendary — NASCAR team owners today:

- ✔ **Richard Childress:** Childress was the long-time car owner of one of the most famous drivers in NASCAR history — seven-time NASCAR Cup champion Dale Earnhardt. Together, the Childress-Earnhardt No. 3 Chevy team won six titles. Childress was a race car driver before deciding to go the ownership route, which turned out quite well for him. He didn't win any NASCAR Cup Series races as a driver, but has won more than 76 races as a car owner.

- **Rick Hendrick:** Hendrick became a NASCAR Cup Series team owner in 1984 with Geoffrey Bodine as driver and then became one of the first multi-car team owners (see the "Multi-car teams — the more the merrier" section) in the series. From 1995 to 1998, Hendrick won four consecutive championships — with Terry Labonte behind the wheel in 1996 and Jeff Gordon winning in the other three years.

- **Roger Penske:** Penske's love for racing began as an open-wheel car driver when he was young. He then branched out into ownership. He owns the teams of Rusty Wallace, Ryan Newman, and Brendan Gaughan, and also owns teams in the IRL series featuring open-wheel cars, where his cars have won a record 13 Indianapolis 500s. (Turn to Chapter 1 for more on open-wheel cars.)

- **Richard Petty:** Petty is known as the king of stock-car racing not only because of his seven NASCAR Cup Series championships and NASCAR-record 200 wins, but also because he's been a successful car owner and has always made himself accessible to the fans throughout his long and famous career. The Petty family has always fielded its own cars, so Richard knows what he's doing as a car owner. When Petty first began driving in 1958, many drivers owned their cars and teams because it was so much less expensive than today, and because they wouldn't have been able to race if they didn't. Petty stayed an owner even as NASCAR changed and costs skyrocketed. It helped that STP oil treatment was his longtime sponsor (replaced now by Cheerios). It's has also helped that he won so many championships and races. Petty Enterprises also fields the No. 45 car driven by his son Kyle.

- **The Wood Brothers:** Len and Eddie Wood have been involved in NASCAR since their father, Glen, began racing in 1953 — just a few years after NASCAR was founded. The two sons continue the family tradition with one of the most famous and longest-running teams in the business. Ricky Rudd drives the Wood Brothers' No. 21 Ford, which has logged at least one victory in each of the last five decades, and almost 100 overall.

- **Robert Yates:** Team owner Robert Yates, perhaps the best engine builder in NASCAR, finally won a championship in 1999 after years of coming close. Dale Jarrett, one of his two drivers, dominated most of the season in the No. 88 Ford to win the title. Some of NASCAR's greatest drivers have driven for Yates since he became a team owner in 1989, including the late Davey Allison, who drove the No. 28 Texaco Havoline Ford. Jarrett and Elliott Sadler are teammates in Yates's two-car operation.

The sponsor doesn't give commands

Even though *sponsors* — the companies that pay for the right to have their names on cars — pay most of the bills, they don't get to hang out at the race shop as much as they may want or give advice to drivers on how to make their cars run faster. Although some sponsors show up at the race shop more often than others, the role of a sponsor is usually limited to paying the bills or handling marketing.

Some sponsors don't like this limited role very much. Considering how much cash their companies are laying out, some sponsors feel they should have a say in how a race team functions, meaning which driver to hire, and which changes should be made to the race car. When a sponsor starts making those sorts of decisions, however, it's almost never good for the race team — unless that sponsor has been a successful NASCAR NEXTEL Cup Series team owner, driver, or crew chief! Running a race team is usually best left to the people involved in racing: Those who know the business and are responsible for a team's performance on the track. Everyone else should just enjoy the results.

Multi-car teams — the more the merrier

In the old days, guys used to haul one car down to the track, gather up whoever was around to change tires or fill up the tank during pit stops, and go racing. Even when the sport got more technical in the 1970s and 1980s, one owner usually employed one driver and had one race team.

When teaming up pays off

When I started racing for Jack Roush in 1988, I was his only driver and my team was the only NASCAR Cup Series team Jack had to worry about. But Jack was one of the first owners to realize the benefits of owning two teams. So in 1992, I had my first teammate — Wally Dallenbach, Jr. And on paper, it paid off. I won twice that year, was second five more times, and had 17 top-ten finishes all together. Today Jack has five NASCAR Cup teams, with myself and drivers Matt Kenseth (the 2003 NASCAR Cup champion), Kurt Busch, Greg Biffle, and Carl Edwards. The five of us have a similar approach to racing, so it's easy to communicate about what's going on with our cars and what we should tell our crew chiefs.

Our crews work well together, too, telling each other what we've learned and making suggestions for how we can each go faster. I've even got my hand in the ownership of one team. I think getting the teams to work together helps all of us have more success.

On the track, the teammate relationship exists — but to a much lesser extent. If I'm leading a race and Matt or another teammate had an earlier problem and is a lap down but still running strong, I may let him get back on the lead lap by allowing him to pass me. Or if one of my teammates has a faster car than I do and I know it, I may not try to fight him off — I'll probably just allow him to pass. But believe me, if I were battling for the win with one of my teammates, I'd race him just as hard as I would anyone else. Even though we're teammates, we still want to kick the pants off each other.

That's not the case any more. One of the most crucial components in being successful in racing is information: what a crew learns about the car and the tracks, what makes a car go faster, and what doesn't. With more money coming into the sport during the 1990s, owners quickly realized that one way to get more information was to use more than one team. When an owner has only one driver and team, he only has one source of information. But when he adds another team, he gets more — and better — information.

NASCAR limits teams to five two-day and four single-day test sessions, so an owner who has multiple teams multiplies his test dates. (Rookies are allowed seven two-day tests and five single-day tests to gain extra experience.) At the racetrack, multi-car teams can do a bit of experimenting. One car can run a particular setup — spring ratios and tire pressures and other things — while another tries something slightly different. As practice goes on, the crews determine which car handles better and which one runs faster. After practice is over, they can exchange the data and determine which setup is best, although different drivers sometimes prefer a different feel to the car, so teams may have to incorporate further adjustments to set up each individual car for a multi-car team.

Because the demand for information has grown so much in recent years, it has become harder and harder for single-car teams to survive. One team owner with one car simply can't learn enough about new tracks and new technologies to compete against the multi-car teams and really hope to contend for a championship. So as stock-car racing moves into the 21st century, expect the majority of owners to field more than one car in each race.

Many multi-car teams have several different owners on paper. Only two teams per owner are eligible for NASCAR's bonus programs. (See Chapter 12 for a list of bonus programs.) Those programs can generate a good deal of money, depending on a team's performance, so every team owner wants to be involved — even it means fudging a bit when it come to team ownership.

Team Managers Organize the Operation

When I started racing, I thought of a team manager as the kid in high school who got water and cleaned towels for the football team. But in racing, the *team manager* serves as the owner's representative in the shop: someone who oversees everything, including ordering equipment, hiring personnel, and organizing test sessions. There are just too many details for the owner and crew chief to deal with, so the team manager position was created. Not every race team has a team manager, but anytime a team can have another experienced person around, it's bound to help. Just don't confuse him with the guy who's supposed to get water for the driver.

The team manager is usually someone with a lot of experience working on race cars, often someone who had been a long-time crew chief, but wanted to step back and take a more administrative role. The team manager isn't hands-on when it comes to how the car is running at a specific time, but is entrusted with hiring candidates for specific jobs.

After the team is assembled, the team manager's job is to get the people to work together, to make sure each individual person is doing his individual job. He works closely with the crew chief in overseeing everyone, and — if the owner owns more than one race team — he makes sure the teams are working together, sharing ideas and information that may benefit both on race day.

The Crew Chief: A Race Team's Head Honcho

No driver can will a lousy car into Victory Lane. It just can't happen. Racing isn't like other sports, where the equipment is the same across the board. Michael Jordan didn't suddenly have to shoot a deflated basketball while the other team got to use the regular kind. Mark McGwire didn't have to swing a hollow bat while everyone else got a solid one. But some days, drivers are presented with race cars that just aren't fast enough to win.

That's where the crew chief comes in. A *crew chief* oversees everyone in the shop to make sure they're building cars that will go fast on the racetrack. He works from his own experience and whatever notes he may keep on how cars have reacted in the past on certain tracks under certain conditions. The crew chief tells each of the workers under him the specifications for doing their jobs, both at the shop and at the racetrack. He determines how the car bodies are built, how the springs and shocks are adjusted, what level of air pressure to run the tires at — everything. It's a big job. Because of that, he usually works longer hours than anyone on the team, looking at numbers and considering possibilities. A great crew chief needs to know everything about a race car, his driver, and the track he's going to run next.

A good crew chief is hard to find

When I raced in the American Speed Association (ASA) Series, a non-NASCAR stock-car series based in the Midwest, I worked with crew chief Jimmy Fennig. We hit it off right away. He was as intensely dedicated to racing as I was, so it was a perfect match. Jimmy and I won the 1986 ASA championship in just our second year together. In those two years, we won nine races and 13 poles, which is amazing considering we hadn't worked with each other for that long. We couldn't stay together forever, though. While he was the crew chief in 1986 when I ran my first five NASCAR Cup races, I wasn't ready to drive full time in the series — and he was, so he had to move on without me. Jimmy, who is from Milwaukee, Wisconsin, worked with NASCAR Cup champion Bobby Allison and almost a dozen other drivers until we decided to work together again in 1996 — and that's one of the best moves either of us ever made, considering what great chemistry there was between us, even after all those years apart. In 1998, we won seven races, the most I've ever won in a season, and finished second in the championship. Without Jimmy, I couldn't have done that.

One thing that doesn't change in NASCAR, however, is that everything *does* change. It's difficult to sustain an ideal driver–crew chief relationship over the long haul, especially during a slump. Jimmy eventually moved on to another of Jack's teams. He is now Kurt Busch's crew chief and they've been terrific together. I've now got Pat Tryson as crew chief, and we work great together, too; plus he's assembled one of the best crews I've ever had.

Although drivers get a lot of attention, crew chiefs have started to become stars in their own right, too. The top crew chiefs have their own trading cards, and they're often asked to sign nearly as many autographs as the drivers — all for doing a job that used to be considered anonymous and not very glamorous. They deserve all the attention they get, though, because they have as much to do with success as anyone involved. Here are two of the better-known crew chiefs:

- **Ray Evernham:** Some people say Jeff Gordon wouldn't have won his first three championships without Evernham setting up his cars and talking him through a race. That may or may not be true, but there's no doubt that Evernham and Gordon had one of the best combinations in racing when they were together. They had that special chemistry that a team needs to win races. Saying he needed a bigger challenge, Evernham left the team in late 1999 to become a car owner and field a multi-car Dodge effort.

- **Robin Pemberton:** Pemberton was my crew chief from 1988 to 1991; his brother, Ryan, also is a crew chief on the circuit, so technical skills run in the Pemberton family. Robin left my team to be Kyle Petty's crew chief, but not because we had a falling out. He just needed to move on with his career and pursue other challenges. In August 2004, Pemberton was named NASCAR's Vice President of Competition.

If You Need Something Done, Go to the Car Chief

Racing has gotten so big over the past few years that owners have had to add another layer of management to their teams — the car chief. The *car chief* is the person who works closely with the crew chief in figuring out setups for the car, but is the actual guy who makes sure it gets done. That allows the crew chief more time to work on a computer or look through notes to figure out better setups and to work on race strategy. When the crew chief does decide on a setup, he discusses it with the car chief — and then the car chief goes to the garage and implements the changes. The car chief gathers other crew members together, tells them what to do, and then rolls up his sleeves and helps get the job done.

Believe It or Not, the Driver Does More Than Drive the Car

The driver often ends up getting all of the credit — and a lot of the blame — for how a race team performs. But when you look at the team picture, the driver is just one part. That's particularly true before the race starts.

During the week leading up to a race, the driver may or may not come to the race shop where the cars are being prepared. The crew chief has conversations with the driver about how the car should be set up, but for the most part, the team does all the work at the shop.

Meeting the team scorer

On race day, each team has its own *scorer* who counts how many laps a car has made around the track. He or she scores laps by hand (using a good, old-fashioned pen and a piece of paper), but computers also are used. For the official tally, NASCAR Timing & Scoring has an electronic system which keeps track of cars on the speedway. Each car has a *transponder* (a small box) attached to its underside. That transponder transmits a signal to NASCAR computers every time it completes a lap. That's how NASCAR knows exactly the position of each car and how many laps it's run, just in case teams question it.

After everyone arrives at the track for a race, teams try to improve their cars during *practice sessions* (when drivers complete laps around the track, and then come into the garage to tell their crew chiefs what the car is doing). Drivers describe whether the car is reacting correctly to the track and where it needs to go faster — on the corners or in the straightaway. The crew chief then determines which adjustments to make.

After the race starts, the driver's role may seem rather obvious — get to the finish line before everyone else. But it's a little more complicated than that. I talk more about the driver's role, and what he has to do during an entire week, in Chapter 7.

Practice for a NASCAR NEXTEL Cup Series race is some of the most important time of the weekend. While the cars may appear to be simply going around in circles, in reality, everyone is involved — the driver, the crew chief, the team manager, and the crew. The team is finding out everything they need to know about how the car will perform under race conditions.

Practice in stock-car racing is a little different than in other sports, in which practice takes place behind closed doors. You don't see the Packers practicing in front of the Broncos before the Super Bowl. But in racing, everybody gets to see how fast everyone else is running. (How a driver runs in practice usually determines how fast he'll be during a race.)

And the Rest of the Team . . .

Besides the owner, the crew chief, the car chief, and the driver, other team members work the garage, too. Those team members do much more than just strut around looking important. Even though they aren't the primary decision makers on a team, they're important components to building a winning program. Keep in mind that not every team member goes to a race, only a set group goes. The others stay at the race shop and work on cars for future races. Here are some that go to the track:

✔ **Engine specialist:** The *engine specialist,* or *engine tuner,* is in charge of taking care of the engines after they get to the racetrack. Engine specialists are the guys you see running around the garage with a tray of spark plugs and a magnifying glass. The engine specialist *reads* a spark plug by examining the insides of it and checking for signs of heat — color variations or spots. After reading spark plugs, the engine specialist determines what he needs do in order to get the optimum power output from the engine. The engine specialist is also responsible for the engine's overall health at the track.

✔ **Tire specialist:** The tire specialist isn't tough to spot — he's the guy who spends the entire day hanging around the team's tires, changing the air pressure, checking the heat buildup, or measuring the wear of a tire after it has taken a few laps on the track. The tire specialist uses an instrument to figure out how the tire has worn in certain places — the inside, middle, and outside of the tread. He also measures the temperature of the tire in these locations to determine the heat buildup. The way a tire wears or how hot it is in certain places reveals how the car is driving on the track. If one tire is too hot in one spot or worn out in one specific place, crew members change the car's setup so that tires touch the racing surface more evenly and smoothly — and many times, that means the car goes faster. The measurements a tire specialist makes are miniscule, so the job may seem insignificant, but it's critical.

✔ **Engineers:** NASCAR racing prides itself on not using any onboard computers to maximize the car's output the way other racing series do. Still, that doesn't mean NASCAR is dead set on staying behind the times. Over the past few years, stock-car racing has seen an influx of engineers who've used their advanced degrees to improve how a car runs. Many teams use engineers to calculate the exact setup for a car on a certain track, including precisely how each shock should be built, which springs should be used, and what tire pressures will be best. Most teams have become so large and specialized that they have one engineer specifically devoted to the shock absorbers. At first, many old-timers in the sport — and some of the young people — resented the engineers for bringing too much technology to NASCAR, which had traditionally been a grass-roots sport. They felt that stock-car racing should stay as basic as possible, and remain accessible to people without fancy college degrees. But as racing has become more competitive, engineers have become must-have additions to each team.

✔ **General mechanics:** While many team members have specialized titles with specialized jobs, some are all-around workers who can do just about anything. General mechanics can help the car chief set up the car, build shocks back in the trailer, or rework the body of a car after a driver crashes it into the wall. Every team has to have a few general mechanics to get by — and I feel kind of funny saying that because in the past, *everyone* was a general mechanic. But now it seems everything is changing and becoming more specialized. Ask the shock builder how to change an engine and he may laugh at you and run away (hopefully not with your shocks in his hands). So every team has to have some people with versatility.

✔ **Pit crew:** A maximum of seven people are allowed to go over the pit wall and service a car during a pit stop. Although some crew members — mechanics, crew chiefs, car chiefs, and tire specialists — still do double duty by working at the shop and pitting the car, some teams fly specialized pit crew members to the track on race morning. To find out more about pit crews and pit stops, turn to Chapter 10.

✔ **Truck driver:** He isn't the primary pilot, but a team's truck driver has a very important job. If the driver doesn't do his job right, the team may show up at the racetrack and not have any equipment. The driver must be on time and be careful driving the rig with millions of dollars of equipment in it. Once at the track, the truck driver also is responsible for keeping the inside of the truck in order, and maintaining a complete inventory of what is inside, including the following items:

- The primary car

- The backup car

- All the uniforms and equipment of the driver and crews

- Tool chests and the pit cart, which carries extra parts for the chassis and engine from the garage to pit road

- Shock dynamometers to figure out how a shock reacts on the track (see Chapter 4 for further explanation)

- Extra sheet metal, including noses, and rear sections for the car, in case of an accident

- Cabinets and drawers filled with snacks for the team to munch on during long days at the track

The team hauler is the place where the team members hang out when they're not working on the car. It's a place to relax and grab some lunch — as well as a place to hold ultra-serious meetings on how to make the race car better. Most haulers have a lounge in front, equipped with a TV, stereo, desk, table and a couple of comfortable couches. The team hauler is where a crew chief goes to crunch numbers for setups, where a driver goes to take naps and where a team owner goes to fire or hire a driver at the track. It's the only private place in the garage area where team members can sleep, hold meetings, or work in peace.

The team's schedule

A race weekend in the NASCAR NEXTEL Cup Series isn't easy or relaxing for a race team. It consists of several long, grueling days. The weekends usually begin on Thursday for the drivers and teams, when they get on a plane to travel to the racetrack. In the late afternoon or early evening, teams and drivers arrive in the town the race will be held, go to dinner, and then get a good night's sleep for Friday's activities, which usually consist of qualifying and practice sessions. The team needs plenty of sleep because the garage usually opens before dawn and closes past dinnertime. Teams practice and qualify their cars on Friday and Saturday; Sunday is race day, of course.

Race weekends in the NASCAR Busch Series and the NASCAR Craftsman Truck Series aren't quite as exhausting because, most of the time, they aren't as long. Many events in those two series last just two days, with qualifying on the first day and the race on the second day.

The People behind the Scenes

The work doesn't end when the race ends. Dozens of team members wait back at the shop for the car to return from the race so they can fix it up and prepare it for the next race it will run, whether the race is the following week or in a month or two. They also build engines, build car bodies, and test parts. Although the following team members work behind the scenes, they shouldn't be overlooked:

✔ **Fabricators:** *Fabricators* have a special talent. They take stock sheet metal parts provided by the manufacturer and fasten them together on the car frame before molding it all into a sleek, aerodynamic race car. They trim the metal, then make it fit the car's frame precisely — called *hanging a body* in racing terms. If the body isn't hung properly, the aerodynamics of the car won't be as good as they should be. And that slows the car down.

✔ **Engine builders and engine assemblers:** An engine doesn't just show up at a race shop ready to be put into a car. Unless a team leases its engines from another engine builder, the engine builders on a team are in charge of building the engine nearly from scratch. Engine builders figure out how to make the engine as light, but durable, as possible. Then engine assemblers put the engines together. The engine tuner, discussed in the "And the Rest of the Team . . ." section earlier in this chapter, takes over from there.

✔ **Parts specialists:** At the race shop, teams have a specialist for everything. For example, a suspension specialist is responsible for taking apart the suspension from a race car that just raced, and then testing to see which parts need to be replaced. Having tons of specialists running around isn't a bad thing, considering how much pressure there is to win races. Teams can't afford to lose races because some small, insignificant part falls apart after too much use. That's why everybody on the team is so meticulous when building and improving the car.

Chapter 7

Who's in the Driver's Seat?

Despite what you may think, NASCAR drivers do much more than just hop in their cars, drive around in circles, win races, and make money! Much more goes into racing than that, so much so that test sessions, races, sponsor luncheons, and commercial shoots take up nearly every second of a driver's day.

With so many non-racing activities filling a driver's schedule, racers today must be versatile — they must be great drivers, competent public speakers, astute businessmen, and half-decent actors (though not necessarily Oscar winners).

The Role of the Driver on the Racing Team

Even though drivers are super-versatile, their primary job is to get into cars and take chances for three or so hours every Sunday — and nothing will ever change that. Drivers also have a better feel for their cars than anyone else, so their feedback to their crews about how to make the cars race faster and handle better on the track is crucial. My current crew is one of the best I've ever had, but they're not mind-readers, so it's up to me to tell them what I need them to do to make the car better.

A driver isn't just a figurehead who gets all the credit and all the headlines in the newspapers. He has to work to make his money, just like everybody else.

During practice, a driver doesn't shut up

It's not to a driver's advantage to be shy when practice begins. It's his job to jabber about everything his car is doing to his team, face-to-face after he finishes the run or over the in-car radio. The more input the team gets about the car, the better work they can perform.

Here's a scenario of what the driver may say to his team throughout a typical practice:

- ✔ The driver shows up for practice, dressed in his driving uniform, and ready to go. He slides into his car and takes a few laps but notices the car is *loose* as he enters the turns, meaning the rear of the car is starting to fishtail because the rear tires are losing traction. He contacts his crew via the in-car radio, tells them what's going on, and then heads into the garage.

- ✔ After the car rolls into the garage, the crew chief (or maybe the car chief or the engine specialist) runs to the driver's window to talk more about what the car was doing. They may, for example, decide to change the air pressure in one of the tires to see whether that does the trick. Of course, they're working in a rush because they only have a limited time for practice — and it never seems like enough when your car isn't running well and your team is scrambling to find out what's wrong.

- ✔ The driver takes to the track with his new setup but quickly finds that the car isn't driving smoothly and that he's having trouble turning the car. There are several terms drivers and crew use to describe how their car is handling. A car is *loose* when a driver goes through a turn and the rear of his vehicle starts to fishtail, making the driver feel as if he's losing control and about to spin out. The rear tires aren't sticking well to the track and providing enough traction. When the front tires don't turn well through the turns because the front tires are losing traction before the rear tires are, the car is *tight*. When a car is tight, it also means it's *pushing*, and if a driver isn't careful, he will end up zooming into the wall.

Although driver input is critical in preparing the car for qualifying, sometimes — although very rarely — the car runs perfectly after the team unloads it off the truck. The driver has no complaints about the car during the first practice, raving to his team the whole time about how great a job they did. When this happens, a driver usually says his car was great *right off the truck*.

No time for timeouts

NASCAR racing, unlike baseball, football, or basketball, doesn't incorporate timeouts into the competition. That's one of the things that makes stock-car racing so challenging. Drivers can't get out of their cars or take a bathroom break while racing (drivers do get a bottle of water at each pit stop, however). After drivers get in their cars,

they're in there for the long run. That's why you may see drivers running to portable toilets before the race. After that, they just have to hold it until the race is over. Often, though, drivers sweat so much during a race, they don't need to go to the bathroom because they're so dehydrated.

When the race starts, there's no zoning out

When the green flag drops, the driver can't be daydreaming about what he's going to eat for dinner. Not only does he have to concentrate on the racetrack, but he also has to make some pretty important decisions like when to make a pass, when to be patient, when to be aggressive, and when to *save his tires* (to taking it easy through the turns and not running the car too hard). So, even during a 600-mile race like the Coca-Cola 600 at Lowe's Motor Speedway, the longest NASCAR NEXTEL Cup Series race of the year, drivers must stay focused at all times.

Staying focused for three or four hours, the length of a typical 400- or 500-mile race, isn't easy. Drivers must be mentally disciplined — constantly thinking about their cars and how to make them drive better. The driver is in constant contact with his crew chief throughout a race, exchanging information on the car and what the team needs to do during a pit stop to help improve the car's performance. (Check out Chapter 10 for more on the action during pit stops.)

Some drivers talk over the radio during practice and races more than others. I prefer to say one or two things to my crew chief from time to time instead of talking over the radio throughout the race. That lets me concentrate on taking the fastest route around the track. Some drivers try to *hit certain points* on the track — a route they've mapped out in their heads that they think will get them around the track in the fastest time. If it works, they try to repeat the previous lap by hitting the points again — either by picking out a spot on the wall in one corner or choosing a line on the inside of the track in another corner — anything that helps them repeat the same lap every time. Drivers aren't veering all over the place if they don't hit their points, but they may not be running the fastest lap possible if they take different routes around the racetrack. (See Chapter 9 for the lowdown on strategizing the driving of a race.)

Why Drivers Are Athletes

Some people think drivers aren't athletes because many hide their muscles under their uniforms and after a long race sometimes climb out of their cars gasping for breath. Others think drivers aren't athletes because stock-car racing doesn't involve a ball, a bat, or a hoop — all drivers do is sit in a car and drive around, right? But if those people were to get into a race car on a typical summer day and weave through traffic at 180 miles an hour, I'm sure they'd change their minds.

While many drivers aren't perfect physical specimens, they do have to stay in a car where temperatures can exceed 120 degrees for more than three hours at a time, concentrating on the road, their car, and the cars around them without getting distracted. In order to do this successfully, a driver must have lightning-fast reaction times, great coordination, and immense endurance and concentration.

Reacting quickly

Imagine flying down the highway, going about 100 miles an hour, when the car just ahead of you spins out and starts rocketing toward you. You'd probably end up with at least a couple injuries and a damaged car. But most NASCAR drivers have the ability to avoid getting into that wreck. It's called *fast reaction time*.

Drivers have incredibly quick reaction time. It's the same ability pro baseball players have to be able to smack balls out of the park, even when those balls come hurling at them at more than 95 miles an hour. In tests over the years, sports medicine doctors have reported drivers have the fastest hand-eye reaction times second only to airline pilots. Not just anybody can get into a race car and drive inches away from the guy ahead of him. Not just anybody can avoid an accident that happens in a split-second just feet ahead of him. But drivers can; that's why they're able to avoid wrecks every weekend and sometimes make it home without a dent on their cars.

No clumsiness allowed

Driving a race car isn't anything like driving your dad's El Camino to the food mart on the corner. Drivers need much more coordination to operate their manual transmission, high-performance race cars. They have to shift gears quickly, turn the wheel smoothly, step on the brake, and jam on the accelerator — all while driving at breakneck speeds. Sometimes, drivers even control the brake and clutch pedals with their left foot and depress the gas pedal with their right foot, which is different than what you learned in your high school driver's education class. Of course in racing, people break those rules all the time. In most cases, using the two-foot technique — which means you're a *left-footed braker* — is quicker than using the same foot on both the gas and brake pedals. Professional race car drivers can't be klutzes — otherwise, they may find themselves careening headfirst into the car in front of them when they accidentally press the gas instead of the brake.

Endurance is key

Even if you're the best driver in the world, you won't make it as a stock-car driver if you don't have endurance. Drivers may not be in the same shape as long distance runners or cyclists in the Tour de France, but drivers' bodies can endure a lot — heat, mental strain, pressure to avoid an accident, and accidents themselves. Drivers can also handle the intense pressure of competition, racing 42 other drivers who are among the best in the world. Without endurance, we'd never make it through a race. Then again, we wouldn't be drivers in the first place.

Getting into peak condition

Many drivers work out on a consistent basis, and I think staying in shape is imperative to being a successful race car driver. And as the sport becomes more and more competitive, drivers have to be in better physical condition to get an edge over everybody else — especially over the newcomers who may have youth on their side.

No time to pal around

It's no secret that a lot of people consider me the most focused driver around. And I take that as a compliment, although sometimes people can take my ultra-focused attitude the wrong way, especially at the track. When I head for my car just before practice or walk to pit road to start the race, it's not easy for me to smile the whole way or stop and sign autographs every two seconds because I'm already thinking about the race and what I have to accomplish. It's not time for me to pal around with other drivers or joke with fans. Just like any other athlete, it's my time to get in a zone.

Need space and distractions? Don't try racing!

If you're the claustrophobic type, stock-car racing isn't for you. Drivers have to squeeze into their tight-fitting seats and stay strapped in for several hours. You can't stretch, and you don't get much air flow. You contemplate the road ahead, how your car is running, and ways to win a race — and that's pretty much it.

If you have a short attention span, driving a race car isn't for you, either. You won't find a radio or a CD player in a race car. You can't hear much besides the drone of the engine and you don't really see much — just the same scenery over and over again. Drivers are used to that, though. After years of training, they can focus on the track for hours.

As a racer, being in good physical shape helps in several ways:

- Drivers suffer fewer injuries. When drivers get into accidents, if they're in shape, they tend to walk away from scary-looking accidents because their muscles protect their bones and internal organs. If a driver is flabby, he has nothing protecting his insides. A driver who's in good shape also rebounds from an injury faster.

- If a driver is cardiovascularly fit or in shape aerobically, he has an easier time sitting in a steaming-hot car for an afternoon while sweating off pound after pound. The heat makes a driver's pulse rise, so if a driver's heart isn't in shape, making it through a race can be very taxing on his heart.

- A strong upper body helps a driver wrestle the car around a racetrack when it's not handling well. A driver can't just leisurely put one hand on the wheel and expect to steer effectively. If his upper body is weak, he'll have a hard time steering.

Staying in great shape is one of my obsessions, even when I'm at the racetrack. From Monday through Friday, even the Monday after a 500-mile race, I wake up at 5:45 in the morning and get to the gym. When I'm at home, I don't have far to go because I have a gym set up in my airplane hangar, which is connected to my house. When I'm at a race, I work out in a gym set up under a tent in the motor home lot. Wherever I end up working out, my main objective is to lift weights and keep my muscles strong for racing, something I've been doing since the 1980s.

Drivers Are Hot Stuff

Even on cool days, the inside of a stock car gets extremely hot for drivers. Not only does the engine run incredibly hot, but there's also no air conditioning. And on days when the outside temperature is in the 90s — like it is plenty of times at places such as Daytona Beach, Talladega, or Darlington, the temperature inside the car can soar above 120 degrees.

Without air conditioning, drivers get pretty uncomfortable inside their race cars (see Figure 7-1). Although drivers need to wear a suit to protect them from possible fires, a helmet in case of an accident, and gloves to protect them from heat and blisters while grabbing the steering wheel and throwing the stick shift into gear, all that equipment makes the conditions even hotter. It's not uncommon for a driver to lose anywhere from 3 to 10 pounds after sweating during a single race. The car's main exhaust system used to travel through a pipe directly under the driver's seat only adding to the heat produced by the car during a race. Occasionally, the seat would get so unbelievably hot that I would feel it on my back and legs for days afterward. Now that the exhaust system travels under the passenger side of the car, the heat is not as bad.

The floor of the car can get extremely hot. That's why drivers wear special driving shoes with a silvery, aluminum-foil looking cover around the heels and on the soles. But sometimes, drivers need additional help to protect their feet, so they strap extra pieces of insulation — called *heat shields* — onto their heels when the floor is extra hot. Some of the older drivers have figured out alternatives to protecting their feet, claiming the bottom part of a Styrofoam cup works better than anything else to keep their feet cool.

Figure 7-1:
Soon after the race starts, the inside of a race car gets unbearably hot, consistently reaching temperatures above 120 degrees.

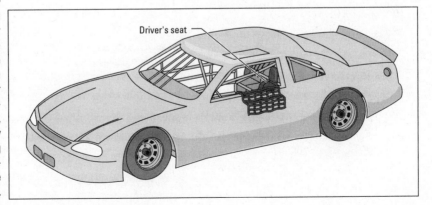

Driver's seat

A family tradition

Many families have been in the sport for generations — including the Frances, who started NASCAR. Here are a few NASCAR racing families involved in the sport:

The Pettys:

- Lee — Winner of the first Daytona 500 in 1959. Won NASCAR Cup championships in 1954, 1958, and 1959.

- Richard (Lee's son) — Holds the NASCAR record for career victories (200) and is tied with the late Dale Earnhardt for the most NASCAR Cup championships (7).

- Kyle (Richard's son) — Races in the NASCAR NEXTEL Cup Series.

- Adam (Kyle's late son) — Raced in the NASCAR Busch Series.

The Earnhardts:

- Ralph — Raced in NASCAR in the late 1950s and early 1960s.

- Dale (Ralph's son) — Shares the NASCAR record for most NASCAR Cup titles (7) with Richard Petty.

- Dale Jr. (Dale's son) — Won two consecutive NASCAR Busch Series championships, including in 1998, his first full season in the series. He advanced to NASCAR Cup Series racing in 2000, was voted the series' Most Popular Driver in 2003, and won the Daytona 500 in 2004.

The Jarretts:

- Ned — Two-time NASCAR Cup champion (1961 and 1965).

- Dale (Ned's son) — Won the 1999 NASCAR Cup title

- Jason (Dale's son) — Races in the Auto Racing Club of America (ARCA) series.

The Labontes:

- Terry — Two-time NASCAR Cup Series champion (1984 and 1996).

- Bobby (Terry's younger brother) — The 2000 NASCAR Cup Series champion.

- Justin (Terry's son) — A NASCAR Busch Series competitor.

The Bodines:

- Geoffrey — The 1986 Daytona 500 winner and part-time NASCAR NEXTEL Cup Series competitor.

- Brett (Geoffrey's brother) — Raced in the NASCAR NEXTEL Cup Series and NASCAR Busch Series; he now works at NASCAR's Research and Development Center as Director of Cost Research.

- Todd (Geoffrey's youngest brother) — Races in the NASCAR NEXTEL Cup Series and NASCAR Busch Series.

The Wallaces:

- Rusty — The 1989 NASCAR Cup champion, who is retiring in 2005.

- Mike — Races in the NASCAR Craftsman Truck Series.

- Kenny — Races in the NASCAR NEXTEL Cup Series.

While plenty of family members have competed in NASCAR over the years, nobody beats the Pettys in longevity and racing lineage. Adam Petty was the fourth generation of the family to race in NASCAR — and no other pro sport can say that they had a fourth-generation athlete in their ranks.

While drivers can't turn on the air conditioner or roll down the window for a shot of cold air, they're not left to suffer without fresh air flow: all teams have a cooling system inside the car that injects air into the driver's helmet and up through holes in the seat (see Figure 7-2). It's a system of tubing that flows from a box with a fan (and sometimes dry ice) in it — without this air flow, drivers would have trouble staying conscious on hot days.

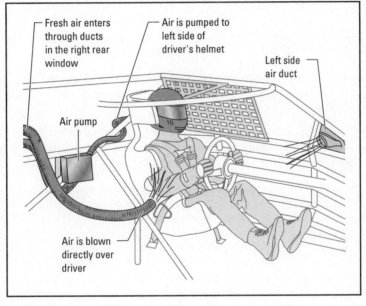

Fresh air enters through ducts in the right rear window

Air is pumped to left side of driver's helmet

Left side air duct

Air pump

Air is blown directly over driver

Figure 7-2: Without a cooling system, drivers may not be able to survive a three- or four-hour race in temperatures above 100 degrees.

Ricky Rudd, a veteran racer who began his NASCAR Cup Series career in 1974, found out the hard way how important an in-car ventilation system is on a hot day. His "air conditioner" malfunctioned during the fall race at Martinsville Speedway in 1998. It was more than 90 degrees outside that day and approached 150 degrees in the car, with no cool air blowing into his helmet or up through his seat. Even so, he held on to win the race, but had to be helped out of his car in Victory Lane. He fell to the ground, with blisters and burns on his backside, and paramedics gave him oxygen so he wouldn't pass out. Even though he felt awful and could barely talk, Rudd still gave post-race interviews while lying down. Later, he was given intravenous fluids because he was so dehydrated.

Racing All over the Nation

When drivers aren't racing, they're probably not lounging at home watching a TV shopping network or pulling weeds in the yard. Their schedules are so packed, they barely have enough time to sneeze after they get home from a race before they have to take off for another event. In 2004, the NASCAR NEXTEL Cup Series had 36 points races (see Chapter 13 for a list of the tracks that hold NASCAR races).

On top of the points races are two exhibition races every year that don't count toward the NASCAR NEXTEL Cup championship:

- ✔ **The Budweiser Shootout at Daytona International Speedway** in February, which includes the previous season's pole winners and one wildcard driver.

- ✔ **The NASCAR NEXTEL Cup All-Star Challenge** held in May at Lowe's Motor Speedway in Concord, North Carolina, which features past winners, the support-race victor, and a wildcard entry.

With 38 weekends of the year accounted for, drivers still have plenty of time for themselves during their off weekends, right? Wrong. With test sessions, sponsor commitments, commercial shoots, and series banquets, those additional weekends are spoken for.

The days of the week before the driver goes to a race are filled with things to do, too. At most, a driver has one day at home to handle his personal business before he's off to a test or to an autograph session someplace far from home.

Here's a snapshot of a typical week for a driver:

- ✔ **Monday:** If he's lucky, a driver gets to sleep in on Monday after what's usually a long day at the races. Most of the time, it's the only day a driver can spend with his family at home and take care of personal business. More often than not, though, he has to go to a sponsor appearance and sign autographs — many times hundreds and even thousands of miles away.

- ✔ **Tuesday:** Teams often conduct two-day testing sessions at racetracks where the teams will race in a few weeks, with the sessions beginning on Tuesday. (See Chapter 5 for more on testing.) For example, drivers and teams test at Daytona International Speedway for several days in January, but the Daytona 500 isn't until mid-February. It's just like preparing for an exam. Teams experiment with their cars, trying different setups in order to find just the right one for the upcoming qualifying session and race. They talk about the fastest way to get around the track and discuss what they'll do when they return for the real thing.

During a test, the driver has to be at the track early in the morning, prepared to slip into the driver's seat and start the session. Even though he's not racing against 42 other drivers during the session, testing a race car isn't easy and may require running hundreds of laps. A session usually lasts from dawn until dark, and teams use every minute of the precious time.

✔ **Wednesday:** Frequently, Wednesday is the second day of a two-day test session. But if a driver isn't testing that day, he's at an appearance for one of his sponsors. Ideally, those appearances are held near a racetrack (at a car dealership or an auto parts store) where the series is racing that weekend.

✔ **Thursday:** This is usually a travel day for drivers because most racetracks open for practice on Friday. Drivers fly to the town where a race is held and then head for the racetrack where their motor homes are already prepared for their arrival. (See the section "(Motor) home away from home".)

Occasionally, drivers are already at the tracks on Thursday for pre-race events.

✔ **Friday:** The NASCAR NEXTEL Cup Series drivers qualify their cars for the Sunday race on Fridays (see Chapter 8). They also participate in several practice sessions during the day. After the garage closes, drivers often meet with fans and sponsors at an appearance, making the drivers' days quite long.

✔ **Saturday:** Drivers don't get Saturday off. They've got to go to the track and practice, making final changes on the car's engine or its setup for race day.

Happy Hour is the final hour of practice for the race, usually held the afternoon before race day. During this time, drivers and teams make last-minute — and sometimes harried — changes on their cars. Because of the urgency, Happy Hour is a crazed 60 minutes of cars whizzing in and out of the garage after running laps on the track. Not all teams leave the track happy after Happy Hour, however — especially the ones whose cars ran slowly or whose drivers got into a late-practice accident.

✔ **Sunday:** Most races are held on Sunday (although a few are on Saturday night). On race days, drivers have much more than just a race to drive in:

- **Sponsors' meeting:** On race days, drivers get dressed in nice pants and a shirt with their sponsor's logo on it and then head for the garage. Most of the time, they have a prescheduled appearance — called *hospitality* — with a group of employees of one of their sponsors. Drivers give a talk and answer questions. It's a little strange for the driver to give a pep talk to *fans* only a few hours before the race, but that's all a part of racing and having a sponsor paying the bills. You don't see football players talking to people in the suites a couple of hours before game time, but that's the difference between racing and football.

Sometimes, thousands of employees from a sponsor's company show up at hospitality, where the sponsor sets up a tent and serves breakfast or lunch. So as a driver, I have to be ready to address all those people, even though I may be nervous about the race or thinking about my race car. As soon as a driver finishes his talk, he signs autographs for a while before heading back to the garage for the drivers' meeting.

- **Drivers' meeting:** The most important thing on race days is to make it to the drivers' meeting, held two hours before each event. (I discuss the meeting in detail in Chapter 5.) If a driver or his crew chief misses the meeting, the driver must start the race in last position, no matter where he qualified.

- **Church service:** Right after the drivers' meeting, many drivers, teams, and their families stay for a brief church service that's held race morning.

- **Driver introductions:** About a half hour before the race, drivers assemble for driver introductions at a stage near the start/finish line. At this time, awards may be given out for teams who did well the week before or for the team that won the pole for that day's race. Each driver's name is then announced as he walks across the stage, waving to fans. Drivers sometimes ride in the back of a car or truck, taking a lap around the track to wave at all the fans.

- **The race:** The main event; what drivers do all the other stuff for.

  If a driver is severely injured prior to the race, as Dale Earnhardt Jr. was while competing in a sports-car race in the summer of 2004, a substitute must be found. In Earnhardt's case, the ride went to Martin Truex, Jr., who drives for Dale Earnhardt, Inc. in NASCAR's Busch Series. Earnhardt didn't lose any points because he managed to drive at least one lap before turning the car over to Truex.

- **Post-race:** When a driver wins, he spends nearly an hour in Victory Lane celebrating and taking pictures. Then he answers the questions of the print media for another half-hour in the press box, followed by TV interviews. Drivers who come in second or third also give interviews with the press, explaining how their cars performed and what they saw during the race. Even drivers who didn't finish well usually stick around to make a few quick comments. If a driver crashed, he can expect to be bombarded with questions when he emerges from the infield care center. (Every driver who crashes has to make a mandatory trip to the infield care center for a check-up before doing anything else.)

  Throughout a race weekend, drivers must deal with reporters — TV reporters wielding cameras and microphones; newspaper reporters with pens, pads, and tape recorders; and radio reporters with headsets and microphones. Whoever they are, the driver has to talk to them at some point during the weekend — or at several points: Before practice, after practice, during practice, before qualifying, after qualifying, just after crashing during qualifying, after winning the pole, after losing the race, or after winning the race.

- **Getting home:** Because the racing season is long and the schedule is packed, almost most teams and most drivers have their own planes. Some teams have as many as three, for those crew members who have to stay after the race to re-pack equipment. Immediately following the race, the driver (if he's not in Victory Lane) heads for a local airport and is in the air within the hour. The biggest problem is the traffic on the runway because nearly all the other teams are trying to leave at the same time.

(Motor) home away from home

Drivers and their families spend at least three days and nights at each race. Three nights multiplied by 36 (the number of NASCAR NEXTEL Cup points races per season) is 108 nights away from home! In the past dozen years or so, drivers, owners, and some crew chiefs got tired of spending all those nights in a hotel room, so they began bringing motor homes to the races.

The kind of motor homes you find in the driver and owner motor home area (called the *motor home lot*) at the races aren't at all like a pop-up camper. Many times, they're quite luxurious with more amenities than the typical home. Most of them have TVs (connected to satellite dishes), a bedroom, a living room with leather couches, good-sized showers, glass cabinets, full-sized refrigerators, kitchen tables, and music systems. This way, drivers and their families are quite comfortable.

A motor home driver, who works for the race car driver, drives the vehicle from track to track. After he gets to a certain track for a race weekend, the motor home driver stocks it with food, extra uniforms, and other essentials and then checks into a hotel.

Drivers don't get fancy motor homes to show off. They just want to make things as cozy as possible. The motor homes also make it possible for the drivers to bring their wives and children to the races — and have them at the racetrack at all times. In the past, drivers were stuck at the track between practice and qualifying with nowhere to go or hang out, while their families were biding time in the hotel room or staying at home because they didn't think going to races was worth the trouble. Now, drivers have a private place to go to be with their families at any point of the day and not have to deal with traffic, crowds, or rowdy fans.

The motor home lot is a small, mobile village with all the same people traveling from race to race. It's also kept safe by security guards who protect the entrances and monitor the grounds.

Meeting Richard Petty

To give you an idea of how easy it was — and still is — to meet a driver, here's how I met Richard Petty, NASCAR's King. Petty is NASCAR's winningest driver, with 200 victories and seven NASCAR Cup championships. He was just hanging out in his race shop when my dad and I went to visit. I was a teen-ager then and, of course, my jaw dropped when I saw him, but my dad was bold enough to approach him and introduce us.

Richard Petty was the most gracious guy I'd ever met and he talked to us for about ten minutes. Meeting Petty, who was, in my mind, the ultimate human being next to my dad, was one of the best things I'd ever experienced. There he was, the most famous stock-car driver in the world, just chatting with us about racing! To this day, that's one of the most memorable moments of my life.

Motor Racing Outreach

Because of the popularity of NASCAR racing, drivers usually can't go casually strolling through town looking for new restaurants, gyms to work out in, or places to go to church because they'd be swarmed by fans. In order to help out drivers and their families during all the weekends away from home, *Motor Racing Outreach* (MRO) provides many services for drivers and their families at the track. I don't know what drivers would do without it.

The following are the services MRO provides:

- ✔ Church services are held every race morning, just after the drivers' meeting. Drivers don't have time to go to a regular church on race day, especially with all the traffic headed toward the track, so the MRO interdenominational Christian church services give them a chance to keep their faith alive. MRO also organizes prayer groups throughout the weekend, held in the motor home lot.

- ✔ When the drivers are in the garage area, their kids aren't stuck in the motor home watching TV. MRO has a day care center in a motor home, bought with funds donated by drivers and their wives and corporations, where children read and learn — all under the care of MRO volunteers.

- ✔ For those racing team members and families who want to stay in shape, there is a little workout center in the motor home lot that travels to every race. It's set up next to the MRO motor home and has a few treadmills, stationary bikes, and free weights.

Part III

What Happens on (and off) the Track

The 5th Wave   By Rich Tennant

"No, really—thank the engineers at Nerf, but I don't think it'll get past the inspectors."

In this part . . .

NASCAR races aren't the simplest events to follow. They're not like football games where two teams play for 60 minutes and are done. NASCAR events last several days, beginning with qualifying for the race (usually on Friday) and ending with a celebration in Victory Lane on Sunday.

This part decodes every move that teams and drivers make on the track and in the garage during a race weekend, including race strategies and pit stops. I also explain why a driver can bump into another competitor without getting even a scratch.

If you want to know what's going on during every moment of race weekend — or even just race day — you'll have fun reading this part. Like a good mystery novel, you won't be able to put it down.

Chapter 8

First, They Gotta Qualify

*B*efore drivers hear the famous command, "Gentlemen, start your engines!" they must qualify for the race. That means they're not going anywhere unless they prove they're worthy to start — and to do that, they have to show that their cars are fast enough. Regardless of how fast a car is, qualifying is nerve-wracking.

Drivers have to *qualify* for a certain race by completing one (or in rare cases, two) full-speed lap around the track without crashing or losing control of their cars. Qualifying, which is normally held on the Friday before Sunday's race, sets the starting lineup and, if there are more cars attempting to qualify than the 43 allowed for each race, weeds out the slowest. Just about every week a few drivers fail to qualify, which is especially depressing for drivers and teams who travel across the nation for a race, and then don't even compete in it. It's like driving to California from the East Coast for a concert, only to find that the concert is sold out.

The Importance of Qualifying Well

Qualifying isn't easy. Drivers have to map out a specific route — or line — around the track that he thinks will be the fastest, although that fast qualifying lap is still like riding a runaway roller coaster that may derail at any second. Teams also tinker with their cars to provide that extra burst of speed for that one lap. While in a race, drivers must be patient and careful over 400 or

500 miles in order to make it to the finish line and win. If a driver also isn't patient and careful during qualifying, he will most likely be watching the race from his living room sofa rather than competing in it. Driving one lap may seem like an easy job, but lose your concentration and nick the wall just once, and you may not qualify and instead be heading home.

Starting up front is groovy

A lot of work goes into making a car qualify well because, depending on the track, starting up front could be the difference between winning and losing the actual race. Tracks in NASCAR racing all race a little differently — especially when it comes to letting a driver pass other cars (see Chapter 13 for more on the different tracks). Some tracks are *one-groove racetracks,* which means there's only one comfortable way to get around a track fast without putting a driver at risk of crashing. (A *groove* is a part of the track where the car's tires get the best grip, and if the car drifts out of that groove, it becomes less stable and more difficult to control.) These one-groove racetracks, such as New Hampshire International Speedway, make passing another car very difficult because when a driver pulls out of the groove to attempt a pass, his car doesn't handle well. And a car that doesn't handle well doesn't go very fast. Other tracks have a *high groove* and a *low groove,* meaning cars can run side-by-side or two-wide around the track, while some tracks let cars race easily on just about any part of the track.

Qualifying well is especially important at one-groove racetracks because passing is so difficult. So, if a driver starts fifth, he has a chance of making it to the front. If he starts 25th, though, advancing is more difficult, unless the cars ahead of him have problems, because getting out of the groove to pass that many cars will slow him down too much.

Qualifying well is also important when racing on a smaller track, such as the .526-mile Martinsville Speedway. Most short tracks physically just don't have enough room for cars to race two-wide, so passing is difficult. Starting up front makes the day much less stressful.

Winning the pole

Drivers and crews scramble during the practice before qualifying to get the car just right for the run, one they hope will be fast enough for them to win the pole. The *pole winner* (or *pole sitter*) is the driver who runs the fastest lap during qualifying, which means he starts the race in the front row and gets to pick either the inside or outside starting position. (NASCAR races start with only two cars in each row; so you have 21 two-driver rows and a single driver starting from the rear of the field in the final "row.") The pole winner starts from the inside, or closest to the grass, giving him a slight edge as the field enters the first turn. The second-fastest qualifier usually starts the race on the outside of the front row, which is the *outside pole.* It's an honor to win the pole because you go to Victory Lane, take photos, and accept awards — and your competition respects you a little more for it. They know how hard it is to be the best qualifier, considering the fastest car (1st) and the slowest car (43rd) are often separated by less than one second.

Winning the pole is a big deal because that driver is in the best position to lead and win the race — even before the race starts. For at least a few moments, that driver has the best view of the racetrack. He also wins at least $5,000 for winning the pole, even if he gets passed right after the green flag drops.

Mapping Out a Track Attack

Most tracks are *ovals,* with two long strips of racetrack connected by sweeping turns at both ends. People started labeling the turns so that drivers and crew chiefs could talk about the race track — and have some landmarks to help them figure out where the car is doing what and where to make to make their moves — see Figure 8-1. Now they can say, "The car scraped the wall in Turn two," and everyone can immediately picture what happened. Drivers compete on the track by circling it counter-clockwise. The section of racetrack where the start/finish line is located is called the *frontstretch, front straight,* or *front straightaway.* It's where you see cars racing each other to the finish in the last seconds of a race. The strip of racetrack on the opposite side of the track is called the *backstretch, back straight,* or *back straightaway.* The turns connect the two straightaways in the following way:

- ✔ Turn 1 is located at the end of the front straightaway and is the first turn the racers make during a race.

- ✔ Turn 2 is at the beginning of the backstretch.

- ✔ Turn 3 is at the end of the backstretch.

- ✔ Turn 4 is at the beginning of the frontstretch.

On most NASCAR ovals, turns 1 and 2, as well as turns 3 and 4, are directly connected, with no straightaway between them to make each turn its own separate corner, like those at the Indianapolis Motor Speedway. Still, that single, big, banked turn that you see at each end of most NASCAR ovals is considered to be *two* different turns.

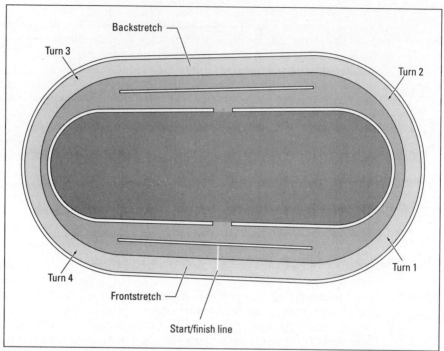

Figure 8-1:
The standard oval track.

Although most NASCAR tracks are ovals, they have several variations in shape, as well a few oddball tracks. And drivers and teams have to adjust to each in order to make sure they get the fastest qualifying time possible. (For more information on the NASCAR NEXTEL Cup Series' different tracks, turn to Chapter 13.) Here are the different types of tracks:

- **Standard ovals** are the most common track shape in the NASCAR NEXTEL Cup Series.

- **D-shaped ovals** are modified ovals that have one long sweeping arc of a turn for a frontstretch instead of a straightaway. (Even so, you'll hear many fans at these tracks refer to the frontstretch as the "frontstraight," even though it's not straight at all.)

- **Tri-ovals** are modified ovals where the frontstretch consists of two sections of angled straightaways connected in the center by a slight corner.

- **Quad ovals** have two slight corners in the middle of the frontstretch.

- **A triangle track,** like the Pocono Raceway, is in its own category. It has three straights, each of a different length, and three corners, each with a different length and degree of banking.

- **Road courses** more or less resemble a winding country highway and have a number of sharp, difficult turns.

Qualifying butterflies

As the years have gone by, I've gotten more and more nervous on qualifying day — literally to the point where I'm on the verge of getting sick to my stomach. I guess that's because getting a good spot in the starting field has become more difficult as the sport grows. Every time I go out to qualify, I have to drive close to the edge in order to get the best possible starting position. It's a tremendously intense experience because the expectations, especially my own, are so high. Maybe that's why I've always been known as a pretty good qualifier. I've also gained confidence from the fact I've never failed to qualify for a NASCAR race.

Getting the Car Ready for the Run

Winning the pole isn't the same as winning the race, but in NASCAR, every aspect of racing is competitive. Drivers, crews, and team owners put a lot of effort into running the fastest lap in qualifying.

Preparing the car for a qualifying run is hard work. First, the driver takes the car on the track during practice to see how fast it is and how it handles. After every practice session, NASCAR puts out a time sheet that ranks the cars from fastest to slowest. Then the scrambling starts. If a driver's car isn't at the top or near the top of the list, he has to change something so that his car can go faster. Some of the things drivers and crews change or fine-tune during practice include the following:

✔ **Balance:** The most important thing to perfect during practice for qualifying is the car's balance. A driver doesn't want one end of the car to *stick to the track* or have more traction than the other end because an unbalanced car is a slow and hard to handle. Teams can adjust the balance by inserting lead weights into the frame rails of the car. Then, depending on how the driver says the car is driving, they can move these chunks of lead within the frame rails to redistribute weight toward any of the four corners of the cars in order to get the traction as even as possible.

✔ **The engine:** In order to have a fast qualifying lap, a car's engine must run perfectly. So while taking practice laps, a driver looks at his *tachometer* (the gauge that measures how many revolutions an engine is making per minute) in order to see how hard the engine is working. If the engine is working too hard or not hard enough, a team changes the car's gears to maximize the engine's output. Teams also must consider the weather when deciding what gears to put in their cars. Usually, when it's really hot, a lower gear ratio is required, and vice versa.

Drivers listen to the engine to find out how it's working. They know exactly how it should sound when it's working right. If it sounds funny — too high-pitched or not smooth — they take the car right into the garage and have the crew look at it.

✔ **The shock and spring combination:** In qualifying, particularly at superspeedways where aerodynamics play such a crucial role, the closer the car is to the ground, the faster it cuts through the air. Whenever air gets beneath a car, it slows it down. So teams try to figure out the right shock absorber and spring combination to get the car as close to the ground as possible without letting it *bottom out* (getting too close to the ground). (For more on aerodynamics, turn to Chapter 13. To find out about different components of the suspension, flip to Chapter 4.)

✔ **Taping off:** When a team wants to see exactly how they'll do in qualifying, they prepare the car for an all-out run. Part of that preparation is *taping the car off*. This means the team places heavy-duty tape over the car's *grille* (which is the screen at the front of the car leading to the radiator), in order to keep air from going through the grille and slowing the car down. A car runs fastest when air is flowing over it, instead of through it or under it. That way, the car is sleeker and faster as it moves through the air.

Even though taping off allows a car to go faster, teams can't do this during the actual race. With no air flowing into the radiator to cool the engine, a taped-off car wouldn't last very long in a 500-mile race. The engine would just go kaput after a certain point when it became too hot.

Picking the Qualifying Order

Drivers don't just drive randomly onto the track to make their qualifying laps. The whole process is precisely orchestrated — it has to be. The qualifying times of all the drivers are frequently separated by less than one second. So if even one element is amiss, a driver's qualifying time could easily put him at the back of the pack.

To start the process, representatives from each NASCAR NEXTEL Cup Series team gather to determine the qualifying order. Each representative (in order of car owners' points — see Chapter 12 for the lowdown on points) picks a ball with a number on it out of a small rotating sphere — just like the ones used in your local bingo parlor. But instead of yelling, "BINGO!," the representative returns to his driver and crew to announce when the driver will go out to qualify. Why does everyone care so much about when their driver qualifies? It's not because they want to get done early so they can catch the evening news.

Sometimes, qualifying order can be crucial because weather plays a key role in how fast the cars run on the track. In hot weather the track is slippery, so the car doesn't stick very well, particularly going through turns. That means the driver must slow down to keep from losing control. In normal weather, the track is cooler and the tires adhere to the track better, so the drivers can go fast through the turns without worrying about crashing. (In cool weather, though, the tires may be cold, which results in little traction and often in a crash. That's why you see drivers swerving back and forth on the racetrack before a race. They're warming up their tires.)

In hot weather, the driver who picks the No. 1 qualifying spot and qualifies at the usual mid-afternoon time, may run at the hottest — and slowest — time of the day, while the driver who picks the last qualifying spot may be in luck, especially if the sun goes down some by the time he qualifies, and the track is faster. At times, though, choosing the first qualifying position isn't bad. For example, if a cloud just happens to float over the track at the right time, cooling the track's surface, a driver may get a fast lap. But if that cloud floats quickly away, the next driver may be out of luck. That's how delicate a situation it is — the passing clouds can and do make the difference between winning the pole or starting 20th.

Sometimes things go wrong right before a qualifying. The team unloads the car off the truck, hits the track for practice, runs top speeds, and then as it lines up for qualifying, something goes wrong. It can be as small as a lug nut coming loose, or as major as having a transmission suddenly going south. So instead of starting the race from the front, where he and his crew were fairly sure they would, the driver now has 40-plus cars in front of him.

The days before qualifying

In the old days, there were no limits on the number of cars that started a race. For example, 75 cars started the first Southern 500 back in 1950. They crammed onto the 1.2-mile track, running perilously close to one another. Today, though, NASCAR is much more safety-oriented and limits the number of cars that compete in a race to 43.

The Moment of Truth: Racing the Qualifying Lap

Drivers take one or two qualifying laps, depending on which track they're on. They each get one lap of warm-up on the track before they take the green flag at the start/finish line. At that point, the car, with a transmitter attached to its fuel cell, runs over a sensor in the track to start the timed lap. During the lap, drivers push the car as much as they dare, hoping the tires have enough traction and stick to the track — and hoping the car doesn't spin out and crash. It's quite a relief when it's all over and the car zooms over that sensor again to end the lap. Sometimes we drivers joke about holding our breath during the entire lap. Following a qualifying run, as well as at other times during the weekend, cars have to go back through inspection. (For more information on inspection procedures, see Chapter 5.)

After qualifying ends, cars are ranked by the speed recorded by NASCAR officials, who score all of the races and time all the qualifying laps with sophisticated, high-tech equipment. The driver with the fastest lap starts the race on the inside of the front row, or the *pole position*. If two cars log the exact same qualifying time, the driver highest in the NASCAR points race starts from the pole. A double-car lineup means the third-fastest car lines up behind the pole sitter and the fourth-fastest behind the outside-pole winner, and so on throughout the field. Only the fastest 38 teams are guaranteed a spot in the race. The final five race entries are provisional entries, which I discuss in the next section.

Daytona is different

Instead of holding a single round of qualifying, NASCAR does things differently for the Daytona 500, the sport's season-opening event. The Daytona 500 is considered NASCAR's Super Bowl. For that top race, drivers have several rounds of qualifying — but not all of them are held the usual way.

Unlike at other events, the contest for the prestigious the Daytona 500 pole position is held a week before the actual race. Drivers complete two laps around the speedway, but only the fastest two drivers lock in their Daytona 500 starting spots. Four days later, all drivers must run in one of two qualifying races, called the

Gatorade Twin 125s (because they are each 125 miles long). Remember, even if the pole winner and outside pole winner finish last in their Twin 125, they still "own" the first two starting spots in the Daytona 500. At the end of the Gatorade Twin qualifying races, 30 spots are now "set" for the Daytona 500. The next eight positions for the Daytona 500 go to those drivers who did not qualify well enough through the Twin 125s, but had the fastest times (among those not yet qualified). The final five spots in the 43-car field are given to teams that are entitled to provisional entries, including past champions.

A Second Chance: Provisional Entries

NASCAR has a built-in safety valve for regular week-to-week drivers that have a bad qualifying weekend. It's called a *provisional entry* (often just *provisionals*) — and it guarantees spots in a race for regular series competitors whose cars weren't one of the 38 fastest during qualifying. The provisional system guarantees that star drivers get into the race. So even if Jeff Gordon or Dale Earnhardt Jr. has a poor qualifying run, fans still get to see them race because they use provisional entries to make the field.

NASCAR allots five provisionals for each race, with those drivers starting 39th through 43rd. A "champion's" provisional spot, if needed, is reserved for the 43rd and final starting position. A champion's provisional is reserved for past champions who are still active drivers.

Provisional entries are allotted based on *car owner points*. (Owners receive points for each race, based on the finishing positions of their cars in a particular race, no matter who's driving.) Car owners in the top 45 positions of the previous season's owner championship standings each get four provisionals at the outset of the season, and an additional one after attempting to qualify for six events with a season maximum of ten provisionals. Car owners not among the top 45, including new car owners, are ineligible for provisional starting positions until after they make an attempt to qualify at four events. After attempting to qualify for four events, the car owner gets two provisional starting positions and additional ones can be earned after attempting to qualify for six events with a season maximum of eight. Each provisional actually used by a car owner during the season counts against the owner's season allotment.

How the champion's provisionals got started

Champions haven't always had special provisionals set aside for them. NASCAR instituted the champion's provisional in 1989 when the king of the sport, Richard Petty, failed to make a NASCAR Cup race at Richmond International Raceway. It was a shocking day for fans, drivers, and crew members to see NASCAR's winningest driver fail to make the cut. NASCAR officials devised a system to prevent something like that from happening again, instituting champion's provisionals the next year so that drivers who had reached the pinnacle of the sport could make every race, even when they had poor qualifying days. Right away,

it was dubbed the "Petty Rule." Champion's provisionals worked flawlessly for several years until former champion Darrell Waltrip went home from the UAW-GM Quality 500 in 1997 because former champ Terry Labonte used the provisional because he was higher in points than Waltrip. In 1998 Waltrip ended up using 20 champion's provisionals in 33 races. It was supposed to be an occasional fall-back for a past champion, something used rarely and in an emergency. So NASCAR changed the rule once again at the beginning of 2004, this time stating each champion would be limited to ten provisional per year.

Note: Should qualifying be rained out, drivers line up on the grid according to owner's points in positions one through 38, with spots 39 through 43 lined up on the grid according to owners' provisional points.

Chapter 9

Passing, Drafting, and Other Race Day Strategies

In This Chapter

▶ Passing other cars

▶ Listening to spotters

▶ Driving aggressively or hanging back

▶ Gambling during a pit stop

▶ Drafting at superspeedways

▶ Dealing with accidents

*I*n stock-car racing, there's no such thing as drawing up a precise game plan before a race starts — a set, pre-planned strategy gets you nowhere. Racing changes by the minute — or even by the second — with caution flags coming out because of accidents, blown tires, mechanical failures, and even rain. It would be silly to devise a plan before a race when that plan may be useless the minute something unexpected happens.

Strategy, however, is very still important as the race unfolds. For example, when drivers take a pit stop near the end of the race, teams have to figure out whether to change two tires or four, depending on whether they want to gain track position (with a faster two-tire stop) or have the best tires (with a slower, four-tire stop) in order to have the fastest possible car after the race resumes. Or if a race has *gone green* for a long time near the end of the race (the race has been under a green flag, without a caution flag coming out — see Chapter 5), teams may tell their drivers to conserve fuel by easing off the gas. They do that because they think their drivers may be able to avoid having to make another pit stop before the race is over. Also, on superspeedways (see Chapter 13), drivers have to know how to use the technique of drafting if they want to go fast and win.

In this chapter, I discuss a variety of these and other racing strategies.

The Art of Passing

One of the most obvious strategies in NASCAR racing is to pass as many cars as you can by coming up on either the right or left side of the car in front of you (see Figure 9-1). But passing during a race isn't like driving around a slow car on the highway. Even if the driver is trying to pass someone on the straight, wide part of the track, it may be difficult because the target doesn't want anyone to pass him. And that driver will do all he can to stay in front.

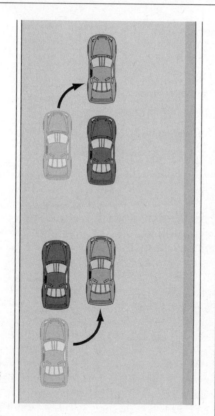

Figure 9-1:
Even on a straight-away, passing another car can be difficult.

Depending on the track and conditions, the easiest pass may be on the left (inside) or the right (outside).

Waiting for a passing chance

Making a pass is much more strenuous than it may seem, especially if the car a driver is trying to pass is on the lead lap or if he's battling for position. *Being on the lead lap* means that a driver has completed the same number of laps as the leader. (If the driver is a *lap down,* that means he has completed one less lap than the leader.) *Battling for position* means the car that the driver is trying to pass is on the same lap as the driver. For example, a driver is battling for position with a car ahead of him when he's in fourth place and that car is in third.

The driver being passed is probably going to try to *block,* meaning he will try to put his car exactly where he thinks another driver is going to try to pass him. That requires plenty of concentration and plenty of glances into the rear-view mirror, but when a driver knows how to throw a good block, even the best cars can't get by him. When a driver tries to pass another car, he has to be patient and stay right on the bumper of the car in front.

Passes frequently occur in the turns, where cars tend to become difficult to drive — and easy for other cars to pass — particularly if the car in front isn't set up correctly. If a driver can't zoom by and easily pass, he has to wait for the driver ahead to make a mistake, even a small one, in order to get by. This may happen when the driver of the car in front takes a turn too wide (see Figure 9-2) and slides up the track when coming out of a turn. Or it can happen when that driver takes his car into a turn too quickly and loses control for a split-second. Going through turns, especially while entering and exiting them, are good places to make a move.

Bumping your way forward

At short tracks, passing isn't as much of an art as it is a technique. Cars at short tracks are going relatively slowly and there is plenty of *downforce* — which means the cars stick to the track — so drivers can be very aggressive without causing a big accident. In order to pass a car in front, the driver doesn't necessarily have to go below him or above him on the track. All he has to do is give the car a tap — called a *bump* — on the rear bumper, as Figure 9-3 shows. Most of the time that causes the car to float up the track and give the other driver enough room to pass.

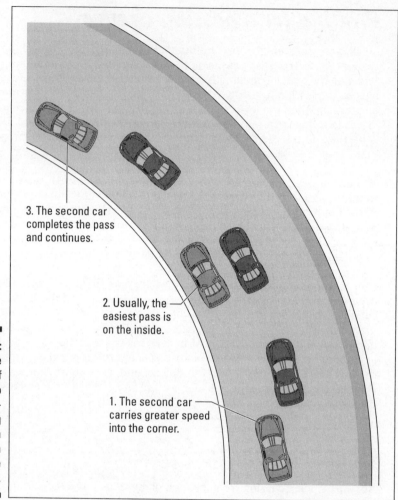

3. The second car completes the pass and continues.

2. Usually, the easiest pass is on the inside.

1. The second car carries greater speed into the corner.

Figure 9-2:
When the car ahead of you drifts up the race-track going through a turn, it's a perfect time to pass.

Passing the slowpokes

The driver in the lead wants to get as much space between him and the second-place car as possible. This becomes a problem — and a big pain in the neck — when the leader comes up on lapped traffic. *Lapped traffic* is a bunch cars that have fallen off the lead lap either because they're considerably slower than the leaders or because they've had problems or penalties. So when the leader is trucking around the speedway, the last thing he needs is a bunch of slower cars getting in his way. This is when the blue with diagonal yellow stripe flag comes into play, cautioning all cars not on the lead lap to look out for those cars that are on the lead lap. (See Chapter 5 for more on flags.) It's sort of like driving in the fast lane on the highway and having to slow down when there's a slow car ahead of you that just won't switch lanes. You could pass on the right, but what if another slow car is in the right lane? You're stuck behind those cars until one or both of them decide to move out of the way. Drivers have the same problem in racing. When the lead car gets caught behind lapped traffic, the driver in second — who has no one ahead of him to slow him down — has more time to catch up to the leader's back bumper.

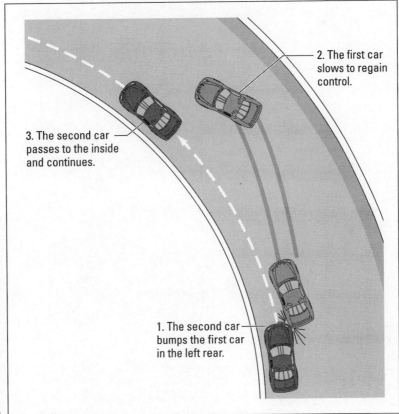

2. The first car slows to regain control.

3. The second car passes to the inside and continues.

1. The second car bumps the first car in the left rear.

Figure 9-3:
At short tracks, the technique is brutally simple. If a driver doesn't move out of the way, someone bumps him.

On the other hand, if the lead driver can pass the lapped car just before going into a turn, the second-place car gets stuck behind the lapped car (see Figure 9-4).

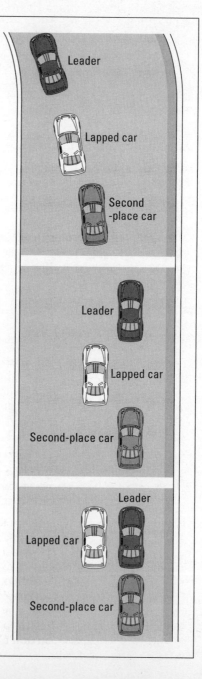

3. As the cars approach the turn, the second car must slow and fall behind the lapped car in order to get through the corner. The lead car can extend his lead.

2. The lead car moves to pass the lapped car.

1. The leaders approach a slower, lapped car.

Figure 9-4:
When lapped traffic gets in the way of a second-place car, the leader has a chance to gain ground.

Staying on the lead lap

Sometimes lapped cars aren't that much slower than the lead cars. They may have blown a tire, spun out, or been penalized for speeding on pit road or doing something else illegal earlier in the race. Those drivers want to get back on the lead lap so that they can have a chance to win. If they can get back on the lead lap, these drivers have a chance at a good finish, especially if a caution flag comes out. As much as they want to return to the front of the field, however, drivers who are a lap or more down usually still follow a "gentleman's agreement," allowing a driver in contention for the victory the right of way.

Under a caution flag (see Chapter 5 for the lowdown on the different flags), all the cars on the lead lap are bunched up single-file, almost bumper to bumper, behind the pace car. Even if the lead car had a substantial edge over the second-place car or the last car on the lead lap was looking at the leader in his rear-view mirror and about to get lapped, everyone's brought together under the great equalizing caution flag. So if you're on the lead lap, you always have hope to get up near the front.

The problem is getting on the lead lap if you're a lap or two down. Here are some ways a driver can get back on the lead lap:

✔ **Pass the leader under green-flag conditions.** Sometimes a driver may be a lap down only because his tire went flat or he ran out of gas — not because he has a slow car. In that case, that driver may be fast enough to pass the leaders and get back on the lead lap.

✔ **Stay on the track when the leaders make a pit stop under the green flag.** And then hope that something causes a caution flag so that you can pit when cars are moving around the track slowly. That gives you enough time to make a pit stop and then catch up to the tail end of the field. If you pit when everybody else does, it's hard to gain position and you'll still be a lap down.

✔ **Be designated the "Lucky Dog" driver.** The Lucky Dog Rule provides that each time there is a caution, the first driver in the one-lap down position gets an automatic wave up to the end of the lead lap. The Lucky Dog Rule is not in effect when there are only 10 laps remaining.

✔ **Have teammates or friends on the track.** Sometimes one driver lets another driver get his laps back by letting the driver who is a lap down pass the driver who's on the lead lap. It all depends on how the lead-lap driver feels about the other driver. If they're friends, teammates, or if they've worked well with each other in the past, the lead-lap driver may let the other driver pass. If they're not friends and have had previous on-track problems, you can bet that the driver who's down a lap isn't going to be able to pass. It's like stopping to let someone into your lane on the highway or on a road. You don't know why you do it. It kind of depends on what mood you're in.

Listening to the Spotter

Unlike passenger cars, race cars don't have side-view mirrors. So passing another car when you're going 180 mph and running inches away from the car in front and behind you isn't the easiest thing to do. That's why teams have spotters perched high above the racetrack.

A *spotter* is a team member who watches a race from atop the press box or the grandstands where he can get a full view of the racetrack. His job is to be the driver's second set of eyes. As soon as the spotter sees there's enough room for a driver to pass another car, he tells the driver, "Clear high!" or "Clear low!" which means, "There are no cars on the high side of the track (the part closest to the grandstands)" or "There are no cars on the low side of the track (the part closest to the infield)." A driver knows he's clear to move around the track in those areas and pass cars.

Although drivers use spotters at every race, spotters are absolutely indispensable at certain tracks in the series. At short tracks, for example, drivers are lapping the track so fast, they can't even tell where they are at times — and they don't have a lot of time to avoid accidents. So, at places like the half-mile Bristol Motor Speedway, where it takes cars only about 15 seconds to go around the track, spotters need to stay alert and notify their drivers of accidents as soon as they happen. If the spotters aren't quick enough, their driver may become a part of the wreck, too. The same thing goes for superspeedways, where cars run in excess of 180 mph just a few feet, or even inches, apart. For example, if an accident happens at the top of the racetrack coming out of turn 4, the spotter notifies the driver and tells him whether to go low or high on the track to avoid it. (See Chapter 8 for an explanation of the turns on the track.)

At the bigger tracks, such as the 2.66-mile Talladega Superspeedway, every team has more than one spotter. One usually sits above the frontstretch and one above the backstretch because one spotter can't see the entire track, even from a high vantage point. This is also true at Indianapolis and the Watkins Glen road course. Sometimes a team may use several spotters, with each one taking responsibility for a certain section of track.

From time to time, spotters communicate with people other than those on their team. If a spotter is working with a driver who is leading the race and coming up on a lapped car, he may walk over to the lapped car's spotter and tell him to ask that driver to move over. The spotter then relays the other driver's request, but that driver doesn't necessarily have to move over if he doesn't want to. It all depends on the relationship between those two drivers. If they've worked well together before, maybe the lapped car will give the leader a break — possibly hoping the driver will remember the favor in the future. At superspeedways, where cars go faster when they work together than they do separately, a spotter may make a deal with another spotter to get two drivers to work together and draft to the front (see the "There's a Draft in Here" section, later in this chapter, for more information on drafting).

Using Your Driving Style to Get an Advantage

Not every driver is aggressive from the start of the race to the finish. Some like to zoom to the front as soon as the green flag drops; others like to hang behind the leaders. It all depends on the race they're in, the racetrack they're on, and their race strategy.

Saving your engine

In a long race such as the Coca-Cola 600, drivers don't like to push their cars and engines too hard at the beginning. They know it's wiser to conserve the car for when they'll need it most, which is the last 50 to 100 laps. If you push the car too hard at the beginning of the race, you risk *blowing an engine* — which means you won't finish the race because your engine failed beyond immediate repair. It's amazing how often an engine blows during that last 100 miles of the Coca-Cola 600 because the driver pushed it too hard throughout the race. Sometimes the configuration of a particular track can wear on an engine. Blown engines are common at the Pocono Raceway because the sharp turns of the triangular track causes frequent and severe accelerating and braking, which puts a lot of strain on an engine.

Taking care of your tires

One reason drivers don't go full-bore around a track all the time is that they must take care of their tires. No question — tires are sturdy: Goodyear Tire & Rubber Company creates tires for each racetrack and are working hard to devise new tires that last longer during a race and don't blister, pop, or go flat easily.

However, tires aren't indestructible. Drivers must be careful not to wear out their tires too quickly during a race. This is called *tire management*. At sandpaper-rough tracks such as Darlington Raceway, drivers make sure not to push their cars too fast through the turns because the tires wear out more quickly. Even on smoother tracks, tires don't last very long, so drivers take it easy when they can. Otherwise, the tires may wear out and provide less traction, which means the car will be more difficult to control. When tires wear out or suddenly go flat, the driver can end up in the infield, up against the speedway wall, or flying down the track.

Drivers also run the risk of blowing a tire if they wear them down too much — and that may be dangerous if their car veers into a wall. Figure 9-5 shows what can happens when a right-front tire blows: the car is carried to the outside wall unless the driver can get the car under control.

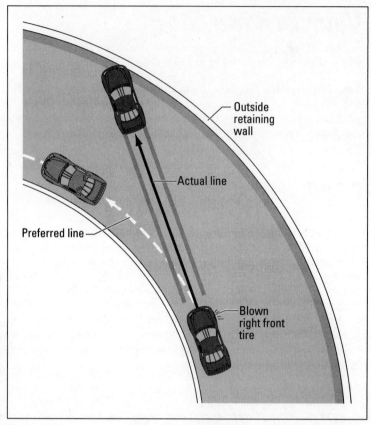

Outside retaining wall

Actual line

Preferred line

Blown right front tire

Figure 9-5:
When a car's right-front tire blows, it's headed toward the wall.

Going easy on the brakes

Brakes can become a problem — a dangerous problem — at short tracks because the turns are so tight that drivers have to brake hard to keep from hitting the wall, especially if they enter the turn too hard. A small track also means that drivers have to brake more frequently. That's a lot of extra strain on the brakes, which wears them down faster.

To compensate for tracks like Martinsville Speedway where races last 500 laps around the .526-mile oval, mechanics put extra thick brake pads and extra durable brake parts on their cars. And drivers make sure to conserve their brakes when they can — especially early in a race when driving aggressively usually doesn't pay off.

Bringing a spare

Every team brings more than one car to the racetrack, just in case the driver crashes one of them irreparably. The best car for that track is the *primary car,* which is the car a driver starts out driving during a race weekend. If something happens to that car, however, a team must unload the *backup car* from the truck. This is never a good sign for a team because the backup car isn't their first choice for their driver to use at that racetrack. It's usually another car out of the team's fleet of about a dozen at the race shop, and a car used on tracks similar to the one they're at. But the backup car isn't setup exactly like the primary car. And if the driver crashes the backup car, too, he may be in trouble at another racetrack — the track where the backup car was supposed to be the primary car.

Gambling with Pit Stops

Pit stops play the greatest role in race strategy. When do you pit? When do you stay on the track? When should you come in for a gas-and-go? When should you make an air pressure adjustment in the tires — and which tires should you change — in order to get the car handling better? It's the crew chief's job to make those decisions, which puts a lot of pressure on him, especially in the final laps when his driver is contending for the victory. A good pit stop can get the driver out in front; a bad one can cost the driver a victory (see Chapter 10 for a lot more on pit stops).

Not running on empty

Even though crew chiefs, engineers, and team members figure out how many laps they can get out of one tank before a race begins, sometimes they make mistakes. In 1998, Dale Jarrett paid dearly for that. Jarrett was leading the Brickyard 400, and his team thought he could make it just beyond the halfway point before making a pit stop. They wanted to lead the race at halfway in order to pick up the $10,000 bonus. The gamble wasn't worth the $10,000, though, when Jarrett ran out of gas on the backstretch of the huge, 2.5-mile track. Obviously, he lost his lead in a hurry while coasting back to pit road — but his car didn't make it all the way to his pit stall. It stopped just at the entrance to pit road, which was quite an unfortunate place to come to a halt because his pit stall was all the way at the other end of pit road. His crew had to run down pit road to the car so they could push it back to their pit. They started out sprinting, but, because it was a good half-mile to the car, the crew came back huffing and puffing. Jarrett lost several laps and finished 16th, loosing the $1 million bonus he could have won for finishing first.

The most important result of a pit stop is *track position* (a car's position in relation to the front of the pack). Teams can improve their cars' track position if they have a quicker pit stop than the teams who came into the pits ahead of them.

Tire gambles

Drivers can improve their track position by changing only two tires instead of four during a pit stop. The few extra seconds gained gets them out on the track while other drivers are still on pit road. But changing just two tires instead of all four is a gamble. Although a two-tire stop is several seconds shorter than a four-tire stop, a driver may not be as fast on the track as a driver who took four tires. Older tires don't provide as much traction — meaning the car doesn't stick to the track as well. The gamble is in estimating how much slower will the car be. If you get out of the pit stop first after taking on two tires with 10 laps left, and the driver who takes on four tires is 10th — perhaps those four new tires will make him so fast that he'll catch up to you before the race is over. It's a guessing game that depends on the track and how the team prepared the car for the race. Many times, crew chiefs won't commit to two or four tires until the last second. They watch the other leading cars on pit road to see how many tires they're getting before making their own decision.

Another question that arises is whether to use sticker tires or scuffs. *Sticker tires* are new tires that still have the manufacturer's sticker on them. *Scuffs* have been previously mounted on the car and "scuffed" on the track surface during practice for a lap or two. Both affect the handling of a race car in different ways, depending on the weather and the temperature of the racetrack. Crew chiefs are better able to predict how scuffed tires will perform, as they already have practice miles on them, but sticker tires are usually more dependable. The choice of which tires to mount depends largely on track conditions and weather, as well as the crew chief. It's all about strategy!

Tires affect a race car's handling more than you may think. That's why drivers often state during a race (over the in-car radio) that they don't like a particular set of tires. For some reason, the tires don't work well together, perhaps because of a miniscule imbalance between them. This mismatched set of tires may make the car more difficult to turn, or they may make the car feel wiggly in the rear-end as it goes though the turns. The foremost thing on a driver's mind then is getting back into the pits for a new, hopefully better set.

Fuel and mileage gambles

Fuel mileage isn't an issue in all races, only the ones where there aren't many caution flags. Long periods of green-flag racing mean that cars are on the track until they need gas instead of staying on the track until there's an accident, which allows all drivers to make a pit stop while cars are slowed on the track during the clean-up.

Michigan International Speedway, which traditionally has long green-flag runs, is a track where fuel mileage is often an issue. With fewer caution laps, tanks quickly run dry. Drivers need to get as many laps from one tank of fuel as they can, in order to utilize every last drop of gas in their tanks. If they consistently get good mileage out of each tank of gas, they may not have to make as many pit stops as the next driver — meaning they'll have a better chance at winning. Sometimes a driver may drive slower to conserve gas, pushing the fuel mileage as far as it will go and hoping he can make it to the finish without running out of gas. However, if a late-race caution flag goes up because of an accident or debris on the track, all that fuel mileage calculation goes out the window because all the cars come into the pits for more gas.

Teams figure out their fuel mileage before a race begins, determining how many laps the car can make around the track before it runs out of gas. They then decide on a *pit window,* which is when they'll need to make a pit stop to refuel. At some tracks, the pit window may be 55 to 60 laps, at others it may be 70 to 125, depending on the length of the track.

Obviously, teams don't want their cars to run out of gas — so they have a system of keeping tabs on the situation. To calculate their fuel mileage, they weigh the gas can when it's full, and then again after a pit stop to find out how much gas is left in the can and the catch can (which catches the overflow of gas) after a pit stop. (Flip to Chapter 10 for more on pit stops.) The gas in the cans reveals how much gas was dumped into the gas tank — which, in turn, reveals how long the car can go without sputtering and stopping. While this sounds like an exact science, it isn't. For one reason or another, cars can run out of gas in the final laps of a race, even when a team thinks it has enough gas to last much longer.

Tony Stewart was leading the Jiffy Lube 300 at New Hampshire International Speedway in 1999, looking as if he was about to win for the first time in his rookie year. What he didn't expect — especially after dominating the race — was his car to run out of gas with just two laps to go. Jeff Burton ended up winning instead. It happens to the best of us, including me a few times. After a while, though, you realize that you lose some races that way and you win some that way. For example, Jeff Gordon was leading the 1999 NASCAR NEXTEL Cup All-Star Challenge by nearly half a lap at Lowe's Motor Speedway, but ran out of gas with one lap to go. I was in second place at the time and couldn't have been happier to hear the news on my radio. The next thing I knew, I was in Victory Lane celebrating a surprise win while Gordon was steaming over the loss (and the lack of gas in his car).

If there's a caution late in the race and a team thinks that once it's lifted the race will be under a green flag until the end, you may see a car dive onto pit road just before the green flag is raised again. This is called a *splash-and-go stop* — a pit stop in which the pit crew doesn't change tires; instead, they just fill the gas tank with a smidgen of fuel before the driver peels back out onto the track. Teams do this when they think that without that small additional amount of fuel, their car will run out of gas. It's better to lose a lap or two than to run out of gas on the track and lose several laps or possibly not finish.

There's a Draft in Here

Have you ever been cruising right behind a semi-truck on the highway and felt like the truck was pulling your forward? But then when you try to pass it, your car bounces all around because of the air flowing off the front, back and sides of the truck? This pull of the truck on your car is called *drafting*.

Drafting is a very important strategy on superspeedways and some of the larger intermediate tracks that are so large and have turns so sweeping that *aerodynamics,* or the way air flows over a car, greatly influences how well a car does. (For more on aerodynamics and superspeedways, turn to Chapter 13.) In racing, drafting is when drivers share airflow among them by racing in single file. The first car in line punches an imaginary hole in the air and the cars behind it slip more easily through that hole. Thus their engines don't have to work as hard to battle oncoming air. The car in front benefits, too. It gets "pushed" by the cars behind it. Figure 9-6 demonstrates how drafting works.

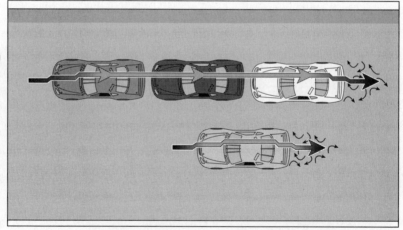

Figure 9-6: Understanding the way that air flows over and under is key to success at superspeedways.

The line of cars racing down the track in single file is known as the *draft*. The first group of cars going single file is called the *lead draft*. If a driver loses the draft and has to race by itself with no other cars around — or if he accidentally falls out of the single-file line — he's in big trouble because his car is so much slower. That goes to show you that, at superspeedways, drivers need help from other drivers in order to get around the track in the quickest way.

Dale Earnhardt was known as the master of superspeedways because, as legend has it, he could "see" air flowing off the car ahead of him. It's exactly this sixth sense drivers need to make smart, thought-out moves on a superspeedway in order to win.

Making a pass at a superspeedway takes a special skill because of the drafting aspect. It's not like passing a car at short or intermediate tracks, where you can roar past someone through a turn or tap the rear bumper of a car to try to move it up the track. Try that at a superspeedway, and you'll probably send that car flying into the wall or spinning around and cause a major accident — cars run too fast for that sort of trick. Instead, in order to pass someone, a driver has to team up with one or more other drivers because two or more cars go faster together than they do separately.

Suppose a driver dives to the inside of the track to pass the leader, and the driver behind him follows. Both drivers most likely will draft past the leader because they are pushing and pulling each other through the pass and probably leaving the leader with no one directly behind him to push him on.

The tricky part of this scenario is that a driver can never be sure whether another driver is going to follow him when he makes a move. His spotter can make all the deals he wants with another spotter (see the "Listening to the Spotter" section, earlier in this chapter) in order to convince another driver to team up with his driver to pass the leader. The problem is, these impromptu deals are never guaranteed. The risk is that the driver dives out of the draft to the inside and no one backs him up — this is called *getting hung out to dry*. No car is ahead of him; no car is behind him. He has no draft. Now the entire line of cars in the draft may pass him because he's running much more slowly.

At superspeedways it's not unusual to see a driver go from first to tenth if he's hung out to dry. It's also not unusual to see drivers struggling to get back in line after they've fallen out of line and lost the draft. Cars run so close together, there isn't much room to squeeze in, and most of the time, your competitors show no mercy. Still, every driver tries desperately to get back into line and back into the draft. If he falls too far back, though, he may lose the lead draft altogether. In that case, he's doomed unless he catches up to the pack (which isn't likely unless he has help from other cars) or a caution flag comes out to bunch the cars back together.

A *slingshot move* is a special technique drivers use to pass cars on superspeedways, but only experienced, savvy drivers have enough guts to try it and enough talent to do it successfully. A driver has to utilize the air flowing off the car ahead of him very carefully, allowing his car to get sucked in by that car (see Figure 9-7). The driver then turns abruptly to one side or the other and gets shot through the air right by the car he is trying to pass. The catch is, the driver making the move has to know exactly where to position his car before and as he makes the pass. For the move to work, he must use the air flowing off the opposing car to his advantage. While the move doesn't work as well today as it did in the days before carburetor restrictor plates, which slow the cars down, Dale Earnhardt, the superspeedway guru, was known to pull it off from time to time. (Turn to Chapter 13 for more on restrictor-plate racing.)

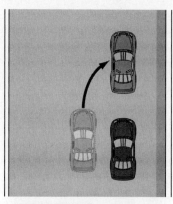

3. His momentum carries him around the first car as he completes the pass.

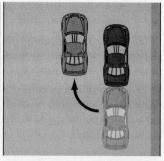

2. The second car accelerates behind the first car and slingshots out around.

Figure 9-7:
Drivers can "slingshot" their way past a car in front of them by tucking behind that car, gaining speed, and then ducking to the inside or outside.

1. The second car is able to go as fast as the first car while only using a portion of his available power due to the lower wind resistance.

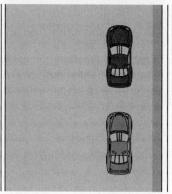

Accidents Happen

No matter how careful drivers are during a race, accidents happen. Sometimes drivers lose control of their cars. Sometimes they blow a tire. Sometimes they blow an engine, and the car behind them slips in the oil they dropped and spins out. Sometimes two cars inadvertently touch coming out of a turn and send each other reeling into incoming traffic. Sometimes a driver hits another car's back bumper and sends that car flying. You can never tell when it will happen next. All you can do is hope you miss the mayhem.

When at all possible, the spotter alerts the driver to an accident and tells him where to go on the track to avoid it. But sometimes if smoke is billowing into the air, neither the spotter nor the driver can see anything. So the best technique in that situation is for a driver to grit his teeth and hope to make it through unscathed. While it's not failsafe, there's often nothing else a driver can do.

Sometimes, though, drivers can see an accident in the making and avoid it before it happens. Maybe a car isn't really stable as it comes out of the turns and its back end is wobbling. Maybe a driver is taking too many chances by cutting off cars and coming close to the wall. Or maybe one car is riding too close to the back of another car and disturbs the airflow off the car in front. Instead of the air flowing onto the lead car's spoiler, it flows off the first car and onto the second car's front end. That leaves the lead car with little rear-end downforce, meaning it doesn't have much traction or control of its back-end. This is called *taking the air off another car's spoiler* and it often ends in the lead car spinning out and getting into an accident — and sometimes taking out other cars with it (see Figure 9-8).

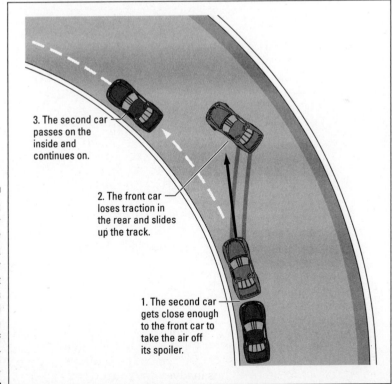

Figure 9-8: When a car runs closely to the back of another car, it disturbs airflow and makes the back-end of that car unstable.

3. The second car passes on the inside and continues on.

2. The front car loses traction in the rear and slides up the track.

1. The second car gets close enough to the front car to take the air off its spoiler.

Chapter 10

Making Pit Stops

The car that wins the race isn't necessarily the fastest one on the track. Many other factors go into making it to Victory Lane. One of the most important components is efficient pit stops.

A bad pit stop can cost a driver valuable time on the track. Wasting even one second during a pit stop can mean the difference between winning and losing, especially when races are frequently won by just fractions of a second.

In this chapter, I run down all the elements of an effective pit stop.

What Is a Pit Stop?

You can't drive several hundred miles without stopping for gas with the small fuel tanks used in race cars. A *pit stop* is when a driver pulls off the racetrack and into the pits so the members of his crew can service his car with gas, change tires, make mechanical repairs or adjustments to improve a car's performance, especially after an accident. Several factors go into how often a car comes in for a pit stop, including how quickly the tires wear down and what kind of fuel mileage the car is getting.

While Goodyear, the company that manufactures all the tires for NASCAR's top series, builds racing tires that last a full tank of fuel, some tires — due to track conditions or debris — develop problems before the tank is empty. Sometimes, the tires wear down more quickly than the fuel dwindles, so the teams have to make a pit stop before their gas tanks are empty. On the average, cars usually go about 100 miles per full tank of gas, which is 22 gallons. That's a little over four miles per gallon. Your typical economy car gets 30 miles per gallon or more on the highway. A stock car's gas mileage varies from track to track and also depends on the driver's driving style. If a driver is rough and pumps the gas pedal frequently, he gets worse gas mileage than a driver who is smooth and steady with the gas pedal.

Pulling off on pit road

When a car needs to make a pit stop, the driver pulls off on *pit road,* which is a separate road inside the racetrack that usually runs parallel to a track's frontstretch between the final turn and the first turn. Only one short track, the half-mile Bristol Motor Speedway in Tennessee, has two pit roads; the 43 cars are too many to stop on a 650-feet front row. (Check out a typical pit road in Figure 10-1.)

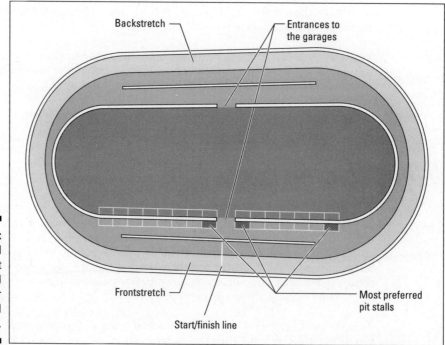

Figure 10-1:
Cars pull off on pit road and into their assigned pit stall.

Backstretch

Entrances to the garages

Frontstretch

Start/finish line

Most preferred pit stalls

Pit road is a haven, like the shoulder on a highway, where drivers go get away from the most hectic action on the track to have their car serviced. But that doesn't mean things don't get busy on pit road. Along pit road, *pit stalls* of equal size are marked off with yellow lines for each of the 43 cars in the race. The drivers have to pull into the box completely to avoid receiving a penalty (see the later section "The Rules of Pit Road" for more on pit stop penalties). Some tracks have smaller pit stalls than others, depending on the size of the racetrack itself, so pulling in and out of a pit stall can be difficult business. It also can be dangerous for the crewmen who service the cars, as they can be bumped by a car pitting in front or behind them or hit by a flying tire or part.

Each driver/crew chief combination has their favorite *pit stall* at each track. Jimmie Johnson and crew chief Chad Knaus, for example, prefer the pit stall closest to the exit of pit road. Other teams would rather have the first pit stall upon entering pit road. With most pit road speeds between 35 and 55 miles per hour, some teams would rather drive slowly the length of pit road and exit quickly, while others prefer to stop in the first stall in an effort to avoid colliding with other cars heading down pit road. Pit stalls are allotted according to how well a team qualifies. The pole sitter gets first choice.

The *pit wall* separates the pit stalls from the area behind the wall where teams keep their equipment and watch the race. Usually, the crew chief sits on top of a box called a *crash cart,* which is filled with equipment used for quick repairs. The rest of the team hangs out in the area, monitoring lap times or listening to their two-way radios in order to hear their driver talk about the car and the race. When their car come in for a pit stop, the pit crew quickly jumps over the wall to service it.

The backstretch blues

Bristol Motor Speedway has two pit roads — one on the frontstretch and one on the backstretch. The double pit roads put teams pitting on the backstretch at a big disadvantage. Those teams are the ones that qualified at the back of the pack, and the ones who lose several positions every time teams make pit stops during a caution period.

Teams pitting on the backstretch can't dive onto pit road when everybody on the frontstretch does under a caution flag. They have to follow the pace car all the way to the other side of the racetrack before heading down their pit road. It's an agonizing wait because by the time they get there, the cars on the frontstretch may already be done with their pit stops and are headed back to the racetrack. Cars on the backstretch often lose positions on the track, even when they have fast pit stops. It's very difficult to win the race if you've got a backstretch pit at Bristol, but it's not impossible, as Elliott Sadler proved in 2001, winning from the 38th starting spot. It was his first victory, too!

Makin' a quick pit stop

Besides filling the car with gas and changing the tires, members of a pit crew are quickly performing the following tasks (see Figure 10-2):

- ✔ Repair the body of a car after an accident, as long as it didn't sustain major damage.

- ✔ Fix a broken component on the car if it doesn't require a major overhaul.

- ✔ Clean the grille.

- ✔ Remove a *tear-off* from the front windshield to improve the driver's view. This procedure has replaced washing the window with a squeegee.

- ✔ Make adjustments on the car to improve the handling.

- ✔ Give the driver a bottle of water.

If a driver says his car is handling terribly, the pit crew makes adjustments to the car during a pit stop. Usually you see the rear tire carrier insert a long *ratchet,* which is similar to a wrench, into a hole on the roof of the car to the front of the rear tires. He cranks the ratchet one way or the other to change the pressure on one of the rear springs in order to improve the handling (this is called putting in or taking out rounds of wedge). A team also can change a car's handling by adjusting the air pressure in the tires, raising or lowering the sway bar, or raising or lowering the track bar (see Chapter 4 for descriptions of these parts of a car).

Figure 10-2:
The pit crew for the Army Chevrolet car quickly perform their pit stop tasks at Daytona International Speedway.

Copyright Sherryl Creekmore/NASCAR

The camera's watching

All pit crews film their stops and review the tape as soon as their car rejoins the race so that they can see what they did correctly and what they did wrong.

The films can be useful in another way, too. Sometimes, when NASCAR fines a team for something the pit crew thinks it didn't do, the team refers to the video of the pit stop to try to prove their innocence.

A pit crew accomplishes many tasks in a short time. A good pit stop can take as little as 14 seconds — not much time, considering the crew changes four tires and fills the gas tank with two 11-gallon cans. If there's the smallest of problems, say the tire changer fumbles the air wrench, the stop may last 17 or 18 seconds, and the driver will undoubtedly lose a number of positions because other drivers behind him completed their stops in 14 seconds and got out ahead of him. There are several types of pit stops, including:

- **A four-tire stop:** The crew changes all four tires and fills the gas tank.
- **A two-tire stop:** The team changes just two tires, usually the two right-side tires.
- **A gas-and-go:** The team adds gas to the car but doesn't change any tires.
- **A splash-and-go:** The team adds just enough gas to make it to the end of the race.

Going behind the wall

A driver also makes a pit stop whenever his team needs to repair his car after an accident or mechanical problem. If the team has to make major repairs to the car, including substantial repairs to the engine or suspension or to replace major pieces of sheet metal or parts, NASCAR rules say the team must perform those repairs behind the wall. *Going behind the wall* means leaving pit road and going into a safe area in the infield or garage where the crew can work on the car and repair it. Also, if the car is leaking fluids, a driver usually brings it behind the wall so that the car doesn't completely mess up pit road.

Pit Crews: Ballet without the Tutus

While the pit crew performing a pit stop looks smooth and choreographed, the moves aren't easy. Crews spend as much as one hour a day practicing pit stops at their shop with a pit crew coach who times and videotapes their stops and analyzes everyone's technique. Crews lift weights usually with the help of a personal trainer at a gym set up in their race shop. Being in top physical shape allows them to lift tires with ease and scramble around the car quickly. Everybody knows that the faster the pit stop, the better chance the driver has of moving toward the front — and to Victory Lane.

While an unlimited number of crew members are allowed to wait behind the wall during a race, only seven can come over the pit wall to work on the car during a pit stop. That's why the crew members who service the car are often called the *over-the-wall crew*. These teammates crouch atop the pit wall and wait for their car to come down pit road. Even before the car comes to a stop, the crew jump off the wall, carrying their equipment, and scramble around the car to change tires, make adjustments, and fill the gas tank.

The seven crew members have specific jobs to do after they leap over the wall (see Figure 10-3).

- ✔ **Tire changers (2):** The crew has one tire changer for the front tires and one for the rear tires. They leap off the pit wall with air wrenches in their hands and rush to the right side of the car (during a four-tire stop). They drop to their knees (wearing knee pads) and remove the five lug nuts holding the tire to the car. They take off the right tire and wheel, place a new tire and wheel on the car, tighten the lug nuts (which are previously glued onto the wheel), and then scurry to the left side to do the same thing.

- ✔ **Tire carriers (2):** Each tire carrier hands two 75-pound tires (already mounted onto wheels) at one time to the tire changers and takes the used tires away. When handing the fresh tire to the tire changer, the carrier is responsible for helping line up the tire onto the car, so that the changer can tighten the lug nuts right away, without having to lift the tire and wheel onto the axle. On the way to the left side, the tire carriers roll the used tire to a crew member who is waiting at the pit wall to take the tire away. Also, the front tire carrier sometimes cleans the grille as he goes past the nose of the car.

- ✔ **Jackman (1):** The jackman usually is one of the strongest people on the pit crew because he has to jump off the pit wall with a hydraulic jack that weighs about 35 pounds in his arms— and then use it to hoist a 3,400-pound car off the ground. He first runs to the right side of the car, positioning the jack under a specific spot (usually delineated by an arrow or a line), and uses the jack to lift the car off the ground. The jackman has to lift the car with one or two pumps of the handle, enough so that the tires are off the ground — weaklings wouldn't fare too well. After raising the right side of the car, the jackman runs to the left side and does the same thing. The driver gets the signal to leave the pits when the jackman drops the jack and lowers the left side of the car and gives the driver a thumbs-up.

✔ **Gas man (1):** The gas man doesn't have to be nimble, but he does have to be strong. He must step over the pit wall carrying a 90-pound, 11-gallon can of gas and then fill the gas tank. When the first can empties, he usually gets a second can from the second gas man (who doesn't go over the wall) and fills the tank with that gas as well. Each can has a special valve on it so that the gas shoots down into the gas tank quickly. You can recognize the gas man easily because he usually wears a helmet and a fireproof apron to protect him from fumes, spillage, and possible fires.

✔ **Catch can man (1):** The catch can man stands behind the car on the left side and holds a special container to collect gas that overflows from the gas tank. That keeps the gas from spilling onto the ground and possibly catching fire as the car takes off.

Even though only seven crew members are allowed over the wall, other people can help service the car — as long as they don't step onto pit road. Those team members use a long pole with a squeegee or cloth on the end to wipe off any rubber or debris that has gathered on the car's grille (to keep the car from overheating if air isn't getting through the grille and cooling its engine). Another team member may use a pole with a handy basket on the end to hand the driver a bottle of water. Until recent years, a crew member also used to wash and squeegee the windshield with a long pole from behind the pit wall. But stock-car windshields now come equipped with several layers of a thin plastic film. Each layer is called a *tear off* because that's what a crew member does to give the driver a nice, new, clear windshield.

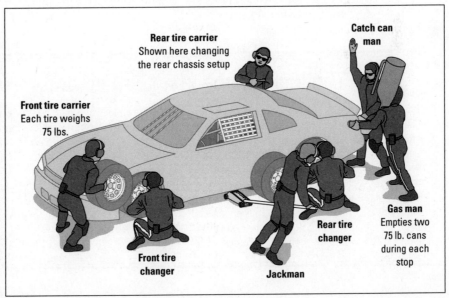

Figure 10-3: The over-the-wall gang is a group of seven pit crew members who service a car during a pit stop. They change four tires and add gas in about 14 seconds.

Rear tire carrier
Shown here changing the rear chassis setup

Catch can man

Front tire carrier
Each tire weighs 75 lbs.

Front tire changer

Jackman

Rear tire changer

Gas man
Empties two 75 lb. cans during each stop

Pit Crews for Hire

Some over-the-wall pit crews are regular members of the team — mechanics, crew chiefs, car chiefs, or truck drivers. Others are specially hired employees who fly to the track on race day solely to pit the car. Some team owners don't want to risk using regular team members to pit the car because they may be tired from working on the car all weekend or they just aren't athletic enough. Being a good pit crew member takes special skill, agility, and physical fitness, which makes these guys hot commodities in the garage. They have to try out and show their talents in order to get a job.

The following are some of the qualities that make a good candidate for a pit crew member:

- Agility to maneuver around a car when six other pit crew members are trying to do the same thing.
- Strength to carry heavy tires or to pump the jack handle and hoist the car off the ground.
- Fast reaction time to get lug nuts off a wheel without hesitation.
- Ability to remain calm under pressure, even when winning a race is on the line.
- Excellent hand-eye coordination, especially for the tire changers.
- The ability to remain focused when people are screaming and cars are zooming by just inches away.

The importance of a good pit crew

Drivers never underestimate the power of a good, fast pit crew. At least I never have. Suppose I've been running second to Jeff Gordon all day long and I've tried everything to pass him but can't do it. During previous pit stops, I've gone into the pits in second place and come out in second place. I've been about one second behind him all day and just can't catch him. In the next pit stop, though, my crew bangs out the fastest pit stop they've ever had, finishes before Gordon's crew, and I beat Gordon off pit road and take the lead. Gaining a second on pit road is much easier than gaining it on the track, especially in the final laps of a race when a driver doesn't have much time to make up ground with his car. That's why a good pit crew is invaluable, and that's why, many times, they're the first team members that I mention when I climb out of my car in Victory Lane.

The Rules of Pit Road

Just like everything else in racing, rules and more rules govern pit stops. NASCAR officials, sitting above the track in the control tower, monitor cars as they travel down pit road. Each team also has an official standing in their pit, watching them as they perform the pit stop to make sure it's all done legally. If it's not, the official penalizes them.

Slow down: Speeding penalties

While speeding on the racetrack goes with the territory, speeding on pit road doesn't. A driver can't just drive like a maniac coming off the racetrack and onto pit road. Although that's what drivers used to do, NASCAR now has a rule that limits the speed on pit road, to protect the crews working on the cars.

The speed limit on pit road ranges from 35 to 55 miles per hour, depending on the size of the speedway. But drivers can't look at their speedometers to make sure they aren't speeding because they don't have them — instead they have *tachometers,* which measure the number of revolutions per minute that the engine is turning. During a pace lap, a pace car drives the pit road speed while the drivers behind the pace car look at their tachometers to check how many rpm (revolutions per minute) they're turning. When a driver later crosses the line that begins pit road during a race, he checks his tachometer to make sure it reads the same as it did during the pace lap.

When a driver is caught speeding while coming down pit road under green-flag conditions, NASCAR officials direct him to "pass through pit road" on his next lap as a penalty. If NASCAR officials in the control tower catch him speeding during a pit stop, he has to come down pit road again for a *stop-and-go penalty,* which means that he has to come back to his pit box another time and stop before heading back on the racetrack. If a driver speeds down pit road under a caution, he has to start on the tail of the longest line on the restart. The worst penalty is when NASCAR docks a driver a lap or two, meaning he has to stay in the pits while other drivers continue to complete laps around the track.

NASCAR generally checks for speeding on pit road with a stopwatch, checking the amount of time it takes for a car to go from one predetermined spot on pit road to another. NASCAR officials already know ahead of time that it will take, for example, three seconds for a car going the speed limit to travel between the two points. If a NASCAR official times a car and the stopwatch shows less than three seconds, they know the car is speeding, and they throw the black flag on that car.

Other pit road no-nos

NASCAR has a list of other no-nos regarding pit stops during a race. If drivers disregard these, NASCAR penalizes them in some way:

- ✔ Drivers can't pass other drivers when the field is under a caution flag (see Chapter 5) or when they're preparing to go onto pit road.

- ✔ When a driver pulls into his pit box, the car must be completely within the box. A pit box is delineated by yellow lines.

- ✔ Only seven crew members are allowed over the pit wall at once. After a pit crew member returns to the pit stall, no other pit crew member can replace him in order to work on the car.

- ✔ Teams may use only two air guns per stop. The air guns remove lug nuts from the wheel hub and tighten the lug nuts after a new tire and wheel are mounted on the car. If one of the air guns malfunctions, the team must complete the stop with the one working air gun. Teams must take both air guns back over the pit wall after they change the tires and before the car leaves the pit box.

- ✔ Teams may use only one jack per pit stop. If a car falls off the jack, however, team members can use a second jack to help raise the car back up.

- ✔ A catch can man has to be on pit road to catch fuel overflow whenever gas is being added to the car.

- ✔ When a team changes tires, the tire changer has to tighten all the lug nuts before the car leaves the pit.

- ✔ Teams can't let their tires roll across pit road or into another team's pit box.

- ✔ Drivers can't run over their air hoses or any other equipment when they exit the pit box.

To Pit or Not to Pit

A driver's crew chief stays in radio contact with him throughout the race and tells him exactly when to make a pit stop. Teams always try to make a pit stop under a caution flag, which comes out an average of three or four times during a race after an accident, an oil spill, or debris accumulation on the track. If drivers duck onto pit road under a caution flag — when traffic is slow on the track behind the pace car — most of the time they don't lose a lap. That's because crews can bang out a pit stop and get the driver down pit road and onto the racetrack before the rest of the field passes him to put him a lap down.

Deciding when to make a pit stop under green-flag conditions is a little more difficult. In some cases, a driver can get himself into all sorts of trouble by pitting under a green flag because a driver loses valuable laps on the track when he's sitting in the pits while the other cars are whizzing by. Pitting under a green flag is fine if everyone else pits with you because everyone is losing the same number of laps. But when a caution flag comes out and a driver is in the middle of or has just finished a pit stop, that driver has a big problem. He already lost laps while pitting, but the caution flag gives other drivers the opportunity to avoid pitting under green — meaning they won't lose any laps because the field isn't driving top speed around the track.

Teams make it easy for drivers to find their pit box when they're driving down pit road by posting a big metal sign with the team name, logo, or car number above the pit. One of the crew members also holds out a long pole with a big metal sign attached to it. He waves the sign up and down so that his driver can see it even through all the traffic. Sometimes, even with that sign, a driver needs help because of all the cars and activity on pit road. That's when a crew chief calls the driver on the radio and coaches him to his pit box, counting the seconds until he arrives at it. He says, "Five, four, three, two, one!" as the driver pulls closer to the pit box, just to give the driver a precise time reference of how close he is.

Chapter 11

Keeping Racing Safe

. . . .

In This Chapter

▶ Walking away from an accident

▶ Understanding the safety features inside a stock car

▶ Seeing how uniforms protect the drivers

. . . .

*W*hile nose-to-tail racing is fascinating because it's so competitive, it also creates a risk of accidents. Lucky for drivers, though, the cars are built for safety and to protect drivers. Safety standards in NASCAR racing didn't just pop out of nowhere. They've evolved and improved as the sport has grown. In NASCAR's infancy, the cars weren't equipped as they are now to ensure drivers were able to walk away from a wreck. Back then, drivers raced regular cars like the ones your parents drove to work, so when they collided, it sometimes wasn't pretty. Those cars didn't have the extra safety features they do now — safety features that save lives and protect drivers. I talk about these features in this chapter.

Stock Car Safety 101

NASCAR NEXTEL Cup Series cars are made to protect the drivers. Here are some of the most basic safety features on a stock car:

✔ Stock cars have no glass, which would shatter upon impact. That means no headlights, taillights, or side windows.

✔ The front and rear windshields are made of Lexan, a hard, shatterproof plastic, as well as side windows when they are used.

✔ The doors can't swing open during an accident because there aren't any. That's why drivers squeeze through the window to get into the driver's seat.

✔ Tires have an inner liner so they don't explode when they run over something on the racetrack. The inner liner gives the drivers some time to notice that a tire is going flat, perhaps giving them enough time to make a pit stop for new tires.

Rusty's wild ride

While most drivers know first hand how safe today's cars are, Rusty Wallace has perhaps the best story to tell after surviving one of the most spectacular accidents in NASCAR history. In 1993, he was racing on the last lap at Talladega Superspeedway when Dale Earnhardt smacked into Rusty's back bumper and sent him flying. Literally. His car began spinning and was sliding backwards when air got under his car and lifted the rear end off the ground. That's when the roller-coaster ride began.

Wallace's car tumbled down the frontstretch, flipping eight or nine times before rolling to a stop in the infield. Not much was left of his car — just the steel frame and a mangled heap of sheet metal and steaming engine parts spread across the ground. "I just wanted it to stop," Wallace said. "I was thinking, man, this is going to be real bad."

Surprisingly, though, in a testament to how safe NASCAR stock cars are, Wallace ended up with only minor injuries. Examples like that keep racers from worrying as they climb into their race cars, knowing that drivers usually come away with only minor injuries, or none at all.

Fastening Those Superior Seat Belts

Stock cars have added safety features that allow many drivers to walk away from accidents. Seat belts are one of the most obvious additions.

When a driver slides into his car, he doesn't have the luxury of one of those automatic seat belts strapping him in for safety. It's much more complicated that that, but when you're traveling at full speed with 42 other cars on the track, it has to be.

Most drivers use *five-point seat belts,* which are five belts that come together at the center of a driver's chest, as Figure 11-1 shows. (Some drivers have a six-point system.) In the five-point best system, each of the belts passes through a steel guide that is welded onto the car's frame. One belt goes over a driver's left shoulder, one goes over his right shoulder, another comes from the left side of the seat, one comes from the right side of the seat, and still another comes up between a driver's legs. They're all latched together at a single point at mid-chest, where a quick-release buckle locks them into place. Although it takes a little while to gather all the belts and buckle up, a driver can release the seat belts in a fraction of a second when he lifts up on the latch that holds all five belts in place. This is an important feature because drivers may need to exit their cars quickly (see the "Putting out fires" sidebar for information on how drivers handle fires).

The NASCAR NEXTEL Cup season begins under the lights with the Budweiser Shootout each February at Daytona International Speedway.

Only the drivers and their cars separate the thousands of fans in the grandstands and the team haulers in the infield.

Mark Martin and crew chief Pat Tryson hold a meeting with members of their crew to plan race strategy.

Mark Martin, Matt Kenseth, and Dale Earnhardt Jr. share a laugh before the race.

One of the most impressive sights at any NASCAR race is the line of drivers and crewmen standing at attention for the national anthem.

Mark Martin in full concentration mode before the signal, "Gentlemen, start your engines!"

Drivers line up double file behind the pace car as the race is ready to begin.

Jeff Gordon takes an early lead with a pack of rivals just behind his bumper.

Pit road is controlled chaos, with each driver trying to find his stall. A crewman holds up the car number to help the driver.

Matt Kenseth's crew, called the "killer bees," prepares to service the car of the 2003 series champion.

Pit crews can change four tires in less than 15 seconds.

A crewman for NASCAR Craftsman Truck driver Travis Kvapil makes sure a tire isn't rubbing against the fender.

Race tracks may look clean from afar, but up close, rubber from tire wear is scattered everywhere.

Drivers make the first turn in the NASCAR Craftsman Truck Series.

NASCAR fans come in every shape, size, age, and gender to enjoy the fast-paced action.

Tens of thousands of fans pack the stands during NASCAR races across the nation.

Cars slow down and line up single file when the caution flag flies.

Jeff Gordon (No. 24) gets a half-car edge on the inside groove over Michael Waltrip (No. 15).

Fans arrive early and party hearty in the infield as drivers zoom around them.

At many tracks, not even the cheers of more than 100,000 fans can drown out the sound of 43 racing engines.

One of the most dangerous parts of a race? The high-five huddle of a winning pit crew.

Mark Martin climbs from his car, definitely the number-one driver this day.

bubbles is the traditional way to a winning effort.

The race isn't over for winner Mark Martin when he takes the checkered flag; the nation wants to know how he did it.

The ten proud drivers vying for the 2004 NASCAR NEXTEL Cup championship get friendly — for the moment — at Richmond International Raceway in Virginia.

NASCAR fans are known to be as proud of the American flag as they are of their favorite driver.

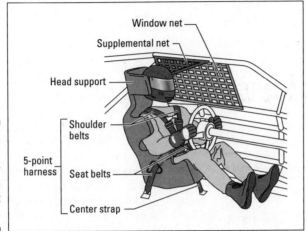

Window net

Supplemental net

Head support

Shoulder belts

5-point harness

Seat belts

Center strap

Figure 11-1:
Stock cars have safety features that protect drivers.

Racing seat belts don't work the way the ones in a passenger car do. The ones in your regular car activate when the car jolts forward or stops abruptly. The seat belts in a race car are working at all times. Drivers get into their seats, lock their seat belts, and then give the belts an extra tug, making them as snug as possible. In case of an accident, a driver wants to be strapped in tightly because the less he moves around, the less likely he'll be injured.

If you're listening in on a radio scanner during a race, you may hear a crew chief tell his driver to "give one more tug" on his seat belts during a race. Why? No matter how cool it is outside, a driver's seat belts become looser and looser during a race because of the extreme heat inside the car. Drivers can lose as much as five to ten pounds during a race as they perspire, so they need to keep tightening their seat belts — during caution periods, not while going full speed — in order for the seat belts to provide optimum protection.

Putting out fires

In the early years of NASCAR racing, fires were a serious problem for drivers. To improve safety, NASCAR officials mandated that all drivers use rubber gas tanks — containers that were far less likely to puncture, burst, or explode upon impact. Now fire is rarely a problem in NASCAR — cars are built with fire walls between the trunk where the gas tank is located and the driver's compartment, as well as between the driver and the engine.

According to NASCAR rules, every car must have a fire extinguisher installed within the driver's reach. NASCAR has also mandated that the crewman who fuels the car wears fire-resistant gear — a suit, gloves, shoes, and helmet with face protection. (See Chapter 10 for more on gassing up a car during a pit stop.)

Preventing Flailing Limbs with Window Nets

While seat belts keep a driver secured to the seat, they don't keep a driver's head and arms inside a race car when the car tumbles. That's exactly what Richard Petty found out when his car flipped several times in May 1970 at Darlington Raceway after slamming into the inside wall along the frontstretch. When his car began to flip, Petty's left arm and head came flopping out the window as the car flew through the air. Petty survived the accident with only a dislocated shoulder, but NASCAR officials made sure nobody else would have to face the same threat by instituting the use of *window nets,* which are screens made of a nylon mesh material and cover the driver's side window (refer to Figure 11-1). They help keep the driver's arms and head in the car during an accident.

Drivers hook the window nets to the top of the window openings with a pair of latches similar to the one used in their seat belts. It's a quick-release latch that takes only a second to unhook. During a race, drivers unhook the window net after an accident, which signals they aren't hurt badly. In a multi-car accident, that signal helps safety workers determine which driver needs help first.

Window nets are used only on the driver's side of the car. On the passenger side, there sometimes is a clear, shatterproof plastic window that protects the driver and provides for better aerodynamics — but only at tracks one and a half miles or more in length. This window doesn't roll down because it's just a shield that fits into and is secured in the window opening. On smaller tracks and on road courses, however, cars don't use the passenger-side window — there's just a big opening.

Holding Your Head Still: Helmets and Head Protectors

Helmets are the number one piece of protective gear that drivers can't do without. Drivers don't just go to the local sporting goods store to buy their helmets, however. They get them from special manufacturers who fit the helmet specifically to a driver's head and put special padding inside the helmet to reduce impact during an accident. After an accident, these manufacturers examine the helmet and X-ray it to see whether there are any internal cracks. If there are, the driver has to replace the helmet.

Starting in 2002, NASCAR became the world's first major auto racing sanctioning body to mandate use of an approved head and neck restraints by all drivers on every type of race circuit. These head and neck restraints, called the HANS Device and the Hutchens Device, help reduce extreme head motion during incidents and sudden stops. The HANS Device utilizes tethers that are attached from the HANS collar to both sides of the driver's helmet. In the Hutchens Device, tethers are attached from the Hutchens body harness to both sides of the driver's helmet. Head protectors vary because each seat is customized to fit a driver's body.

Keeping Your Wheels on the Ground

After cars start spinning, they usually don't become airborne — despite being so aerodynamic. Cars have roof flaps on them designed to keep them on the ground. *Roof flaps* are rectangular pieces of metal attached to the roof of a car that are designed to lie flat when the car is moving forward, but pop into the air when a car spins backwards or sideways (see Figure 11-2). Roof flaps keep a car from lifting into the air.

NASCAR NEXTEL Cup Series cars also have a *roof hatch,* which is like a trap-door on the roof of the car. This hatch allows a driver to exit the car if his window opening is blocked somehow.

Figure 11-2:
Roof flaps and a roof hatch provide extra stability for the car and an escape hatch for the driver.

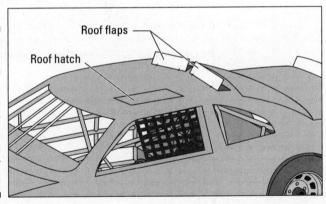

Staying Safe inside the Roll Cage

Drivers can walk away from accidents because a protective cage surrounds the driver, safeguarding him during impact. This *roll cage* of protective steel tubing called *roll bars* keeps the driver from getting crushed if the car flips on its roof or side (see Figure 11-3).

While regular passenger cars have a simple frame, the roll cage of a stock car is very extensive. For example, the driver's side door is reinforced with roll bars installed to protect the driver from a driver's side impact. Another bar travels through the center of a car's windshield, going from the top of the dashboard to the roof of the car. It keeps the roof from collapsing on a driver. All the roll bars within a driver's reach inside the car are wrapped in padding. With protective bars and padding nearly overdone to ensure safety, drivers can survive crashes at full speed, sometimes even without a scrape.

NASCAR officials make sure the roll bars that make up the roll cage are thick enough to keep a driver safe. During a routine inspection, they climb inside the car and use special instruments to determine the thickness of the steel. (Most of the roll bars are in plain view inside the car.) They also examine the roll bars to make sure teams haven't drilled holes in them to make the car lighter in certain areas. Officials also make sure that roll bars are made of steel and not a lighter, softer, or less-durable metal. (See Chapter 5 for more information about inspections and ways teams try to get around the rules to gain an advantage.)

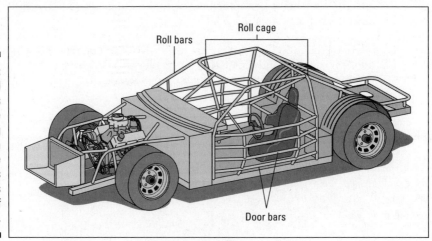

Figure 11-3:
The roll cage is protective steel tubing that keeps a driver safe in case his car rolls on its roof or side.

Roll cage

Roll bars

Door bars

Racing Uniforms: Not Your Ordinary Sunday Outfit

Just like other professional athletes, NASCAR drivers have uniforms. But in racing, those uniforms serve many more functions than simply identifying who is who outside of the race car. The uniforms have a special, protective use in case of a fire in the car.

Drivers wear a fire-resistant suit that's similar to a jumpsuit (see Figure 11-4). It covers their legs and their arms and zips up from their waist to their neck. Under those suits, drivers wear fire-retardant long underwear. While these suits make drivers hotter and more uncomfortable inside the car, the benefits are worth it. In the rare instance of a fire, the uniform can be a lifesaver by preventing burns.

In addition to their firesuits, drivers also wear special, space-age gloves and boots that protect their hands and feet from the heat and possible fires inside the car. While the boots are insulated to keep out heat, drivers often also wear heat shields over their boots because the floorboards and pedals get so hot that the heat's unbearable without additional protection. Sometimes even those heat shields don't provide enough protection. Some of the more creative drivers cut out the bottom of Styrofoam cups and stick them on their heels. But other drivers try to tough it out. Dave Marcis for many years hopped into his car wearing old-fashioned, wing-tip street shoes with no extra protection.

To give you an example of how hot the floorboards can get, Tony Stewart forgot to put on his heat shields for one race in 1999 and ended up with burns and blisters on his heels, which kept him out of commission for more than a week. After a race in 1998, Johnny Benson gave his post-race interviews with his feet stuck inside a bucket of ice water.

Figure 11-4:
Drivers wear special jumpsuits, shoes, and gloves that protect them from possible fires in the car.

Chapter 12

Winning It All: Making It to Victory Lane and the Championship

In This Chapter

▶ Making the trip to Victory Lane

▶ Taking home the paycheck

▶ Understanding NASCAR's point system

▶ Winning a championship

*W*inning a NASCAR NEXTEL Cup Series race is every stock-car driver's goal. Some never get there, but those talented enough and lucky enough to win are certainly grateful when they finally reach the pinnacle of the sport. In some cases it takes years; in others just a few seasons. No matter how long it takes, the satisfaction of finally getting to Victory Lane makes the wait worthwhile. This chapter shows you what's involved in making it to Victory Lane and also how drivers compete in the Chase for the NASCAR NEXTEL Cup Series Championship.

Making a Grand Entrance: Heading into Victory Lane

Victory Lane isn't really a lane — it's more like a circle or square in a fenced-in area somewhere near pit road — but it's where a driver goes to celebrate after winning a race. After the winner crosses the finish line, he circles the track one more time for a cool-down lap and then drives down pit road toward Victory Lane. Before getting there, some drivers like to add some panache to their win by doing doughnuts — spinning the car in circles — in the infield or on the frontstretch. The car's wheels spin out, burn rubber, and send smoke into the air, leaving behind a bunch of tire marks and a bunch of screaming fans.

Some drivers go even further than just doing doughnuts as part of their celebration. The late Alan Kulwicki, the 1992 NASCAR Cup champion, who was of Polish descent, used to drive the opposite way around the track to celebrate a win. That way, his driver's side window faced the crowd so they could see him smile and pump his arm — and he could see the crowd cheer. It became known as Kulwicki's trademark "Polish Victory Lap" before he died in a plane crash in April 1993. (See Chapter 16 for more on Kulwicki.) Several drivers who admired Kulwicki continue to drive a "backward" victory lap in honor of their friend.

Whatever unique celebration the driver thinks up, at some point he must start driving toward Victory Lane. On his way there, other crews may wait on pit road to give the winner a high-five, as they did in 1998 when Dale Earnhardt finally won the Daytona 500 on his 20th try. The winner's crew also usually waits just outside of Victory Lane to guide the driver in and greet their hero.

Who's in there?

Victory Lane is packed with all sorts of people. Of course, the winning team and the winning owner are in there, along with the driver's family, TV reporters, photographers, sponsor representatives, NASCAR media representatives, NASCAR officials, track officials, and track public relations people. (See Figure 12-1.) Fans often pack the fencing outside of Victory Lane to take pictures, but credentials, which allow you entrance into the garage area, cannot be purchased.

Figure 12-1: Driver Matt Kenseth celebrates with his family and team in Victory Lane after winning the Daimler Chrysler 400.

© Sherryl Creekmore/NASCAR

Live network TV (and radio) coverage

Ever notice when you're watching a race that you come back from a commercial and see the driver getting out of his car just in time for cameras to catch it on live TV? It's not luck; it's staged that way. A driver may drive into Victory Lane and pull his car up to the awaiting crowd, but he can't get out until the network TV crew tells him to. Even if he is about to burst with excitement over the win or is exhausted from the heat of the day, he has to sit in the car and wait a few seconds until the commercial break is over. Then, and only then, can the driver dramatically emerge from his car, climb on the roof, and start spraying people with champagne or any other available liquid.

After that, the winner has time only to give his crew chief or owner a quick handshake and his wife a quick peck on the cheek before he gets interviewed on live TV. After TV is done, he gets interviewed on live radio, which most of the time is broadcast throughout the grandstands. After TV and radio interviews are done, the photo session begins.

Photos and the hectic hat dance

A hoard of photographers wait somewhere inside Victory Lane to take pictures of the winner, his crew, his family, and his sponsors. But it's not just a quick snap-and-go photo shoot as you may expect. A driver poses with the following people each time he wins:

- His team
- His car owner
- His family
- His car owner's family
- Each of his sponsors
- The event sponsors, such as Coca-Cola employees at the Coca-Cola 600
- Representatives from his car manufacturer

The photo shoot is especially complex because a driver has to do the *hat dance*. He must put on and take off dozens of caps each with different sponsor logos on them. Each time the driver puts on a cap, the photographers snap photos to send or sell to the sponsor. Those photos are one of the perks a sponsor gets for being involved with the team and in the sport. While a driver appreciates all the sponsors' involvement, you can bet that it's a challenge to smile as big at the end of the hat dance as at the beginning. Still, even after posing for his 45th picture, the driver doesn't have too tough a time smiling. After all, he's just won a NASCAR NEXTEL Cup Series race! And that's not an easy thing to do.

Newspaper and magazine reporters

The Victory Lane proceedings may last more than an hour, depending on the race, but even then the driver isn't free to go celebrate with his crew. Track public relations representatives whisk the driver away to the press box where he and his crew chief or car owner talk to newspaper and magazine reporters for about a half hour. There's always a question-and-answer session in front of the group and often another session in which reporters get to ask the driver questions in a small group.

Stopping by the suites

After that's done, the afternoon or night still isn't over. The winner goes to the suites where employees from sponsoring companies await him. He answers a few questions and then signs autographs. Champagne flows freely for everyone there in order to celebrate the victory some more. At some tracks, the driver also may go to the track owner's suite or a NASCAR suite after winning.

The Growing Race Purse

NASCAR racing has become more and more lucrative over the years. Just look at how much today's drivers win each season. In the years that NASCAR legend Richard Petty raced (from 1958 through 1992) he won 200 races, seven NASCAR Cup championships, seven Daytona 500s, and $7,755,409 — making him the most successful NASCAR driver in history. That means he averaged about $221,580 per season in on-track winnings for 35 years. While other drivers during the modern era (since 1972) have earned more money then Petty, it is not likely that any driver will ever again win 200 races.

Today, however, even the non-winning drivers average much more than that every year:

- ✔ From 1994 to 1998, Ward Burton won one race and averaged $866,820 per season.

- ✔ In that same time, Ward's brother, Jeff, won five races and averaged $1,407,774 per season.

- ✔ In 1997 and 1998, David Green competed in 41 NASCAR Cup Series races — finishing only 30 of them and failing to record any top-ten finishes. Still, he averaged $476,852 each season.

- ✔ Jeff Gordon tops everyone. From 1993 through 2003 he won 64 races, four NASCAR Cup championships, and $58,525,057. In 1998 alone, he won $9,306,584 — more than Richard Petty won in a 35-year career.

When a driver wins a race, NASCAR publishes the amount they've won. That's the number you see in the newspaper the next day. But drivers don't leave the racetrack with all that cash stuffed into their driver's suit. They have to share the winnings. Depending on their contract with their team owner, drivers get up to 50 percent of the money they win.

Winning a race can be very lucrative, but so can just starting a race. Michael Waltrip won $1.4 million for his 2003 Daytona 500 triumph, while last-place finisher Ryan Newman went home disappointed but $195,663 richer. Not all races are as financially rewarding as the Daytona 500. A *race purse*, which is the money the track pays to drivers who start the race, varies from event to event and track to track. Some races, such as the Brickyard 400, pay the highest purses because they draw the largest crowds.

A breakdown of winnings

Ever wonder where all the prize money comes from when a driver wins a race? Table 12-1 shows a breakdown of the purse that Jeff Gordon won when he earned $1,637,625 at the 1998 Brickyard 400 at Indianapolis Motor Speedway. It was one of the highest payouts in auto racing history.

Table 12-1 Jeff Gordon's $1.6 Million Purse	
Source	*Amount*
Race purse and TV money (both from the track)	$270,875
NASCAR car owners "Winner's Circle" award (The ten most recent winners qualify for this program)	$10,200
NASCAR car owners "Plan 1" award (The top 30 teams from the prior season qualify for this program)	$7,000
Winston Leader Bonus (Awarded to any driver who wins a race and leads the series point standings at the conclusion of that event. The bonus starts out at $10,000, then increases $10,000 for each race it goes unclaimed. Jeff Gordon won $160,000, the record pay-out for this award, when he won the DieHard 500 at Talladega Superspeedway in 1996. Two years later, Gordon won $290,000 of a possible $330,000 after winning the bonus 11 times.)	$10,000
Third place qualifying award	$2,500
Defending NASCAR Winston Cup Series Champion Award (Given to the defending NASCAR Winston Cup Series champion each time he starts a race)	$5,000
PPG "Winner's Trophy" Award (from the track)	$225,000

(continued)

Table 12-1 *(continued)*	
Source	**Amount**
Lap leader bonus (for leading the most laps)	$10,000
Kodak "Photo Finish" Award (to winner)	$10,000
Herff Jones "Champion of Champions" Award (to winner)	$10,000
Ameritech "Youngest Driver" Award	$5,000
Premier Farnell Corp. Race Team Excellence Award (to winner)	$5,000
Premier Farnell Corp. Mechanical Excellence Award (to winner)	$5,000
Snap-On Tools "Top Five" Award (for drivers finishing in the top 5)	$2,500
"No Bull 5" $1 Million Bonus	$1,000,000

Picking up contingency awards

NASCAR and its sponsoring companies award special funds called *contingency awards*. Table 12-2 lists some of the contingency award sponsors and the awards they give. (The amounts listed are per race). Not all drivers participate in all the available awards, especially if they have contingency sponsors whose participation is deemed a conflict of interest. (See Chapter 2 for more on contingency awards.)

Table 12-2	Contingency Awards*
Sponsor	**Award**
Budweiser Pole: The fastest qualifier, who starts the race from the No. 1 position	$5,000
McDonald's/Powerade Drive-Thru Pit Championship: Goes to the driver with the shortest cumulative (year-long) time on pit road	$20,000
MBNA Mid-Race Leader: Goes to the driver who leads at the mid-point of a race	$10,000
Goodyear Gatorback Fastest Lap: Awarded to driver to turns the fastest lap while leading the race	$5,100
Mobil 1 Oil: Awarded to the race winner	$5,000
Outback Steakhouse: Awarded to the race winner	$5,000

Sponsor	Award
USG Driver of the Race: Goes to the race winner	$5,000
WIX Filters: Awarded to driver who leads the most laps in a race	$5,000
Clevite Engine Builder of the Year: Goes to engine builder whose car qualifies and finishes best at each race	$5,000
Raybestos Brakes: Goes to the highest-finishing rookie at each race	$1,500
Waste Management: Goes to driver who picks up most positions between qualifying and the end of the race	$5,000

Given by companies whose products a driver uses or whose decals a driver displays on his car.

Understanding the Points System

After every event, points are given to drivers and their car owners, depending on where they finish in a race. The system used today was put into place in 1975, so that drivers and teams could vie for a series championship.

The formula for doling out points was designed to reward teams and drivers who support the series by racing in it on a consistent basis. At the time it was designed in 1972, a significant number of NASCAR teams didn't run the entire series. The winner of a race gets 180 points, and the last-place finisher receives 34 points. You can see how somebody can lose a lot of ground in the NASCAR NEXTEL Cup Series championship if he blows an engine and finishes last.

Earning points

Both car owners and driver earn points, but do so in slightly different ways. A driver accrues points (called *driver points*) for the races he competes in, whatever car he drives. But a car owner accrues points — called *car owner points* — whenever his car is in a race, no matter who's driving it. This ensures that teams reap benefits from running in a race and investing in the sport. Driver points accumulate toward the championship, while owner points accumulate to help teams obtain provisional qualifying entries (see Chapter 8 for more on how provisional entries work).

This points system is the reason you sometimes see drivers with the flu, broken bones, or other maladies slide into their cars on race day just to complete one lap. They don't do that because they love pain but because a driver needs to complete one lap of a race in order to earn points. (NASCAR awards points to the driver who starts the race.) After that lap (or after he can't take the pain anymore), he pulls onto pit road where a relief driver replaces him.

The *relief driver* may be a driver who had mechanical problems with his car and retired from the race early. Or he may be a NASCAR Busch Series driver who just happens to be at the race that day. Regardless of the relief driver's experience, he's someone who gets in the car because the primary driver isn't healthy enough to finish the race. The relief driver may hop in the car for free or may charge a one-day fee for his services, depending on how well the driver and team owner know the relief driver and whether that relief driver is willing to do the team a favor. Whatever it costs, the injured driver or the team owner is happy to pay. If that relief driver finishes well, the injured driver ends up with the championship points because he started the race. And the car owner accumulated those points, too, no matter who drives his car.

Breaking down the point earnings

Here is a breakdown of each finishing position and how many points the driver and car owner earn for that race:

- 1st place — 180 points
- 2nd place — 170 points
- 3rd place — 165 points
- 4th place — 160 points
- 5th place — 155 points
- 6th place — 150 points
- 7th place — 146 points
- 8th place — 142 points
- 9th place — 138 points
- 10th place — 134 points
- 11th place — 130 points
- 12th place — 127 points
- 13th place — 124 points
- 14th place — 121 points
- 15th place — 118 points
- 16th place — 115 points
- 17th place — 112 points
- 18th place — 109 points

- 19th place — 106 points
- 20th place — 103 points
- 21st place — 100 points
- 22nd place — 97 points
- 23rd place — 94 points
- 24th place — 91 points
- 25th place — 88 points
- 26th place — 85 points
- 27th place — 82 points
- 28th place — 79 points
- 29th place — 76 points
- 30th place — 73 points
- 31st place — 70 points
- 32nd place — 67 points
- 33rd place — 64 points
- 34th place — 61 points
- 35th place — 58 points
- 36th place — 55 points
- 37th place — 52 points
- 38th place — 49 points
- 39th place — 46 points
- 40th place — 43 points
- 41st place — 40 points
- 42nd place — 37 points
- 43rd place — 34 points

Racking up bonus points

In addition to the regular points that drivers and teams get for competing in a race, they also can earn bonus points in a couple of different ways:

- **Any driver who leads a lap gets five extra points.** That means he must be in front of the field when crossing the start/finish line. So, a race winner gets a minimum of 180 points for winning a race because, at the very least, he led the final lap. Sometimes a driver stays out when the rest of the field makes a pit stop just so he can lead one lap and pick up those five extra points. A driver may do this when he's scrounging for points because he is in the chase for the championship or because he is fighting to get in the top 25 in the standings so that his team can get unlimited provisionals (see Chapter 8 for info on provisionals for qualifying).

✔ **The driver who leads the most laps gets five bonus points.** A race winner potentially can earn 190 points for winning — 180 for the victory, five for leading a lap, and five more for leading the most laps. Sometimes it doesn't work that way, and a race winner leads only one lap — the last.

Winning the NASCAR NEXTEL Cup Series Championship

Winning the NASCAR NEXTEL Cup Series championship — stock-car racing's version of the World Series, the Stanley Cup, or an Olympic gold medal — isn't necessarily about winning the most races, although that certainly helps. It's about winning the most points during a season.

Beginning in 2004, NASCAR introduced the Chase for the NASCAR NEXTEL Cup Series championship, a completely new system for crowning a champion. Following the fall race at Richmond International Raceway, only the top 10 drivers in the point standings — or any driver within 400 points of the leader — are eligible to contend for the series title. With 10 races remaining, starting at New Hampshire International Speedway, the points leader starts over with 5,050 points; the other contending drivers start over with totals in decreasing five-point increments according to their rank. The revamped points among the top-10 drivers not only closes the points race, but means a driver who has an accident or technical failure can quickly be eliminated from the title race, although they are guaranteed finishing 10th or better.

The race for the championship is hectic, nerve-wracking business. In 1997, the championship came down to the last race of the season, the NAPA 500 at Atlanta Motor Speedway. Before the race began, nobody knew who would be the champion — Jeff Gordon, Dale Jarrett, or me. Gordon had to finish 18th or better to win the title, otherwise Dale or I would have had a chance. As it turned out — unfortunately for me — Gordon finished 17th in the race and won his second title. Jarrett finished second in the championship, just 14 points behind Gordon. I finished third in the championship, just 29 points out of first.

A driver doesn't always clinch the championship at the final race of the season, however. If his lead is big enough, he can clinch the title with two or three races to go. That means he's gained enough points that the driver in second place has no mathematical chance at catching him. The first-place driver could finish last in the remaining races — and sometimes not even start those races — and he still would walk away the champion.

What it means to be the best

In 2003, NASCAR Cup champion Matt Kenseth earned $9,422,764; by comparison 1998 champion Jeff Gordon took home a championship check made out for about $2 million. But although that mega money prize may be the most obvious perk of winning the championship, there are many others:

- **Media exposure:** After winning the NASCAR NEXTEL Cup Series championship, the driver goes on a whirlwind media tour. Reporters interview him, and photographers take thousands of photos. He traditionally is invited to visit *Late Night with David Letterman* and *Live! With Regis & Kelly*. It's a thrill from the moment he wins until the end of the next season when his reign ends (unless he wins the title again). A driver's sponsors are ecstatic about the media blitz, which gives them even more exposure than usual.

- **Prestige:** Winning the championship means that you're the best stock-car driver on the best team that year. And no matter how your career unfolds after you win NASCAR's top honor, you'll always be known as a NASCAR NEXTEL Cup champion. Fans and other drivers never forget it — and the record books don't erase it.

- **Respect:** When you win a championship, other drivers and teams look at you differently. It doesn't matter whether they like you as a person; they respect you for your accomplishment. They know how good a team must be *throughout* the season — not just *part* of a season — to win the title. Drivers can't just win a majority of the races and expect to win the championship. They have to record good finishes week after week and finish every race — or nearly every race. If a driver wins half the races in a year, but gets into accidents and fails to finish the other half — which are called *DNFs* because a driver *did not finish* — he isn't going to win the championship. Terry Labonte is a perfect example of the consistency required. He had won only two races when he won the 1984 championship, and then only won two races when he won the championship again in 1996, proving race wins don't win championships; consistency does.

- **A great parking spot:** The reigning champion gets to park his team hauler in the No. 1 spot in the garage and also uses the best garage stall at each track for the entire year. The rest of the teams line up their haulers and use garage stalls according to where they rank in the points championship.

But of all the perks a driver gets for winning the NASCAR NEXTEL Cup Series championship, the end-of-the-year banquet may be the most fun. Each year during the first weekend in December, NASCAR holds an award banquet at the luxurious Waldorf-Astoria Hotel in New York City. That's where NASCAR pays tribute to the champion and his team. It's also where NASCAR and NEXTEL hand the drivers checks for their year-long performance, from the champion's $5 million to the $1 million awarded the driver who finishes 11th.

Numerous trophies are also awarded, including the one for the series champion and the rookie of year. The spouse of the champion traditionally also receives nice gifts, including a replica of the winner's ring.

In the week preceding the banquet, the champion is ferried around the city in a limousine. He goes to photo shoots, newspaper interviews, and live TV programs. Broadway shows are a top draw, as are meals at New York's finest restaurants. He and his family stay in the most glamorous suite at the Waldorf, which can cost more than $7,000 a night.

After the driver finishes his media tour of New York City, he dresses up and heads for the banquet. It's a black-tie function where everybody celebrates the end of the season. Drivers, team owners, and crew members wear tuxedos instead of their driving suits or uniforms (you'd be amazed at how they clean up), and wives and girlfriends dress in sparkling gowns. While all drivers are invited to the year-end ceremony, only those who finish in the top 10 in NASCAR NEXTEL Cup Series points give speeches to the crowd packed into the Grand Ballroom. That's one big difference between finishing 10th and 11th in points; only the top-10 are called up on stage.

Winning the Raybestos Rookie of the Year Award

The Raybestos Rookie of the Year Award is one of the honors given out at the NASCAR NEXTEL Cup Series banquet. All the drivers running their first full season on the circuit are eligible, unless they've run more than five races in the series during another year. Some of the best drivers in NASCAR history are former Rookies of the Year, including NASCAR Cup Series champions Dale Earnhardt, Jeff Gordon, and Rusty Wallace.

NASCAR and Raybestos award Rookie of the Year honors to the first-year driver whose best 15 finishes are higher than any other first-year driver in a complex scoring system that gives one point to every rookie who makes a race, ten points to the highest finishing rookie, and nine points to the next highest finishing rookie. Top-ten finishes are awarded extra points.

Rookies get bonus points three times a season, which NASCAR awards after the 10th race, the 20th race, and the season's last race. The highest rookie at those times gets ten bonus points, the next highest one gets nine bonus points, and so on.

NASCAR also doles out discretionary points at the end of the year based on how a driver conducts himself with the fans, the media, and his fellow competitors. This way, NASCAR officials have the final word on which rookie wins the award.

Part IV
Keeping Up with NASCAR Events

The 5th Wave   By Rich Tennant

"I'm a big fan of Mark Martin too, but when did they start televising his drives to the mall?"

In this part . . .

This part is completely dedicated to budding NASCAR fans — and even some who have been around a while and want to be on the cutting edge of fandom. Whether you're a NASCAR novice or a NASCAR expert, you'll find this part handy because it tells you all about each of the tracks that host NASCAR NEXTEL Cup Series races, which are the top races in NASCAR. The rest of this part explains the dos and don'ts for NASCAR fans: what to wear, what not to wear; what to bring, what not to bring; which driver to root for, which driver not to root for (anyone but me)! You can also find listings of NASCAR TV shows, radio programs, and Web sites so that you can explore and discover the sport from the comfort of your own home.

Chapter 13

Getting the Lowdown on Each NASCAR Track

Some people think NASCAR drivers just drive in circles all the time. They get into cars, go fast, and turn left — doing the same thing week after week without any variance or scenery changes. That couldn't be farther from the truth.

The races are always different, even though drivers do go fast and turn left most of the time. It's hard to tell from the grandstands, but each track has its own characteristics that make it challenging. One track may be *high-banked* in the turns — which means the racing surface is steeply sloped — while another track may be nearly flat. One may have a smooth surface, while another has plenty of bumps. One may have a wide *straightaway*, which is the long section of track between the turns, while another may have a narrow straightaway.

Not only does each track feel different to drive on, but each looks different, too. You can find superspeedways (the longest of all NASCAR tracks), intermediate tracks, short tracks, and road courses. All have different sizes and shapes — and if a driver wants to be successful, he must be able to negotiate every track with skill. Drivers have to be versatile and able to adapt quickly to different tracks each week.

NASCAR's wide range of racetracks does more than pose a challenge for the drivers — it also gives fans variety. If watching the bump-and-pass moves on a short track doesn't thrill you, perhaps you're drawn to the high speeds of a superspeedway. Or maybe you find watching a racer's agility on a road course more thrilling. Whatever your taste, NASCAR has a track for you. Each track also has a seat for you. Many racetracks seat more than 100,000 fans, not including the infield, which is filled with fans perched atop motor homes and cars to get a glimpse of the action.

This chapter gives you the lowdown on all the different track types and the styles of racing they produce. It also gives you a brief intro to each of the NASCAR tracks.

Superspeedways Are Super Fast

If you're looking for high-speed thrills, you'll love superspeedways. Drivers race in excess of 180 mph down the straightaways while just inches apart from each other, and long conga lines of cars zoom past the start/finish line in a blur of color.

In NASCAR NEXTEL Cup Series racing, only two tracks are technically considered superspeedways. While the previous definition of a superspeedway was any track one mile or more in length, that has changed now that NASCAR has introduced bigger, faster, and higher-banked tracks into its series. Right now, drivers and crew members consider only two tracks in NASCAR as superspeedways: Daytona International Speedway and Talladega Superspeedway. They fall into that category because of their size (2.5 miles or more), because they're high-banked (at least 31 degrees), and because they require use of carburetor restrictor plates.

This section shows you why carburetor restrictor plates are used and how teams prepare for racing on the superspeedways.

Restrictor-plate racing

In the past, cars used to average speeds of more than 200 mph circling these tracks, but in 1988, NASCAR officials decided to slow the cars down to make races safer. The plates were introduced after Bill Elliott turned a qualifying lap of 212 miles per hour in 1987. Knowing the crews would continue to find more speed in newer engines, the plate was added at the fastest superspeedways in the series. Despite the plates, the laps remain some of the fastest of the year, as the frontstretch and backstretch are long enough for car to reach maximum (although still restricted) speeds.

A *carburetor restrictor plate* is a metal plate with four holes drilled into it that NASCAR officials place atop an engine's carburetor (see Chapter 5 for a diagram of the carburetor restrictor plate). The holes in the plate restrict the amount of fuel and air that flows through the carburetor and into the intake manifold, on its way to the combustion chamber. The fuel and air mixture must squeeze through the four small holes before flowing more quickly through the four larger holes in the carburetor.

In short, the plate chokes the flow of air into the engine, which reduces its horsepower. So, instead of cars roaring around the monster tracks with about 750 horsepower, they have about 450. And less horsepower means less speed. Although fans noticed a difference in the type of racing at the plate races (drivers weren't able to pass as easily as previously), the plates also benefited them physically, as incidents at non-supersonic speeds tend to keep debris from flying into the grandstands.

Although fans immediately felt the benefits of restrictor plate racing with the increased safety of grandstand areas, the drivers had to learn a new kind of racing for the superspeedway races: how to break out of packs caused by the cars being set up so equally.

The restrictor plates choke an engine to the point where throttle response is slower. So, instead of cars being able to accelerate away from each other, they drive around the track in packs — sometimes one large, single pack. And that leaves drivers feeling less in control of their cars. Drivers would much rather drive at staggered speeds in order to pass one another. Also, without the ability to zoom past a rival coming off a turn or into the backstretch, it's imperative for drivers and their crew chiefs to make "deals" by radio as the race winds down. Two drivers drafting (see Chapter 9 for a discussion of drafting) one behind the other can give the lead car the extra second needed to win the race.

Unlike other tracks, where drivers decide when to accelerate and when to brake, superspeedways make those decisions easy: drivers always have their foot to the floor and rarely brake (unless they see an accident). This is called *running wide open*. Drivers can do this at restrictor plate superspeedways because the engines are choked down. If the engine didn't have a restrictor plate, the car would be running well over 200 miles an hour even through the corners — and it would be nearly out of control.

Even though the restrictor plates cause cars to bunch in packs, many times you see a group of cars breaking away from the main pack to form a lead pack. However, if one of the drivers makes even the slightest mistake going 200 miles an hour with a train of ten cars behind him, he may inadvertently cause an 11-car pileup in no time.

At those speeds, drivers sometimes are able to react quickly to avoid an accident just ahead of them. Sometimes they miss a wreck by just a few feet. But most of the time, unfortunately, drivers can do nothing if a car just inches ahead of them blows a tire and veers wildly out of control.

The thrill of superspeedways

I'm one of the few drivers in the NASCAR NEXTEL Cup Series garage who knows how it feels to drive a car on a superspeedway without a restricted engine. That's a feeling a driver never forgets. I drove in an Automobile Racing Club of America (ARCA) race in 1981 at Talladega and averaged more than 200 mph per lap. We didn't race in packs back then because we didn't use carburetor restrictor plates and drivers had control over whether they were going to run wide open or not. A driver could go so fast that he needed to brake in certain situations (or else, he crashed) — so a driver and his skill were integral in performing well in the event.

At that time, no one dared run an inch off someone else's bumper because it was frightening. The cars ran fast, and drivers knew they were going fast. Now, though, it's like driving down the highway going 40 mph. Drivers aren't afraid of driving an inch behind the car ahead of them because they don't feel as if they're going fast at all. Drivers feel totally in control. But in a NASCAR NEXTEL Cup Series car, that feeling is deceiving. While we are driving slower, we're still going pretty darn fast. And if a driver crashes, it still hurts.

Aerodynamics: The sleeker the better

Race teams spend many long days working on their cars before arriving at superspeedways. That's because *aerodynamics,* or the airflow over the surfaces of a car, is crucial at those big, high-speed tracks. The long straightaways and wide, sweeping turns provide a perfect arena for cars to go fast. Even with restricted engines, the cars still exceed 180 mph on the straightaways. That means they're cutting through the air pretty fast.

Why is aerodynamics so important at superspeedways? At those tracks, a driver never takes his foot off the gas pedal, so one of the only ways to get an advantage over the competition is to have a car that slips through the air better. A sleeker car means a faster car. That's why race teams are forever refining and reworking the bodies of their cars in preparation for a superspeedway race. While a winning car at a short track may have a banged up side or a crumpled bumper, even the tiniest imperfections on a car costs precious speed on superspeedways — and can cost a win, too.

A physics lesson

Aerodynamics and superspeedways go hand in hand. In fact, you can see a good example of the effect of aerodynamics when you stick your hand out of a car window. When you cup your hand, you feel resistance from the air, and you have trouble keeping your hand still. But when you keep your hand flat like a knife or a wing, the air flows over your hand more easily and much of that pressure from the air is gone. That's the same way that race cars work. The shape of the car is critical when designing for improved aerodynamics. Teams want to make their car as sleek as possible, so that it slips through the air.

Wind tunnels: Laboratories for race cars

In preparation for a superspeedway race, such as the Daytona 500 that kicks off the NASCAR NEXTEL Cup Series season each February, teams take their cars to a *wind tunnel* to figure out how well air is flowing over their car. A wind tunnel is just what it sounds like: a tunnel that shoots wind at a car from all different angles. Just like other kinds of scientific testing, it's a slow and tedious process to get all the data from the wind tunnel, but the information is invaluable. Teams may make one change to the body of the car, and then go to the wind tunnel and compare the results to the last time they went. If the results are worse, then they know the change wasn't a good one and that they must go back a step and rethink their methods. During one day at a wind tunnel, a team may change the car 20 times before coming up with an aerodynamic shape that works for them. Any changes, of course, must remain within the template measurements mandated by NASCAR.

The following are some of the measurements taken at a wind tunnel:

- ✔ **Drag:** When a car moves through the air, the air causes different kinds of pressure on the surfaces of the vehicle. Drag is one of them. Drag also is something race teams can't stand because it slows the car down tremendously. Basically, drag is a major drag.

Drag is caused by several things, including a high amount of air pressure pushing on the front of the car and low air pressure pulling on the back of the car. Other things cause drag, such as air flowing through the cooling system, ducts in the body, and open windows. Air travels into these openings instead of smoothly sliding over the car. Also, friction between a car's body and the air flowing over it causes drag.

With less drag, a car can accelerate faster, especially at higher speeds, because it needs less horsepower to move forward through the air.

✔ **Downforce:** While drag is bad, one type of air pressure is actually good for a race car — and that's downforce. *Downforce* is the air pressure that pushes a car onto the track, giving it better traction at high speeds and on turns. When the air pressure on the top of the body is greater than the air pressure on the bottom of the body, you have downforce.

Even if a car isn't engineered to have a lot of downforce, NASCAR allows cars to have front air dams and rear spoilers, which help create downforce:

- A *front air dam* is a special extension that goes from the bottom of the front bumper and extends nearly to the ground. (See Chapter 4 for an illustration and further explanation.) Most of the time, passenger cars don't have them, but race cars do in order to control the amount of air flowing under the car and the amount of air pressure pushing the front end to the ground. The air dam reduces drag because air has less space to flow beneath the car; instead, the air slides over the car. The air dam also increases downforce because more air is flowing over the car, so more air is pushing down on the car, giving it more traction.

- A *rear spoiler* is a blade that runs along the back of a car's trunk lid. (Turn to Chapter 4 to for an illustration and more explanation.) When air flows over and along the sides of a car, it hits the rear spoiler and gathers in front of it, increasing the pressure on the top of the body. At a superspeedway, the spoiler angle must be 45 degrees, but at other tracks, each team determines the spoiler angle (usually from 60 to 70 degrees) so their car reaches its optimum speed. (That spoiler angle is one of the elements that teams test for when spending time at a wind tunnel test. They move the spoiler up and down, searching for the best combination of drag and downforce at a specific kind of track. The trick is finding a way to increase downforce while minimizing the resulting increase in drag.)

The trip to the wind tunnel is never a cozy one, and only a few team members go along to conduct the tests. It's a big deal that involves engineers from the manufacturer, wind tunnel engineers, and team owners. In fact, from time to time, NASCAR officials impound several NASCAR NEXTEL Cup Series cars after a race and take them to the wind tunnel themselves in their ongoing efforts to keep the cars as equal as possible. They make sure to bring at least one car from each manufacturer — which means at least one Chevy, one Ford, and one Dodge. These NASCAR tests are different than the private tests teams conduct in the wind tunnel. In private tests, the teams and the manufacturer

Rule changes make things equal

The heights of the spoiler and air dam don't stay the same throughout the year, necessarily. NASCAR officials constantly monitor if one car make has more downforce than another or if it has an aerodynamic advantage over another make. For instance, in 1998, NASCAR officials decided the new Ford Taurus had too much downforce because it was performing better on intermediate tracks than other cars — it could go faster on those tracks because it was sticking to the racing surface better, which allowed Taurus drivers to race through corners without slowing down much, while other drivers had to slow down in order to stay in control of their vehicle. Because NASCAR is forever searching to keep the three car makes as equal as possible (see Chapter 1), it changed the rules and required a smaller spoiler on every Taurus. The smaller spoiler gives the car less downforce and less drag, which makes the car less stable on the track, harder to drive, and slower, too.

are the only ones to see the data — and they pay for that right, too. Wind tunnel time is very expensive, costing about $16,000 for an eight-hour test.

In the group tests, though, NASCAR foots the bill and shares the data with all three manufacturers, just to give them information on whether they're ahead or behind in the area of aerodynamics. It also helps NASCAR keep the three cars in the same ballpark so they can maintain parity among the cars. If one car has great aerodynamics and another one doesn't, the sleeker car would win technically all the superspeedway races — and that wouldn't excite fans very much.

Testing at the racetrack

With all the pressures and forces affecting the way a car drives, NASCAR drivers and teams have to know a lot about physics. They use that knowledge during wind tunnel tests and also at track tests where teams test different body shapes and spoiler heights in order to find a car's maximum speed and best aerodynamic setup. At superspeedways, though, the tests are the most nerve-wracking because aerodynamics plays such a crucial role there. Teams gather information such as lap times, corner speeds, and suspension settings to figure out how to make their cars faster. While the body has to be nearly perfect for the car to cut through the air efficiently, the suspension package must be nearly perfect, too, so that the car can hug the ground as much as possible.

Rough-and-Tumble Short Tracks

While cars have to be nearly impeccable to win a superspeedway race, the opposite applies to short track races. They can, and they have, limped into Victory Lane battered and banged up but still victorious.

Short tracks are less than one mile in length, where aerodynamics and horsepower aren't particularly important in winning the race. That's because the track is so short, there's not much room to accelerate and get into open air, so sometimes drivers are on the brake almost as much as they're on the gas. Also, with little room for cars to move around, short-track races are filled with bumping and banging. Many times, you see the winning race car roll into Victory Lane with a bunch of dents, scratches, and tire marks on it. Even though the car may look pretty sad, it was still strong enough to survive a short-track race — and surviving is the key to winning.

The following speedways are the short tracks in the NASCAR NEXTEL Cup Series. They are the places where cars are bound to get a beating before the race is over:

✔ Bristol Motor Speedway, a high-banked, .533-mile oval located in Bristol, Tennessee.

✔ Martinsville Speedway, a nearly-flat, .526-mile oval located in Martinsville, Virginia.

✔ Richmond International Raceway, a .5-mile, D-shaped track located in Richmond, Virginia.

Short tracks create short tempers

The shorter the track, the less room the cars have to maneuver. And less room invites more contact among cars. So at short tracks, the etiquette changes a bit. Instead of passing someone on the outside or inside, some drivers opt for the bump-and-pass move (see Chapter 9 on racing strategies). They nudge the car ahead of them out of the way by bumping its rear bumper to push it up the track. Sometimes cars get penalized and sometimes they don't. That's the nature of short-track racing. It's high-contact, high-temper, and high-action crammed into one tiny track.

While short-track racing is a lot of fun, it has many accidents because cars don't have much room to move around and get all bunched up together. If one car spins out or loses control, the cars behind it may end up getting collected by the wreck because they have no where to go. Accidents happen really quickly at short tracks because the speeds are so fast and the tracks

MARK SAYS

Where stock-car drivers start out

Most NASCAR drivers started their careers driving on short tracks in the nation's smaller stock-car series, so short tracks are places many of us call home. People just don't grow up learning how to drive on a 2.5-mile paved superspeedway or a high-banked intermediate track. There aren't many around — and that's probably a good thing because a driver needs to have certain skills before he or she drives on those tracks, anyway.

So, beginning racers learn how to drive on small dirt tracks, where they hone their skills and improve their reaction times, and then move up to bigger tracks through the years. Still, that doesn't mean that short tracks are easier to drive — in fact, in many cases, they're more difficult. Just because a driver has a good, fast car doesn't necessarily mean he'll be in Victory Lane at the end of the race. Short tracks require that drivers have keen driving skills to pass or to stay in front, so they're a great place to learn the basics.

are so small. At Bristol, a car can circle the track in about 15 seconds. So when an accident happens, the cars behind the wreck can become a part of it in a fraction of a second.

Qualifying is particularly important at short tracks because passing on tracks so small is difficult. Even if a driver qualifies a decent 15th, he may be stuck there if he can't find a way around the cars ahead of him. Most race winners at these tracks come from the top-ten qualifiers. Most drivers who don't qualify in the top ten are cranky.

Short tracks are NASCAR's roots

Short tracks are special places in NASCAR history because racing started there and many racers started their careers there. Way before NASCAR formed in 1948, short tracks ruled the racing world. There was no such thing as a superspeedway or even 1.5-mile tracks. (In fact, I don't even think asphalt was that popular back then.) Those bigger tracks were too expensive to build, so track owners went with the plain and simple dirt track to get by — and those were the only tracks around. Sure, people always raced on the hard-packed sands of Daytona Beach, but in most parts of the nation, short tracks were all that racers had. Drivers either raced on a short track or they didn't race at all. That's how short tracks became so popular and how they provided a strong foundation for stock-car racing in America.

Intermediate Tracks Are Middle-of-the-Road

Not all racetracks in NASCAR NEXTEL Cup Series racing are superspeedways or short tracks. There are plenty of tracks that fall into a category between those two extremes, combining a diluted version of a superspeedway's high speeds with the rubbing-and-bumping kind of racing found on a short track. These combination tracks, which are usually oval tracks at least one mile but less than two miles long, are called *intermediate tracks*. (Keep in mind that NASCAR technically considers tracks one mile or more in length as super-speedways, but that technical definition isn't what drivers and teams go by.) The following are the intermediate tracks in the NASCAR NEXTEL Cup Series:

✔ Atlanta Motor Speedway, a 1.54-mile oval in Hampton, Georgia, just outside of Atlanta.

✔ California Speedway, a 2-mile oval in Fontana, California, near Los Angeles.

✔ Darlington Raceway, a 1.366-mile, egg-shaped oval in Darlington, South Carolina.

✔ Dover International Speedway, a 1-mile oval in Dover, Delaware.

✔ Homestead-Miami Speedway, a 1.5-mile oval in Homestead, Florida, near Miami.

✔ Indianapolis Motor Speedway, a 2.5-mile oval in Indianapolis, Indiana.

✔ Las Vegas Motor Speedway, a 1.5-mile oval in Las Vegas.

✔ Lowe's Motor Speedway (formerly Charlotte Motor Speedway), a 1.5-mile oval in Concord, North Carolina, just north of Charlotte.

✔ New Hampshire International Speedway, a 1.058-mile oval located in Loudon, New Hampshire.

✔ Michigan International Speedway, a 2-mile oval in Brooklyn, Michigan, just outside of Detroit.

✔ Phoenix International Raceway, a 1-mile oval located in Phoenix, Arizona.

✔ Pocono Raceway, a 2.5-mile triangular track in Long Pond, Pennsylvania.

✔ Texas Motor Speedway, a 1.5-mile oval located in Fort Worth, Texas.

Even though NASCAR's intermediate tracks are all comparable in size, that doesn't mean they host the same kind of races or are the same to drive on. Each racetrack has its own characteristics, such as high *banking* (when the racing surface is at an angle), bumpy racing surfaces, or difficult-to-negotiate turns. That's what makes each intermediate track unique. And that's what makes it challenging for drivers and interesting for fans.

The Dreaded Road Courses

It's not much of an exaggeration to say most NASCAR NEXTEL Cup Series drivers would rather call in sick than drive on a road course. Some drivers, however, are very skilled at road courses, including Jeff Gordon and Robby Gordon. For others, it's just not what they're used to. *Road courses* aren't shaped the way ovals are, with four turns and two straightaways. They're complex configurations of left and right turns of all sorts of angles. While some may be sweeping, gradual turns, others may be *hairpin turns* — which are drastic, sharply-angled turns that make drivers to slow down to a crawl. (These turns are shaped like a hairpin where drivers go into the turn traveling one direction and exit the turn going the opposite direction.) The whole point of it is that there's no consistency to the course — sometimes drivers feel as though they're driving through a great, big, hilly field; other times, they think they're racing through a maze.

Instead of holding the throttle wide open the whole way around the track as a driver does on a superspeedway, racing on a road course entails a lot of shifts in speed — and a lot of shifting gears. Pocono Raceway, which isn't a road course, is the only other track in the NASCAR NEXTEL Cup Series where drivers shift gears during the race. They shift at least two times per lap because of the sharp turns at the triangular track — but the road courses require much more shifting than that because of the many turns and elevation changes during an event.

Road course skills

Racing on road courses is a specialized skill for NASCAR drivers because they are so used to racing on circular tracks. So it's understandable to see stock-car drivers freak out a bit when they show up at a track with long straightaways, short straightaways, wide turns, sharp turns, dips, and slopes. It's just not what most stock-car drivers were trained to do. For me, though, driving on a road course comes more easily than for most stock-car drivers. In fact, it's almost second nature.

I learned how to drive a car — not a go-kart, but a real car — when I was just 14. I drove my car as fast as it would go, not only on paved road, but also on the hilly, curvy dirt roads of Arkansas. That's where I fine-tuned my driving skills, such as how to control a car going through turns and how not to run into ditches (which was important because there were plenty of ditches around to run into).Those lessons have helped me through the years on all tracks, but particularly on road courses. I won three consecutive races at Watkins Glen International from 1993 to 1995, so I can't complain much. Other drivers can't stand them.

NASCAR travels to only two road courses each year, with one race at each of the tracks:

- Infineon Raceway, a 1.95-mile, 11-turn road course in Sonoma, California.
- Watkins Glen International, a 2.45-mile, 11-turn road course in Watkins Glen, New York.

Racing under the Lights

While each NASCAR NEXTEL Cup Series track has its own appeal, some of the tracks have a special allure: night racing. While cars race the same way, the show they put on for fans is much different. When cars bottom out or crash against each other, sparks shoot into the air like fireworks. It's quite a spectacle.

More and more tracks are installing lighting systems so that they can host night races, or so that rain-delayed events can be held at night, if need be. Currently, five speedways host night NASCAR NEXTEL Cup Series events:

- Bristol Motor Speedway hosts night racing each summer at its second NASCAR NEXTEL Cup Series event of the season.
- Daytona International Speedway has a night race every July.
- Lowe's Motor Speedway hosts the NEXTEL All-Star Challenge race in mid-May and then holds the Coca-Cola 600 on Memorial Day weekend, which begins in the late afternoon and ends at night. And in 2004, the UAW-GM 500 in October was held at night.
- Richmond International Raceway holds night races every time NASCAR comes to the track.
- California Speedway outside Los Angeles starts races in the afternoon, with drivers taking the checkered flag at night.

For the drivers, night racing has a slightly different feel from racing during the day. The lighting systems have become so good that drivers actually can see more of the track, including many of the bumps and dips of the racing surface. Also, night races are cooler than daytime racing, especially in the summertime — and comfort means a lot when you're racing in (or watching) a three-hour race in the steam bath of Central Florida in July. The fans love night racing for the same reasons.

MARK SAYS

Night moves

Night races often provide plenty of excitement, with all the sparks flying off the cars and the blur of colors racing by. But drivers and crews also find racing under the lights thrilling for another reason. Racing on Saturday nights gives us Sunday off. So we don't mind that night races last until nearly midnight. After the races, we rush to our planes to get home as soon as possible, so we can go to sleep in our own beds and sleep late the next day. That gives us an extra day to spend with our families, go to our family church, run errands, or do things normal people do on weekends. It's kind of weird waking up on Sunday with no race to drive in, but drivers relish the moment, especially because our schedules are so packed during the week. It's no wonder that my wife and son love Saturday night races, too!

For a fan, night racing isn't too bad, either. After the race, you don't have to drive or fly home early the next morning to be at work on time. You can relax in your hotel or campground for one more night, then leisurely get up the next morning and mosey all the way home without any stress.

Who Owns the Tracks?

In the old days of stock-car racing, big-wig companies didn't own racetracks — people did. Families or individuals with money or land built small tracks in their communities so that people could enjoy racing and watching races there. Now, though, individually owned racetracks, at least on the NASCAR NEXTEL Cup Series level, aren't common. The big companies have taken over.

Two large companies, both publicly-owned with stock traded on the New York Stock Exchange, own most of the 22 tracks hosting NASCAR NEXTEL Cup Series races: International Speedway Corporation (ISC) and Speedway Motorsports, Inc. (SMI).

Here are the owners of the 22 tracks in NASCAR NEXTEL Cup Series races:

✔ **International Speedway Corporation,** or ISC, as it's known in the racing world, is the company that owns most of the tracks that host NASCAR NEXTEL Cup Series races. ISC is based in Daytona Beach, Florida. ISC owns the following NASCAR NEXTEL Cup Series racetracks: California Speedway, Chicagoland Speedway, Darlington Raceway, Daytona International Speedway, Homestead-Miami Speedway, Kansas Speedway, Martinsville Speedway, Michigan International Speedway, Phoenix International Raceway, Richmond International Raceway, Talladega Superspeedway, and Watkins Glen International.

- **Speedway Motorsports Inc.,** or SMI, is NASCAR's second-largest speedway owner. It is based in Concord, North Carolina, and O. Bruton Smith is the CEO. SMI owns the following NASCAR NEXTEL Cup Series tracks: Atlanta Motor Speedway, Bristol Motor Speedway, Infineon Raceway, Las Vegas Motor Speedway, Lowe's Motor Speedway, and Texas Motor Speedway.

- **Dover Motorsports, Inc.,** runs the Dover International Speedway.

- The rest of the NASCAR NEXTEL Cup Series tracks are owned by families who have held onto their tracks and not sold out to huge companies yet:

  - Indianapolis Motor Speedway is owned by the Hulman-George family. (Hulman Co.)

  - New Hampshire International Speedway is owned by the Bahre family.

  - Pocono Raceway is owned by the Mattioli family.

So even though big companies have entered the speedway ownership business, there are families that still own tracks.

A Snapshot of Each NASCAR NEXTEL Cup Track

With 22 tracks in the NASCAR NEXTEL Cup Series, how do you choose which one to go to? NASCAR weekends aren't inexpensive (after including tickets, travel, food, and lodging) so you should consider your options carefully.

Do you like the bumping and banging of a short track? Do the high speeds of a superspeedway get you pumped up? Do the thrills of a night race on an intermediate track get your heart racing? If you're not sure, watch a few races on television before you decide which track to go to. This section gives you the specs on each of the tracks. (Check out Chapter 8 for a description of the different track shapes.)

After you decide which track you like the best, call for tickets right away. Many times, races are sold out months — or even a year — in advance! The same goes for making hotel reservations. Race fans tend to stay at the same hotel year after year, renewing their reservations before they leave to ensure they have a place to stay the next year. So, if you're looking for lodging, start planning way in advance, perhaps by calling the local tourist bureau or chamber of commerce to see what's available. Also, if you want to camp out at the track (in the infield or adjacent to the track), many facilities require reservations — call the track for information. (See Chapter 14 for more info on getting tickets and lodging.)

Atlanta Motor Speedway

Atlanta Motor Speedway hosts two NASCAR NEXTEL Cup Series events each year, one in the spring and one in the fall. Both those events are lightning-fast because the track is high-banked and was repaved and reconfigured into a quad oval in 1997 (see Figure 13-1). The newly-paved track causes cars to stick to the track more so drivers can go faster through the turns without worrying about losing control. For example, Geoffrey Bodine set the track qualifying record for the NAPA 500 in 1997, the first NASCAR NEXTEL Cup Series race after the track was repaved. He went a blistering 197.498 mph, which is ultra-fast and ultra-scary for a driver on a 1.54-mile track.

Track specs

✔ **Shape:** Quad-oval, which is a modified oval with two extra, very slight turns. Those turns are located part-way down the frontstretch, one on each side of the start/finish line.

✔ **Length:** 1.54 miles.

✔ **Banking:** 24 degrees in the turns and 5 degrees in the straightaways.

Dates to watch

Mid-March and late October.

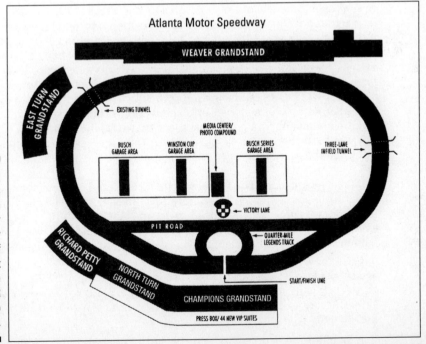

Figure 13-1: Despite its size, Atlanta Motor Speedway is one of the fastest tracks in the NASCAR NEXTEL Cup Series.

Getting to the track

The track is located at Highways 19 and 41 in Hampton, Georgia, about 30 miles south of Atlanta. To get there from I-75 south, take exit 77 south, and go 15 miles to the track. From I-75 north, take exit 70 and follow Georgia 20 for eight miles to get to the track.

Getting tickets

For tickets or information, call 770-946-4211 or check out the track's Web site at www.gospeedway.com.

Finding lodging

- ✔ Henry County Chamber of Commerce: 770-957-5786
- ✔ Atlanta Convention and Visitor's Bureau: 404-521-6600

The key to enjoying a race at Atlanta Motor Speedway is avoiding the traffic. Get to the racetrack extra early if you want to see the green flag fall, otherwise you may be listening to the beginning of the race on your car radio. Also, make sure to bring a raincoat to the spring race because it tends to rain — or perhaps even snow! — at some point during the weekend.

Bristol Motor Speedway

Even though Bristol is one of NASCAR's tiniest tracks at a half-mile, it doesn't lack action. Far from it. In fact, an improved speedway and grandstands and the intense on-track action have made it the hardest ticket to get on the circuit. The track has a concrete racing surface and the steepest banks on the circuit, with a neck-straining 36-degree banking in the turns (see Figure 13-2). People liken it to a Roman coliseum because more than 147,000 seats tower above the small track. Drivers describe racing at the track by comparing it to flying a Learjet around a clothes dryer or maneuvering a speed boat around a toilet. There's not much room on the track, but there's a whole lot of noise in the place — particularly with 43 NASCAR NEXTEL Cup Series cars circling the track and the roar of the engines reverberating off the aluminum grandstands.

Bristol is nicknamed "The World's Fastest Half-Mile" for a reason — cars lap the track in about 15 seconds. Blink a few times, and you've already missed the lead cars going by. The track hosts two NASCAR NEXTEL Cup Series events each year, one in the spring and another in late summer. The late summer event is held at night and is one of racing's hottest tickets.

Track specs

- ✔ **Shape:** Standard oval.
- ✔ **Length:** .533 miles.
- ✔ **Banking:** 36 degrees in the turns and 16 degrees in the straightaways.

Dates to watch

April and August.

Getting to the track

The track is located on Volunteer Parkway, Highway 11E, about five miles south of Bristol, Tennessee. To get there, take Virginia exit 3 off I-81 and follow Volunteer Parkway to the track. Or take Tennessee exit 69 off I-81 and follow Highway 37 to Highway 11E.

Getting tickets

For tickets or information, call 423-764-1161 or check out the track's Web site at www.bristolmotorspeedway.com.

Finding lodging

✔ Bristol Chamber of Commerce: 423-989-4850

✔ Bristol Convention and Visitor's Bureau: 423-989-4850

✔ Camping at the track: 423-764-1161

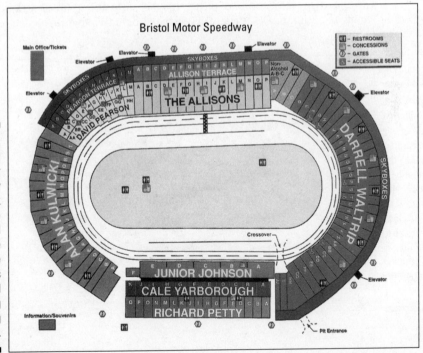

Figure 13-2:
Bristol
Motor
Speedway
isn't a track
for the
fainthearted
because
of all the
incidents
and
bumping
during
races there.

TIP

If you want to go to a race at Bristol, getting tickets may be difficult. Events are sold out years in advance, with most ticket holders keeping their seats from year to year. You can get to a race if you scour the classified section in racing magazines or newspapers for somebody selling tickets. Bristol does reserve tickets for each season that you can enter a drawing for. Check out its Web site for more information. Or you can take your chances and head to Bristol without tickets, hoping to bump into somebody hawking tickets near the track.

California Speedway

You'll find only two NASCAR NEXTEL Cup Series tracks on the West coast, and California Speedway is one of them (see Figure 13-3). The track was built by legendary IndyCar owner Roger Penske and is one of the snazziest tracks around. Drivers love it because it's laid out the way many think a track should be: it's a regular oval, not shaped like a dog's hind leg. Also, the racing surface is nice and smooth, making it a dream to drive on. In fact, the entire facility is a dream. It has meticulously groomed grounds along with neat parking lots and grandstands. The track workers smile and wave, even when they have to get up at 4 a.m. and direct traffic all day. The traffic flow to and from the speedway isn't too bad, either. It's a great place to incorporate into a family vacation to Disneyland. The track hosts two events each season.

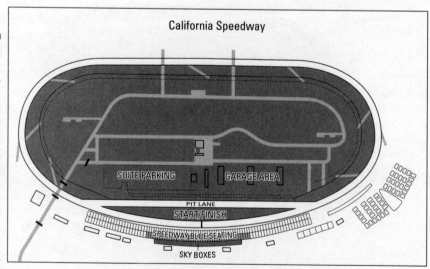

Figure 13-3:
California Speedway is a favorite among the majority of the circuit's drivers, with its close access to Los Angeles and the Pacific Ocean.

Track specs

- ✔ **Shape:** D-shaped oval.

- ✔ **Length:** 2 miles.

- ✔ **Banking:** 14 degrees in the turns, 11 degrees on the frontstretch, and 3 degrees on the backstretch.

Date to watch

End of February and September.

Getting to the track

The track is in Fontana, California, about 40 miles east of Los Angeles. To get there, follow I-10 east from Los Angeles and take the exit for Cherry Avenue. Head north to the speedway.

Getting tickets

For tickets or information, call 800-944-RACE or check out the track's Web site at www.iscmotorsports.com and click on California Speedway.

Finding lodging

- ✔ City of Fontana Chamber of Commerce: 909-822-4433

- ✔ City of Ontario Chamber of Commerce: 909-984-2458

California Speedway is just about an hour east of Los Angeles and Hollywood, the movie-star mecca. If you're in the mood for some people-watching, make this trip. Just give yourself plenty of time to get there and back, as traffic jams are a Southern California staple.

Chicagoland Speedway

One of the newest speedways in the NASCAR NEXTEL Cup Series, Chicagoland Speedway has quickly become a favorite of the drivers (see Figure 13-4). In addition to being a modern facility, it's close to some of the best restaurants in the country. While drivers don't have much time to act as tourists, they enjoy visiting the city and taking in its sites and sounds when they can. Since the track's opening in 2001, Kevin Harvick has been the man to beat, logging back-to-back victories in 2001 and 2002. Ryan Newman was the winner in 2003, and Tony Stewart (considered by many Midwesterners to be a home-town boy) went to Victory Lane in 2004.

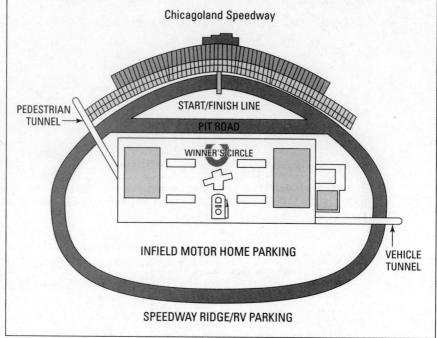

Figure 13-4:
Chicagoland
Speedway
is one of
the newest
tracks in the
NASCAR
NEXTEL Cup
Series.

Track specs

- **Shape:** D-shaped oval.
- **Length:** 1.5 miles.
- **Banking:** 24 degrees in the turns, 11 degrees on the frontstretch, and 5 degrees on the backstretch.

Date to watch

July.

Getting to the track

The track is in Joliet, Illinois. From I-55 southbound, take the I-80 exit east and then Illinois Hwy. 53 (exit 132A) south to track. From I-55 northbound, take River Rd. exit east, and then Hwy. 53 north to Schweitzer Rd. and the track. From I-80, take Hwy. 30 exit 137; go west on Hwy. 30, south on Gouger Road, and then right on Laraway to the track. From I-57 westbound, take Wilmington (exit 327) west, then Hwy. 45 north to Hwy 52, which you take north to Schweitzer Rd. and the track.

Getting tickets

For tickets or information, call Chicagoland Speedway at 815-722-5500 or check out the track's Web site at www.chicagolandspeedway.com.

Finding lodging

For information, call Chicagoland Speedway at 815-722-5500.

Darlington Raceway

Darlington is one of NASCAR's oldest and most ornery tracks. It was built in 1950 and is NASCAR's original superspeedway, which back then was any paved track a mile or longer (see Figure 13-5). Over the years, it earned a nickname as "The Track Too Tough to Tame" and there's a good reason for that. Most drivers can't tame it — and many drivers have trouble driving it.

The speedway is egg shaped, meaning one end (turns 1 and 2) has tighter turns than the other. The banking on the end with the tighter turns is two degrees steeper than the other end. Drivers have to pay attention to keep from smacking into the wall. Then again, smacking the wall at a storied place like Darlington is part of a NASCAR driver's rite of passage. Driving close to the wall is mandatory. Your car drifts up the groove on the racetrack and ends up only inches from the wall, many times scraping it and leaving a stripe on the car from the wall's paint. Over the years, that stripe has become known as the Darlington Stripe — and every driver who has raced there has earned it, whether he's a rookie or a veteran. Although Darlington isn't near a big city like the California Speedway and doesn't have sky boxes, it has its own history. While for many years it hosted a race during Labor Day weekend, beginning in 2005 that event will be held Mother's Day weekend in May.

Track specs

- **Shape:** Egg-shaped oval.
- **Length:** 1.366 miles.
- **Banking:** 25 degrees in turns 1 and 2; 23 degrees in turns 3 and 4; and 2 degrees on the straightaways.

Dates to watch

Saturday of Mother's Day weekend.

Getting to the track

The track is in Darlington, South Carolina, about 75 miles east of Columbia and ten miles north of Florence. To get there from I-95, take Highway 52 to Darlington. From I-20, take 401 east to Darlington. The track is on Highway 151/34, two miles west of Darlington.

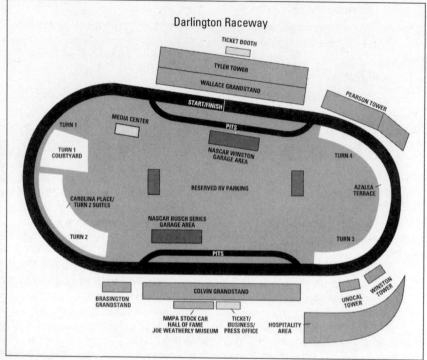

Figure 13-5:
Darlington Raceway, NASCAR's original speedway, is one of the toughest tracks in NASCAR NEXTEL Cup Series racing.

Getting tickets

For tickets or information, call 843-395-8499 or check out the track's Web site at www.darlingtonraceway.com.

Finding lodging

- Darlington County Chamber of Commerce: 843-393-2641
- Florence Chamber of Commerce: 843-665-0515
- Pee Dee Tourism Commission: 800-325-9005
- Camping at the track: 843-395-8499

When buying tickets to a Darlington race, try to get seats close to the turns because a lot of the action happens there. You also may want to plan a trip to the beach during your weekend at Darlington: Myrtle Beach is only 70 miles away, where you can play mini-golf, body surf, or even continue your race-filled weekend and head to the NASCAR Speedpark there, where you can race go-karts.

A preponderance of pond

Why is Darlington shaped so strangely? Well, at first it wasn't to make the track challenging for drivers. When building the track, the original owner, Harold Brasington, wanted his speedway to have sweeping turns all the way around, but a local farmer refused to sell his fish pond — the one that sat right in the way of one end of the proposed track — so Brasington had to squeeze that end of the track to fit it in the allocated spot. He also had to make the banking steeper on that end to make the turn easier for drivers to negotiate. Years later, the fish pond is still there and the track still boasts its weird shape. Good for the fish, tough for the drivers.

Daytona International Speedway

Daytona International Speedway is the most famous track in NASCAR racing, mostly because Daytona Beach is where NASCAR began. Even before NASCAR was founded, racers would flock to Daytona's hard-packed sand beaches to go head-to-head against each other while trying to avoid the incoming tide. Now, though, those racers and millions of fans each year flock to the 2.5-mile superspeedway a few miles inland from where NASCAR stock-car racing started (see Figure 13-6).

The high-banked, high-speed track hosts two official NASCAR NEXTEL Cup Series races each year — the Daytona 500 and the Pepsi 400, formerly known as the Firecracker 400. The track also holds the Budweiser Shootout, which is a non-points race about a week before the Daytona 500 consisting of pole winners from the previous year and one wildcard entry.

For the most part, race fans don't just show up in Daytona Beach the day before the Daytona 500 because there's plenty to see before the big event. The track hosts more than two weeks of racing each February, a time of the year known as *Speedweeks*. The annual series of events starts out with the Rolex 24 at Daytona, a sports-car endurance race. The stock-car portion kicks off with pole qualifying and the Budweiser Shootout. The NASCAR Craftsman Truck Series and the NASCAR Busch Series have their season-opening events — followed by the Daytona 500 on the final Sunday of Speedweeks.

The track decided to give competitors and fans a break from the heat, scheduling the summer Pepsi 400 in the evening.

Track specs

- ✔ **Shape:** Tri-oval.
- ✔ **Length:** 2.5 miles.
- ✔ **Banking:** 31 degrees in the turns, 18 in the tri-oval (frontstretch), and 3 degrees in the back straightaway.

Dates to watch

Mid-February and Fourth of July weekend.

Getting to the track

The track is in Daytona Beach, Florida, about 70 miles northeast of Orlando. From Orlando, take I-4 east to Daytona and exit on U.S. 92 or West International Speedway Boulevard. From I-95, take the U.S. 92 exit toward Daytona Beach.

Getting tickets

For tickets or information, check out the track's Web site at www.daytona intlspeedway.com and also www.nascar.com.

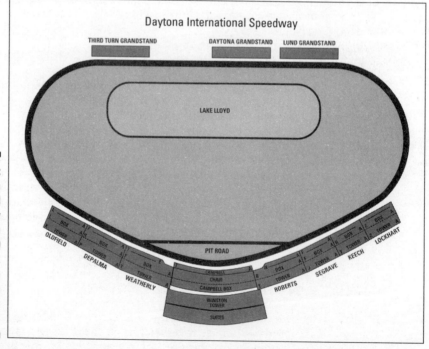

Figure 13-6: Daytona International Speedway hosts the Daytona 500 each year, one of the most famous auto races in the world.

NASCAR's Super Bowl

The Daytona 500, held at Daytona International Speedway each February, is the most famous stock-car race in the world. It's NASCAR's Super Bowl and is the race every driver dreams of winning. Why is it such a big deal? Not only does it pay the most money, but it also has the most prestige.

Some of the most legendary drivers in the world have won the event, including Richard Petty (a record seven times!), Cale Yarborough, and even Indy 500 winners Mario Andretti and A.J. Foyt. Dale Earnhardt considered it the biggest feather in his cap, and son Dale Earnhardt Jr., added it to his resume in 2004. But if you win the Daytona 500, not only do you join that elite group of drivers — but you also get loads of fame. The

winner goes on a whirlwind media tour the week after making it to the famed Victory Lane, making appearances on national TV shows like *Late Night with David Letterman* or the *Tonight Show.* So, if you're not famous when you win it, you will be by the time the week is over.

Winning the Daytona 500 is quite an accomplishment because about 200,000 fans watch it in person and millions of people watch it on TV, but there's something even more special about winning the 500-mile race. The driver who wins it feels pretty darn good about his upcoming season — the Daytona 500 kicks off the NASCAR NEXTEL Cup Series season every year and doing well in the race boosts a driver's (and his team's) confidence heading into the rest of the season.

Finding lodging

✔ Daytona Beach Chamber of Commerce: 904-255-7311

✔ Daytona Beach Area Convention and Visitor's Bureau: 800-854-1234

If you plan on bringing your family to Daytona Beach for the races, you'll find there are plenty of things to do in the area. Orlando, with Walt Disney World and Universal Studios, is just an hour away. The beach is just east of the speedway. But if you're in town, you really don't want to miss Daytona USA, a motorsports attraction right in front of the speedway that's part NASCAR museum, part interactive funhouse. You can watch movies, play video games, and even participate in a real pit stop. Tours of the speedway also are available, so even if you don't get into the infield on race day, you can see everything up close beforehand. Call 904-947-6800.

Dover International Speedway

There's nothing prim or proper about Dover International Speedway (see Figure 13-7). It's loud (with noise reverberating off the aluminum seats) and dirty (with dust kicked up everywhere), and it's good, hard racing (with fast cars running close together). For drivers, though, it's not quite relaxing enough. The racing surface used to be asphalt, but it's concrete now, making the ride bumpier than usual. Imagine driving down a concrete highway and hearing the "Thump-thump! Thump-thump!" of the wheels riding over the concrete seams on the road. Well, that's how drivers feel as their car travels over the rough concrete — and 400 miles of that thump-thumping isn't what I call a mellow afternoon. Most of the time, though, fans get their money's worth at the track dubbed the "Monster Mile," even though the drivers are exhausted and cranky when the day is over. While there's not much passing, the cars go frighteningly fast down the straightaways and into the high-banked turns.

Track specs

- ✔ **Shape:** Regular oval.
- ✔ **Length:** 1 mile.
- ✔ **Banking:** 24 degrees in the turns and 9 degrees on the straightaways.

Dates to watch

Early June and late September.

Getting to the track

The track is in Dover, Delaware, about 65 miles south of Philadelphia and 75 miles away from Baltimore. From New Jersey, take the N.J. Turnpike south across the Delaware Memorial Bridge and follow U.S. 13 south to the track. From Philadelphia, take I-95 south to I-495 south to U.S. 13. From Baltimore or Washington, take U.S. 50/301 east across the Bay Bridge, and then take U.S. 301 north to Maryland 302 east. After that, turn right on Maryland 454 at Templeville, which becomes Delaware 8, and turn left on U.S. 13.

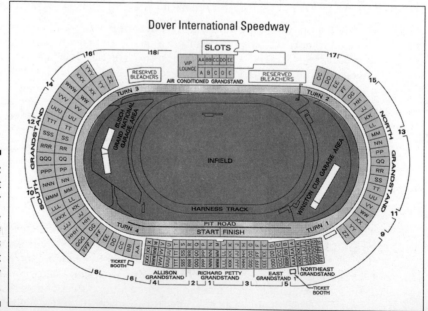

Figure 13-7:
Dover isn't a driver favorite, but the grandstands sell out nearly every time.

Getting tickets

For tickets or information, call 302-674-4600 or check out the track's Web site at www.doverspeedway.com.

Finding lodging

- ✔ Central Delaware Chamber of Commerce: 302-734-7514
- ✔ Delaware Tourism Office: 800-441-8846

Dover isn't the biggest town around and lodging is scarce and expensive, with race teams taking up the rooms at most of the hotels near the track. So when looking for a place to stay, try Newark or Wilmington, two cities north of the track. While the drive may be a bit longer, you'll have a better chance there than with the ones closer to the track.

Homestead-Miami Speedway

The 1.5-mile track south of Miami (see Figure 13-8) used to be called the Metro-Dade Homestead Motorsports Complex, but it was renamed the Homestead-Miami Speedway in mid-1998, just before NASCAR NEXTEL Cup Series' first race there in November 1999. When NASCAR hit south Florida, it was quite a culture clash. NASCAR has a distinctly southern, old-fashioned twinge to it. South Florida, on the other hand, is known for its international flair and the cutting-edge fashion of the South Beach area. But NASCAR racers and fans seemed to enjoy the trip south anyway, especially because of the weather in Homestead, which is normally mild in late November. Many NASCAR Busch Series competitors stay there for vacations after they're done racing because the series' season finale is there.

Track specs

- ✔ **Shape:** Regular oval.
- ✔ **Length:** 1.5 miles.
- ✔ **Banking:** 6 degrees in the turns and 3 degrees in the straightaways.

Dates to watch

November.

Getting to the track

The track is located in Homestead, Florida, 25 miles south of Miami. To get there from the north, take Florida's Turnpike to Speedway Blvd. (SW 137th Avenue) and go south. From the south, take U.S. 1 to Palm Dr.; then go east for 2½ miles. Turn left on SW 142nd Avenue.

Figure 13-8:
Homestead-Miami speedway hosted its first NASCAR NEXTEL Cup Series event in 1999 and is now a regular part of the schedule.

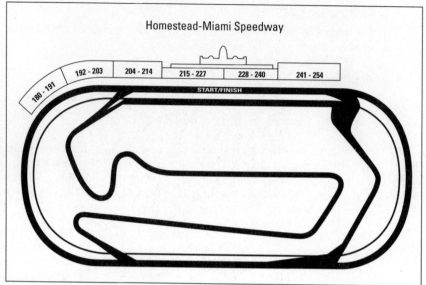

Getting tickets

For tickets or information, call 305-230-RACE or check out the track's Web site at www.racemiami.com.

Finding lodging

✔ Greater Miami Convention and Visitor's Bureau: 800-933-8448

✔ Homestead/Florida City Chamber of Commerce: 305-247-2332

When booking a hotel in the Homestead area, you may be tempted to search in and around Miami but don't forget to look south of the speedway, too. The Florida Keys are just over 45 minutes south of the track, and staying there gives you the opportunity to enjoy gorgeous blue ocean waters and white sand beaches while still staying relatively close to the track. Also, after the race most of the traffic flows north to Miami, so by staying in the Keys, your trip back may be easier.

Indianapolis Motor Speedway

Indianapolis Motor Speedway, nicknamed the "Brickyard" because its racing surface used to be paved with bricks, is hallowed grounds for IndyCar racing. It was built in 1909 and is the oldest continuously operating track in the world. The Brickyard became legendary for hosting the Indianapolis 500, the nation's marquee event for Indy cars, where more than 400,000 fans pack into the grandstands and infield. Because the track is such an IndyCar racing icon, many people thought hell would freeze over before stock cars raced on (and desecrated) the track.

Well, as it turned out, hell did freeze over. In 1994, the NASCAR NEXTEL Cup Series competed at the Brickyard for the first time, breaking tradition at the 2.5-mile track (see Figure 13-9). Now, the Brickyard 400 is one of NASCAR's most prestigious races.

When NASCAR comes to the Brickyard, the race is technically a sell-out, although no infield tickets are sold. Even so, there are almost 300,000 fans in the grandstands to see the Brickyard 400 — which makes it the biggest race, in terms of fan attendance, on the NASCAR circuit. Drivers get to see those fans, too. The turns are nearly 90 degrees, making it seem as if you're going to drive right into the grandstands before easing off the throttle to turn drastically left. It's scary, especially for rookies who aren't used to the sharp turns, high speeds on the straightaways, and racing in on the narrow speedway. As a driver, you just have to get used to it before you feel comfortable, which may take a few years because NASCAR only races once a year at the speedway.

Track specs

- **Shape:** Four-cornered oval, which is nearly a rectangle because the turns are almost at 90-degree angles.
- **Length:** 2.5 miles.
- **Banking:** 9 degrees in the turns and flat straightaways.

Dates to watch

Early August.

The track is at Indianapolis, Indiana (technically in a town called Speedway), and is located about seven miles northwest of downtown Indianapolis. To get there, take Exit 16A (the Speedway/Clermont exit) off I-465 west; then go east on 16th Street to the track.

Getting tickets

Tickets for the Brickyard 400 are primarily sold by mail order. Call 317-484-6700 for an order form or write to P.O. Box 24152, Speedway, IN 46224. The race sells out quickly, so you must call or write for an order form at least one month before the August race if you want to get tickets before they're sold out. In addition, tickets may be available through the speedway's Web site at www.brickyard400.com.

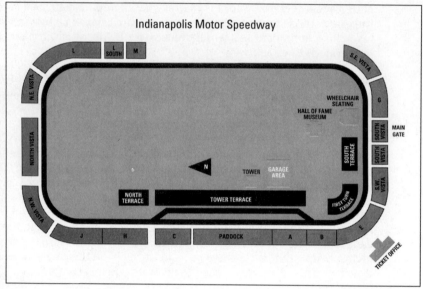

Figure 13-9: Indianapolis Motor Speedway is the home of the famed Indianapolis 500 — but also the Brickyard 400 NASCAR NEXTEL Cup Series race.

Getting to the track

Finding lodging

✔ Indianapolis City Center: 317-237-5200

✔ Indianapolis Convention and Visitors Association: 317-639-4282

✔ Indianapolis Chamber of Commerce: 317-464-2200

✔ Indianapolis Hotel Information Line: 800-323-INDY

No matter how high you get in the grandstands, your view of Indy's huge 2.5-mile track is limited. When buying tickets, your best bet is to sit somewhere in the frontstretch section where you can see cars come out of turn four, race down the straightaway, and then barrel through turn 1. But get the seats facing the infield, not the ones in the infield, if you want to have the best vantage point.

Infineon Raceway

For those mellow, wine-drinking race fans, Infineon Raceway in Sonoma, California, may be the quintessential venue (see Figure 13-10). The track, located in the heart of Sonoma Valley's wine country, is a twisting, turning road course with as many elevation changes as there are wineries nearby. Drivers have to deal with sharp turns, dips, and hills throughout the race, so it's exhausting as much as it is demanding.

Fans have it all together different. They are spread throughout the hills surrounding the track, drinking wine, snacking, and cavorting while watching the race. You can find some grandstand seating, but not much, so be prepared to bring a blanket and food so you can chill out while your wine chills. Then you can watch the race and enjoy the spectacular scenery of the valley. The track hosts one NASCAR NEXTEL Cup Series race each year.

Track specs

- ✔ **Shape:** 11-turn road course.
- ✔ **Length:** 1.95 miles.

Dates to watch

Late June.

Getting to the track

The track is located in Sonoma, California, about 40 miles north of San Francisco. To get there, take Highway 101 north to Route 37, and then take Route 121 to the track.

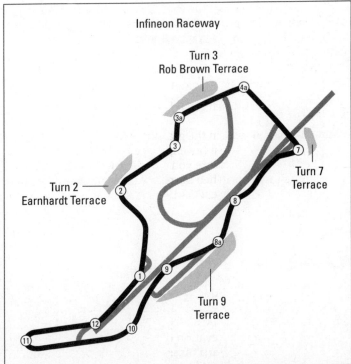

Figure 13-10: Infineon Raceway is one of two road courses in NASCAR NEXTEL Cup Series racing.

Getting tickets

For tickets or information, call 800-870-RACE or check out the track's Web site at www.infineonraceway.com.

Finding lodging

- ✔ Sonoma Valley Visitors Bureau: 707-996-1090
- ✔ Sonoma Valley Chamber of Commerce: 800-899-2623

Don't expect to see the entire racetrack if you're going to an event at Infineon. The track is so big and has so many dips and turns, that there's just no way to see the whole thing. So, when hunkering down to watch the race from the hillside, try to pick a place where you'll see at least one of the turns. That's where you'll find a lot of the action on a road course because a lot of passing is done there.

Kansas Speedway

New to the NASCAR NEXTEL Cup Series in 2001, the modern Kansas Speedway, which plays host to 80,000 fans, quickly became a driver favorite (see Figure 13-11). Located in the heart of the United States, Kansas Speedway is a favorite of multiple winner Jeff Gordon (2001–2002) and 2003 winner Ryan Newman. Although the drivers enjoy racing on tracks with a long history, there also is excitement that comes from racing at a new venue. At Kansas, the accommodations are excellent, including a top-of-the-line garage area and a smooth track surface.

Track specs

- ✔ **Shape:** D-shaped oval.
- ✔ **Length:** 1.5 miles.
- ✔ **Banking:** 15 degrees in the turns and flat straightaways.

Dates to watch

Mid-October.

Getting to the track

From the north: I-435 south to State Ave. Go east on State to north 98th St. Turn right on north 98th St. Turn right on France Family Dr. **From the south,** take I-435 north to State Ave. Go east on State Ave. to 98th St. Turn left on north 98th St. and left on France Family Dr. **From the east,** take I-70 west to I-435 north. Go east on State Ave. to north 98th St. Turn left on north. 98th St. and left on France Family Dr. **From the west,** take I-70 E. to I-435 North. Turn east on State Ave. to N. 98th St. Turn left on N. 98th St. and left on France Family Dr.

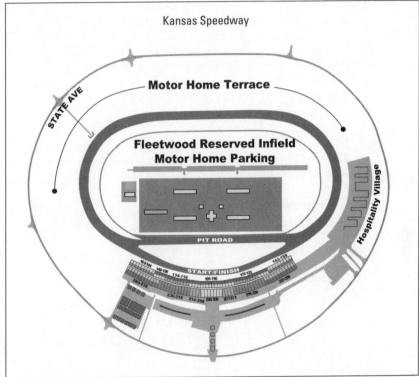

Figure 13-11:
Kansas
Speedway
quickly
became a
favorite of
Jeff Gordon.

Getting tickets

For tickets, contract the speedway at 400 Speedway Blvd., Kansas City, KS 66111 or call 913-328-3300. Also check out the Web site www.kansasspeedway.com.

Las Vegas Motor Speedway

If you're a race fan who loves nightlife, the Las Vegas Motor Speedway is your mecca for NASCAR racing. During the day, you get to watch great racing on a track that drivers love because there's plenty of room to drive (see Figure 13-12). Drivers can run on the bottom, in the middle, or on top — which is great because, as you've probably figured out, racers love having a lot of room to work with so they can pass the cars in front of them. While you're watching the racing, you can't help but notice the track's breathtaking surroundings. The McCullough Mountain Range is in the distance, plus Nellis Air Force Base isn't far, either, often providing a free air show of F-14s flying in formation.

After you're done watching racing, you can get out of your racetrack duds, put on a fancy-schmancy outfit, and explore the town. Las Vegas is nicknamed "The Entertainment Capital of the World" because of its dozens of casinos, hundreds of restaurants, and smorgasbord of shows. But don't stay out too late the night before the race because traffic to the track is challenging. You'll have to get there early to avoid starting your day with congestion on the roads — and to avoid a headache, too. Also, make sure to get your fill of Vegas before the weekend is through. So far, NASCAR only stops there once a year.

Track specs

- ✔ **Shape:** D-shaped oval.
- ✔ **Length:** 1.5 miles.
- ✔ **Banking:** 12 degrees in the turns, 9 degrees on the frontstretch, and 3 degrees on the backstretch.

Dates to watch

Early March.

Getting to the track

The track is located in Las Vegas, 11 miles from the heart of the Vegas Strip. To get there, take I-15 north to exit 54 for Speedway Boulevard.

Getting tickets

For tickets or information, call 702-644-4443 or 800-644-4444. Also, check out the track's Web site at www.lvms.com.

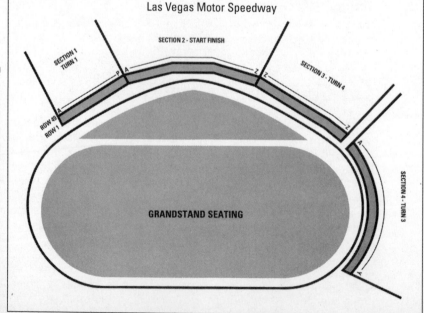

Figure 13-12: Las Vegas Motor Speedway made its NASCAR NEXTEL Cup Series debut in 1998 and quickly has become one of the drivers' favorite tracks.

Finding lodging

- Las Vegas Visitor's Information: 702-892-7576
- Las Vegas Tourist Bureau: 702-739-1482

When Vegas nightlife gets too expensive, perhaps a more down-to-earth option is sticking around the speedway. There's a dirt track around the corner from the track, where you can see even more racing after the NASCAR garages close for the evening. Those races, held under the lights, don't host NASCAR cars. They have other cars and other series, including the World of Outlaws Series, which features sprint cars with a large wing on top.

Lowe's Motor Speedway

Most NASCAR NEXTEL Cup Series drivers live in the Charlotte, North Carolina, area, so it's no wonder they love racing at Lowe's Motor Speedway. Three times per year, many drivers get to sleep in their own beds on race weekends instead of in a hotel or their motor homes. Drivers also like the track because you can pass on it and go very fast (see Figure 13-13).

The 1.5-mile track, formerly known as Charlotte Motor Speedway, is the first NASCAR track to change its name because owners sold its naming rights. Expect many more tracks to change their names in the future due to bigger money being offered by companies to change names. But, whatever the name of the track, the facility hasn't lost any of its glitz. It has many luxury sky boxes just as other tracks do, but it also has two condominiums built at one end of the track, where many drivers and fans own condos overlooking the racetrack. How exciting it must be to wake up in your own condo in the morning and glance out your window to see a group of gritty race teams testing their cars. Or just think, you can have a dinner party and watch races while nibbling on hors d'oeuvres and sipping on chardonnay. You'll also find the ritzy Speedway Club at the track, which is racing's version of a country club. It's a concept dreamed up by Speedway Motorsports CEO Bruton Smith and speedway president H.A. "Humpy" Wheeler, two of the most innovative, creative promoters in the sport.

In addition to hosting the NEXTEL All-Star Challenge event each May, Lowe's Motor Speedway hosts two NASCAR NEXTEL Cup Series events each year, including the Coca-Cola 600 on Memorial Day weekend, which television numbers have shown has more viewers then the Indianapolis 500. By contrast, Lowe's Motor Speedway plays host to approximately 160,000 fans, while Indianapolis brings in a live crowd of 350,000.

Track specs

- **Shape:** Quad-oval.
- **Length:** 1.5 miles.
- **Banking:** 24 degrees in the turns and 5 degrees in the straightaways.

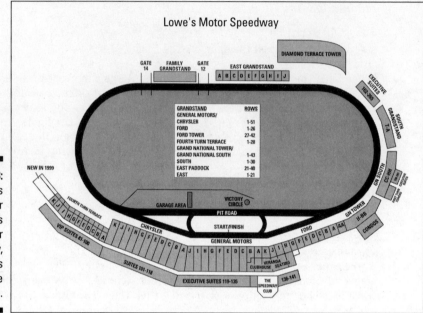

Figure 13-13:
Most drivers
live near
Lowe's
Motor
Speedway,
so drivers
love to race
there.

Lowe's Motor Speedway

GRANDSTAND	ROWS
GENERAL MOTORS/	
CHRYSLER	1-51
FORD	1-26
FORD TOWER	27-42
FOURTH TURN TERRACE	1-28
GRAND NATIONAL TOWER/	
GRAND NATIONAL SOUTH	1-43
SOUTH	1-30
EAST PADDOCK	21-40
EAST	1-21

Dates to watch

Mid- to late May and early October.

Getting to the track

The track is located in Concord, North Carolina, about 12 miles northeast of
Charlotte. To get there, take I-85 north from Charlotte, and take exit 49 for
Speedway Boulevard. The speedway is on Highway 29.

Getting tickets

For tickets or information, call 704-455-3200 or check out the track's Web site
at www.lowesmotorspeedway.com.

Finding lodging

✔ Charlotte Convention & Visitors Bureau: 800-231-4636

✔ Camping at the track: 704-455-4445

If you want to see race teams up close, you can drive to some (or even all, if
you're so inclined) of the race shops in the Charlotte area (see Chapter 15
for race shop addresses). You won't have a hard time finding one because
they're everywhere. The best place to see a group of shops in one visit is
Mooresville, known as "Race City U.S.A.," which is about 20 miles north of the

track. Take exit 36 off I-77 north, go over the highway, and turn left at your first light. Drive down that group of streets, including Rolling Hills Road and Knob Hill Road, and you'll find more race shops than you can visit in one day, including Roush Racing and Penske Racing South. Most race shops have a free visitors' area, where you can take a peek at the race teams preparing cars. Many also have souvenir shops.

Martinsville Speedway

Martinsville's .526-mile oval is the tiniest track in NASCAR NEXTEL Cup Series racing and also is one of the oldest (see Figure 13-14). It was built in 1947 and even pre-dates the NASCAR organization itself. Good old Martinsville is a typical short track with not much room to pass and a bumpy racing surface. The tricky part is that it's concrete through the turns and asphalt in the straightaways. Some drivers lovingly call it two drag strips attached by two U-turns. Some just call it frustrating. With little room to get by the car in front of you, drivers know they must qualify well in order to have a decent finish. But qualifying well doesn't exempt you from finishing the race unscathed. Even though Martinsville isn't high banked the way Bristol is, cars still get bumped and banged during the race. There just isn't anywhere to hide, especially when somebody spins out or wrecks just in front of you.

Track specs

- **Shape:** Regular oval.
- **Length:** .526 miles.
- **Banking:** 12 degrees in the turns and zero in the straightaways.

Dates to watch

Early April and October.

Humpy's pre-race festivities

Humpy Wheeler, president of Lowe's Motor Speedway, is known especially for his pre-race festivities, which border on the outrageous. Nevertheless, they are unforgettable. For instance, before the Coca-Cola 600 (formerly the World 600) each year, he calls in the National Guard to perform a military exercise, filled with loud booms and plenty of billowing smoke. But Wheeler has had some brilliant ideas over the years, including the NEXTEL All-Star Challenge each May, which features NASCAR NEXTEL Cup Series winners. The all-star race has different rules and is not an official points event.

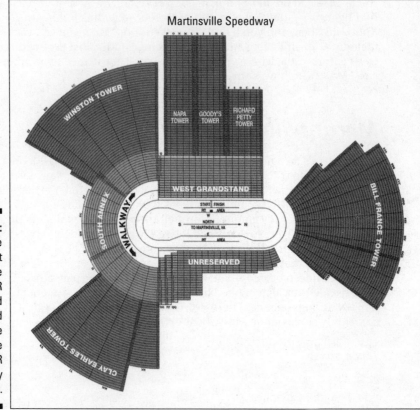

Figure 13-14:
Martinsville
is the tiniest
track in the
NASCAR
Series and
has hosted
races since
before
NASCAR
officially
began.

Getting to the track

The track is located two miles south of Martinsville, Virginia, and about
50 miles south of Roanoke. To get there, take U.S. 220 Business south. From
Greensboro Airport, take Route 68 north to U.S. 220 north to the track.

Getting tickets

For tickets or information, call 540-956-3151 or check out the track's Web site
at www.martinsvillespeedway.com.

Finding lodging

To reach the Martinsville-Henry County Chamber of Commerce, call
540-632-6401.

A trip to Martinsville is a trip into NASCAR's history, but it also can be a culi-
nary thrill. While at the track, it's imperative that you try one of the track's
famous (or infamous, depending on who you ask) Jesse Jones brand hot
dogs. On the outside, they are regular-looking hot dogs, which you can get
with all sorts of toppings, including chili and cheese, but after you bite into

them, you'll notice they have an extraterrestrial pink glow in the middle. Rumor has it, that's what makes them taste so unique. If you have a weak stomach, however, you may want to steer clear.

Michigan International Speedway

With Detroit just about an hour away, executives from the car companies don't have to travel far to see some of the best racing in the sport. That's because many racers deem Michigan International Speedway as one of the best tracks they drive on (see Figure 13-15). There's plenty of room to race on the speedway's wide straightaways and turns, making it easy for drivers to take the low route, the high route, or any route they choose to get by somebody in front of them. Michigan is also one of the fastest tracks in the NASCAR NEXTEL Cup Series because of the long straightaways and the relatively high banking. And unlike cars at Daytona and Talladega, cars at Michigan don't have to use restricted motors that cut down on horsepower and speed.

While drivers love the 2-mile oval, fans may wonder why the track is so alluring. Sure, the wide, fast racing surface is easy to negotiate, but that makes for few accidents and cautions. Many times, races at Michigan come down to a battle of which team gets the best fuel mileage or which team pumps out the fastest pit stop — not which driver makes the most dramatic, thrilling moves on the track to take the lead.

Track specs

- **Shape:** D-shaped oval.
- **Length:** 2 miles.
- **Banking:** 18 degrees in the turns, 12 degrees on the frontstretch, and 5 degrees on the backstretch.

Dates to watch

Early June and late August.

Getting to the track

The track is located in Brooklyn, Michigan, about 70 miles southwest of Detroit. From Detroit, take I-94 west to Highway 12 west (exit 181A). The track is one mile west of U.S. 12 and M-50.

Getting tickets

For tickets or information, call 800-354-1010 or check out the track's Web site at www.michiganspeedway.com.

Figure 13-15: Michigan Speedway's wide straight-aways and high banking make it fun to drive on.

Finding lodging

✔ Greater Jackson Chamber of Commerce: 517-782-8222

✔ Brooklyn-Irish Hills Chamber of Commerce: 517-592-8907

✔ Brooklyn Tourist Bureau: 800-354-1010 or 800-543-2937

Because races at Michigan International Speedway don't have many cautions and accidents, the best place to see the most action is from the north grandstands. Sitting there gives you a good vantage point to see the cars exit turn 3 and enter turn 4 and then barrel down the frontstretch.

New Hampshire International Speedway

Yes, there's hope for New Englanders who want to see a NASCAR NEXTEL Cup Series race but don't want to drive all over creation to do it — a 1-mile track in Loudon, New Hampshire. The speedway (see Figure 13-16) is a huge version of the Martinsville Speedway. It has sharp turns, a slick racing surface, long straightaways, and not enough room in the corners to pass the cars in front, even if the car in back is much faster. In fact, there isn't much room to pass anywhere on the track, which is why qualifying up front is so important.

The NASCAR NEXTEL Cup Series races at the track twice a year, once in the summer when the nights are much cooler and crisper than in the steamy south and once in the fall just as leaves on the trees start to turn colors. The fall race is the first race in which NASCAR's top-10 drivers begin contending for the championship.

By the way, racers never call the track New Hampshire International Speedway. It's just called "Loudon," short and sweet. (There are too many syllables in New Hampshire International Speedway, and racers are always in a rush, rush, rush.)

Track specs

- **Shape:** Regular oval.
- **Length:** 1.058 miles.
- **Banking:** 12 degrees in the turns and 5 degrees in the straightaways.

Dates to watch

Early July and September.

Getting to the track

The track is located in Loudon, New Hampshire, about 70 miles north of Boston, and ten miles north of Concord. To get there, take I-93 north to I-393 east, and then follow Route 106 to the track.

Getting tickets

For tickets or information, call 603-783-4931 or check out the track's Web site at www.nhis.com.

Figure 13-16:
New Hampshire International Speedway is the only NASCAR NEXTEL Cup Series track in New England.

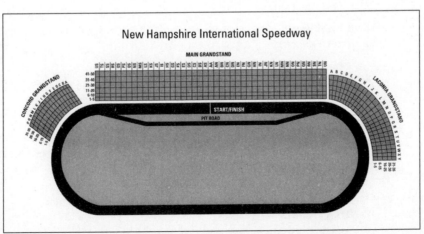

New Hampshire International Speedway

Finding lodging

- Greater Concord Chamber of Commerce: 603-224-2508
- Southern New Hampshire Visitor's Bureau: 800-932-4282

While lodging is available in the nearby towns of Manchester and Concord, race weekend in Loudon is the perfect opportunity to check out small, cozy inns and bed and breakfasts in the New Hampshire Lakes region not far from the track.

Phoenix International Raceway

With the majestic Sierra Estrella Mountains in the background, Phoenix International Raceway is one of the most picturesque tracks in NASCAR racing. It's also one of the most oddly shaped tracks (see Figure 13-17). Instead of being a plain, old oval, Phoenix is shaped like a reverse "D" because the track's owner didn't want to alter the facility's road course to accommodate an oval.

Phoenix isn't a high-banked track and the turns are tricky because turns 1 and 2 have different degrees of banking than turns 3 and 4. Each turn is challenging. Turns 1 and 2 are tight, with the wall coming out of nowhere as you come out of turn 2. Turns 3 and 4 are more sweeping, with a subtle turn (or *dogleg*) in the backstretch just to make things more interesting. The NASCAR NEXTEL Cup Series drivers race here twice each year.

Track specs

- **Shape:** D-shaped oval.
- **Length:** 1 mile.
- **Banking:** 11 degrees in turns 1 and 2; 9 degrees in turns 3 and 4; and zero degrees on the straightaways.

Dates to watch

April and November.

Getting to the track

The track is located in Phoenix, Arizona, about 15 miles southwest of downtown. To get there, take I-10 west to the 115th Avenue exit. Follow the road south for six miles.

Getting tickets

For tickets or information, call 602-252-2227 or check out the track's Web site at www.phoenixintlraceway.com.

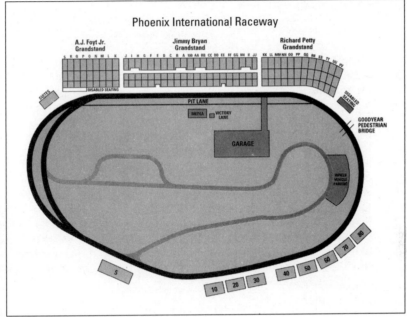

Figure 13-17:
Phoenix's odd shape makes it challenging for drivers.

Finding lodging

To reach the Phoenix & Valley of the Sun Convention & Visitors Bureau, call 602-54-6500.

The track sells general admission tickets for seating on the hillside above turns 3 and 4 — and those may be the best seats at the speedway. It's relatively inexpensive and parking is nearby, which makes hillside seating the best buy at the raceway. Bring a blanket and binoculars if you plan to park yourself on the hill.

Pocono Raceway

Pocono's triangular racetrack, tucked into the Pocono Mountains (a haven for honeymooners in the northeast), may very well be the most difficult and frustrating track in NASCAR. It isn't a regular oval, a D-shaped oval, a road course, or a superspeedway. It's a combination of all those tracks. It has three straights, each a different length, and three corners, each a different length and with a different level of banking (see Figure 13-18). It rivals any superspeedway for pure speed because of its long front straightaway, which is the longest straight stretch of road in NASCAR NEXTEL Cup Series racing. Cars can reach 200 mph as they barrel down that straight. Going into the turns, though, cars aren't going that fast. That's where Pocono the super-speedway turns into Pocono the road course because the turns are so different. In fact, drivers must downshift and upshift at least two times per lap.

The most heart-stopping turn at Pocono is turn 2, known as the "tunnel turn" because the tunnel into the infield is beneath the turn. It's also considered the toughest turn in racing. The groove in the tunnel turn is extremely narrow, so cars must negotiate the turn single file. If they don't, they'll end up smacking into the wall. It's also a relatively flat turn, which makes it tough to negotiate because the cars are still going really fast after the trip down the long frontstretch and through the banked first turn. Turn 3 is relatively easier. It's a wider turn with more racing room.

With those three very different turns on the same course, drivers and teams have to set up their cars carefully. They must learn to make compromises in order to get the best out of their vehicles through each lap. Sometimes, teams choose to set up their cars for turn 3 so the driver is better equipped to make a pass there and carry some momentum down the long stretch. But that means that going through turns 1 and 2 could be interesting.

Track specs

- **Shape:** Triangle.
- **Length:** 2.5 miles.
- **Banking:** 14 degrees in turn 1; 8 degrees in turn 2; 6 degrees in turn 3; and no banking in the straightaways.

Dates to watch

Mid-June and late July.

Getting to the track

The track is located in Long Pond, Pennsylvania, tucked into the Pocono Mountains about 80 miles northwest of Philadelphia. To get there, take exit 43 off I-80, then go south for three miles.

Getting tickets

For tickets or information, call 800-RACEWAY or check out the track's Web site at www.poconoraceway.com.

Finding lodging

- Pocono Mountains Vacation Bureau: 800-646-2300
- Monroe County Chamber of Commerce: 717-421-4433
- Camping at the track: 800-RACEWAY

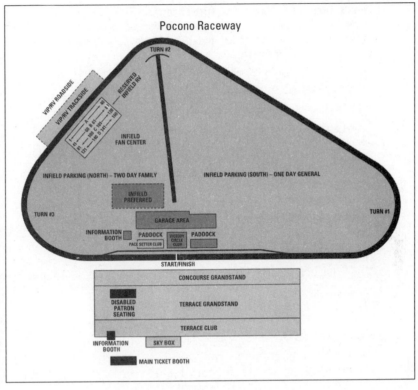

Pocono Raceway

Figure 13-18: Pocono Raceway has the characteristics of both a road course and a superspeedway because of its unique shape and challenging turns.

Looking for an autograph of your favorite driver? On the way from the garage to pit road, there's a small grandstand where fans with pit passes can sit and wait for a glimpse of drivers and crews. It's called "autograph alley" because there are a few windows built into the fence in front of the stands, where fans can hand drivers hats, T-shirts, programs, and other souvenirs to sign. Sit there long enough and a driver is bound to come by and oblige you.

Richmond International Raceway

Many drivers consider Richmond International Raceway the best short track in NASCAR. Even though it's only three-quarters of a mile long, there's still enough room for you to race up high, down low, or in the middle (see Figure 13-19). If drivers want to make a pass, they can do it anywhere they want instead of waiting for a wide enough spot on the racetrack. While drivers love the place, fans don't think it's too shabby, either. It hosts two nighttime NASCAR NEXTEL Cup Series races each year, becoming electric with the cars circling the racetrack under the lights. When fans snap photographs, the flashbulbs make the grandstand look as if it's filled with fireflies. And when the drivers race, their cars throw sparks into the air to electrify the night even more. Since 2004, the fall race is where top-10 drivers, or those within 400 points of the leader, are locked into the Chase for the NASCAR NEXTEL Cup Series championship.

Track specs

✔ **Shape:** D-shaped oval.

✔ **Length:** .750 mile.

✔ **Banking:** 14 degrees in the turns; 8 degrees in the frontstretch; and 2 degrees in the backstretch.

Dates to watch

Mid-May and September.

Getting to the track

The track is located near downtown Richmond on the Virginia State Fairgrounds. To get there, follow signs from I-64 or I-95 for the fairgrounds. The address is 602 East Laburnum Avenue.

Getting tickets

For tickets or information, call 804-345-7223 or check out the track's Web site at www.rir.com.

Figure 13-19: Richmond International Raceway holds two night-time NASCAR NEXTEL Cup Series events each year.

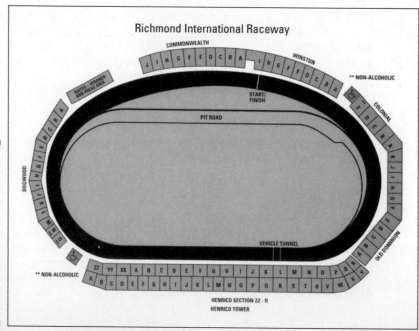

Finding lodging

The speedway publishes its own fan guide, which includes information on local hotels and restaurants. To receive a guide, send a self-addressed, stamped, business-sized envelope (with 78 cents postage) to Fan Friendly Guide, P.O. Box 9257, Richmond, VA 23227-9257.

To reach the Richmond Convention and Visitors Bureau, call 800-365-7272.

The best seats at Richmond are in the turns, but it's hard to be picky about where you sit when tickets are so hard to come by. The track holds a lottery to handle requests for tickets, so take what you can get. But if you have a choice, pick the Dogwood grandstands or the Old Dominion grandstands where you can get a good view of the cars going through the turns.

Talladega Superspeedway

According to legend, Talladega is haunted because it was built on an old Native American burial ground. There's no doubt that Talladega is the biggest, meanest, and fastest track in NASCAR racing. Bill Elliott set the speed record for stock cars in 1987 when he won the pole for the Winston 500 with a 212.809 mph lap. Obviously, that was before NASCAR mandated carburetor restrictor plates (see Chapter 5) to slow down the cars.

Talladega is Daytona International Speedway's sister track, built almost to the same specifications although, at 2.66-miles around, it's slightly bigger (see Figure 13-20).

Track specs

- ✔ **Shape:** Tri-oval.
- ✔ **Length:** 2.66 miles.
- ✔ **Banking:** 33 degrees in the turns and 18 degrees through the tri-oval.

Dates to watch

Late April and October.

Getting to the track

The track is located in Talladega, Alabama, about 40 miles east of Birmingham. To get there from the west, take I-20 east to exit 169 to Speedway Boulevard, and then go about three miles to the track. From the east, take I-20 west to exit 173.

Getting tickets

For tickets or information, call 256-362-RACE or check out the track's Web site at www.talladegasuperspeedway.com.

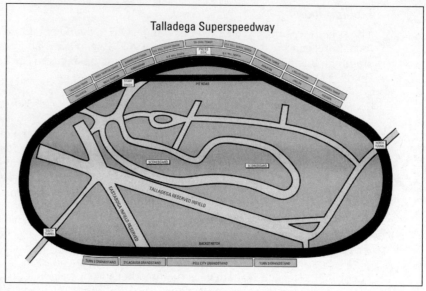

Figure 13-20:
Talladega
Superspeed-
way is
NASCAR
racing's
longest
track.

Finding lodging

▶ Greater Birmingham Convention and Visitors Bureau: 800-458-9064

▶ Calhoun County Chamber of Commerce: 256-237-3536

Texas Motor Speedway

When Texas Motor Speedway opened in 1997, drivers were concerned about the racing surface. But after millions of dollars of renovations and reconfigurations to improve the racing surface and the turns, the track has become popular (see Figure 13-21). Fans have noticed other improved parts of the speedway, such as the Speedway Club and condos at one end of the track. The club houses a gourmet restaurant with dinner and dancing after the race and also holds a state-of-the-art gym for locals to work out in. All that has made the facility one of the most innovative tracks in racing.

Track specs

▶ **Shape:** Quad-oval.

▶ **Length:** 1.5 miles.

▶ **Banking:** 24 degrees in the turns and 5 degrees in the straightaways.

Dates to watch

April and November.

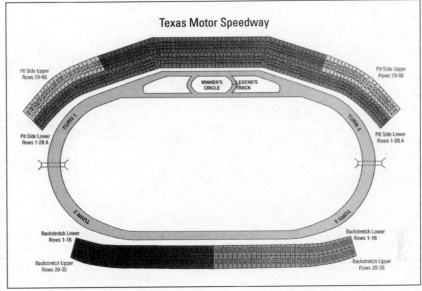

Figure 13-21:
Texas Motor
Speedway
picked up a
second race
date starting
in 2005.

Getting to the track

The track is located in Fort Worth, Texas. To get there, take I-35 west, north of downtown Fort Worth, and then take the exit for Highway 114.

Getting tickets

For tickets or information, call 817-215-8500 or check out the track's Web site at www.texasmotorspeedway.com.

Finding lodging

✔ Fort Worth Convention & Visitors Bureau: 800-433-5747

✔ Dallas Convention & Visitors Bureau: 800-232-5527

Watkins Glen International

Unlike Infineon Raceway, Watkins Glen International is more of a modified oval with mostly right turns instead of left turns (see Figure 13-22). It also doesn't have the drastic sharp turns of Infineon Raceway, so cars can lap the track much faster. One of the best things about "the Glen," as it's affectionately called, is that fans can get a great view of the track by perching themselves at various points around the speedway. Still, you can't see the entire track because it sprawls so much. The track hosted Formula One racing's U.S. Grand Prix from 1961 to 1980, but now its biggest race is when NASCAR comes to the tiny town in the Finger Lakes region of upstate New York.

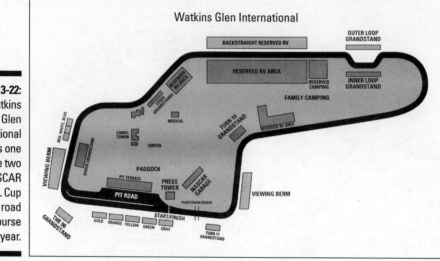

Figure 13-22:
Watkins
Glen
International
hosts one
of the two
NASCAR
NEXTEL Cup
Series road
course
races a year.

Track specs

- **Shape:** 11-turn road course.
- **Length:** 2.45 miles.

Dates to watch

Mid-August.

Getting to the track

The track is located five miles southwest of the village of Watkins Glen, New York, about 80 miles southwest of Syracuse and 18 miles northeast of Corning. Going south, take Route 414 to County Route 16 and go three miles to the track.

Getting tickets

For tickets or information, call 607-535-2481 or check out the track's Web site at www.theglen.com.

Finding lodging

- Schuyler County Chamber of Commerce: 800-607-4552
- Corning Chamber of Commerce: 607-936-4686

Just like at Infineon, the best seats at Watkins Glen are near the turns where drivers most often make their moves. The *esses* is a part of the track where cars snake through the course in a series of turns, and it's an especially good part of the track to watch from because the cars snake right up a hill. Sit at the top of the hill and you'll see plenty of action.

Chapter 14

Heading Out for a Weekend at the Track

. . . .

In This Chapter

▶ Buying tickets for an event

▶ Finding lodging

▶ Getting a list of what to bring to a race, along with some dos and don'ts

▶ Getting a behind-the-scenes view

▶ Listening to races from the grandstands

▶ Picking up souvenirs

. . . .

Going to a NASCAR race isn't like going to a professional basketball game. It's more like going to Woodstock. Fans make pilgrimages to NASCAR races, sometimes driving across the country to their favorite tracks. And when they get there, they enter a unique universe.

Often, NASCAR fans camp out on speedway grounds or near the speedway before an event. They bring their tents, motor homes, campers, and vans to the track and then party like there's no tomorrow. You think tailgating before a college football game is a blast? Well, you haven't seen anything unless you've trekked to a NASCAR race. From 70,000 to 300,000 fans descend on NASCAR tracks during race weekends. They bring their NASCAR hats, NASCAR T-shirts, NASCAR flags, and NASCAR bumper stickers. But most of all, they bring their loyalties to their favorite NASCAR drivers. While fans at basketball games cheer for one team or the other, fans at NASCAR races are cheering for 43 different teams.

If you decide you have to be part of this mania, this chapter's for you. I tell you everything you need to know about having a great race weekend, from getting tickets and lodging, to what to bring on race day, to getting back to meet your favorite drivers.

What a suite deal

Above the grandstands at the majority of tracks are rows of boxes encased in glass where people gather to watch races. These are the *suites* and you can't buy tickets at the box office to sit in them. They're for corporations or people with enough money to rent them out. Usually, companies rent the suites for thousands of dollars each race and then invite employees, colleagues, clients, friends, or family members to watch the race. All the suites have TVs, so you can see all the action, including replays of big wrecks or key passes. Most also have catered lunches or dinners, so you can dine in air-conditioned comfort while the drivers bump and bang on the track. It's a luxurious way to watch a race and a great way to entertain a group.

Getting Your Tickets for a Race

Before you head to a NASCAR race, you want to have tickets for the event in hand. This section offers some different ways to get tickets and also helps you decide what tickets you want to get.

Tips on buying tickets

Most races sell out weeks or months before the event, so tickets are hard to come by. They can also be quite pricey, ranging from $25 to more than $250. Keep in mind that some tracks sell discounted tickets for children. (See Chapter 13 for information on how to get tickets at each of the NASCAR NEXTEL Cup Series tracks.) Here are some tips for getting tickets to events:

✔ **Call the track ticket office as soon as possible,** even a year before an event, to get information on securing tickets for the race you want to see.

Tickets for races go on sale long before the event, so if you call early, you increase your chances of going to an event (and getting the best seats). If the race is sold out, some tracks can put you on a waiting list just in case more seats open up. Or you can stay on the waiting list until a season-ticket holder decides to give up his or her tickets.

✔ **If you're computer-savvy, you can get on the Internet and check to see whether a track sells tickets on its Web site.** (See Chapter 13 for Web site addresses.) Sometimes, tracks reserve a chunk of seats and save them for Internet-based customers. Check the Web sites for details.

✔ **Flip through the classified section of your local newspaper or national racing publication.** Fans sell their tickets to sold-out races all the time, so if you keep your eyes open for tickets to the race or racetrack of your dreams, you may get lucky.

> ✔ **Drive or walk around a racetrack to find fans selling their unused tickets.** Sometimes, fans buy too many tickets and have extras on race day. Beware of scalpers who charge too much and put you at risk for buying counterfeit tickets.

Whenever you buy tickets from a place other than the racetrack, however, you're taking your chances that the tickets may be outrageously priced or even counterfeit. Be aware that in most states, it's illegal for someone to sell tickets to an event if they aren't properly licensed. In other states, it's illegal for someone to charge more than face value for tickets. Still more states have laws about how much a scalper can boost the ticket price over face value. It may be tiresome to find out what the local laws are regarding scalping tickets, but it's worth it. Depending on the jurisdiction, you can get fined or even arrested for buying tickets illegally. To check on specific scalping laws, call that state's chamber of commerce or the police department located closest to the track.

Grandstands or infield?

When buying NASCAR tickets, you have the option of getting tickets for the grandstands or for the infield (for some tracks). Each location gives you a different feel of racing, and one is no better than the other — it just depends on what you want to get out of your trip to the racetrack.

Sitting in the grandstands

Most fans watch races from the grandstands. The grandstands give you the best view of the track, and you ensure yourself a seat because you purchase tickets for specific seats. It's the traditional way to do things. It's just like sitting in the stands at a football game, but much louder — not because of the people around you, but because of the roar of the engines as the cars go around the track. And you get to make friends with the person you're sitting next to, whether you like it or not, because the seats are so close together.

Keep in mind the best seats are the highest seats, which isn't the case in most sporting events. Sitting up higher gives you a better view of the entire track, while sitting lower gives you a perfect view of cars zooming by — and that's about it. All you see is a blur. So this is one sporting event where you don't want to be in the front row.

Camping out in the infield

Not all tracks, and particularly not the smaller ones, allow fans in the infield. The tracks that do offer infield tickets, however, are packed not only on race day, but also throughout the weekend with people camping out. Most fans who choose the infield drive motor homes and park them as close to the track as possible. The tickets are general admission because there are no seats in the infield, so don't expect luxury when you get there. In addition, infield parking passes do not allow access to the garage area, but fans are allowed to line the fences and take pictures of their favorite driver. Watching a race from the infield is an acquired taste, somewhat like caviar or plaid pants. It's a big party from the time the people stream in to the time the people trickle out. Sometimes, you wonder if they even notice whether the race is going on or not.

At larger tracks, the fans who drive their cars or motor homes into the infield watch the race from on top of their vehicles. Even from those vantage points though, fans usually can't see the entire racetrack. You may see a bit of the frontstretch or a turn or two, but that's it. The rest is up to your imagination. However, grandstand tickets usually sell out first, so the infield may be your only option.

Even though infield tickets don't sell out as quickly, you should still contact the track ahead of time. Many parking spaces and camping spaces in the infield are reserved in advance and sold out before the race comes to town. At Daytona International Speedway, for example, motor home spaces are reserved so that you have an exact place to set up camp. The track also has unreserved places, which are doled out on a first-come, first-served basis. As you can guess, the reserved spaces are more expensive and are in a better spot inside the track than the unreserved spaces.

Also, be prepared to spend money on an infield pass for each person in your party because buying a parking spot in the infield doesn't grant you admission. If you have eight people stuffed in your Winnebago, you need eight tickets. The best part about bringing your motor home, camper, or tent into the infield is that you get to sleep in it, so you'll save money on lodging. While staying at a hotel may cost $200 a night (especially on race weekends when hotels tend to hike up their prices), staying in the infield may cost $250 for two nights. The prices for infield camping vary widely, though, depending on whether you get a reserved spot (which is more expensive) and how many spaces are available. So check with the track before driving down in your pop-up camper and $20 in your pocket.

Fans in the infield aren't the types to show up on race day, watch the race, and then head dutifully home right after the checkered flag falls. They usually get to the racetrack two or three days in advance to set up their campers, motor homes, or tents, then slip into their pre-race partying mode. They bring their gas grills, coolers filled with beverages, and lawn chairs, and then cavort like mad. Some cavort more during the race, and keep cavorting even when the race is done. So, if you think you're more apt to be a serious race-watcher who doesn't like distractions during an event, the grandstands may be a better place for you.

Come on and bring the kids

NASCAR promotes itself as a family sport, with participants who don't mind being role models and don't do shocking things that athletes from other sports have been caught doing. I think it's rare to find a sport like NASCAR NEXTEL Cup Series racing these days, and I think that's partly why parents aren't afraid to bring their kids to the races. Families interested in going to NASCAR races should keep the following points in mind, however:

✔ It's not the cheapest event that you can take your kids to, but some tracks may have special, discounted tickets for younger children.

✔ It may not be a wholly G-rated experience. Although most NASCAR fans are well behaved, some aren't.

✔ Drinking alcohol is allowed in the grandstands and in the infield, where fans have been known to carry coolers filled with a variety of beverages (although some tracks do have alcohol-free grandstands).

Not much gallivanting goes on during races, though. Much of it is contained to pre- and post-race activities, so if you want to protect your children from that hubbub, show up at the racetrack and head straight for your seats.

Racing started out as a family sport for me back in Arkansas. Even though my parents were divorced, racing was one way my family would get together and have fun. So, some of my best memories with my family were at the racetrack. Now I'm also creating some of those same memories for my 8-year-old son, Matt, who is starting to race quarter midgets at a small track near where I live in Florida. Quarter midgets are open-wheel cars small enough for young children to drive. My wife, Arlene, and I watch him race and always have a blast. It's just like old times.

The infield is pretty much an adult playground, so if you want to bring the family and make a weekend out of it, ask the track if it has a family camping area. Many tracks have staked out camping areas for families, complete with curfews and noise limits.

Make sure to bring a gas grill if you want to cook out in the infield. Many tracks don't allow open fires in the camping areas.

Finding Lodging Well in Advance

Suppose you have tickets to a NASCAR race and are ready to head to the event. If you're making a day trip out of it, the only thing you need to worry about is traffic. If you want to stay over a night or two, you have a bigger challenge.

Finding a place to stay near a racetrack during a NASCAR race weekend may not be easy. Most racetracks aren't in metropolitan cities with hotels on every corner. They're in smaller towns away from cities, like Talladega, Alabama, or Dover, Delaware. There just aren't that many hotel rooms available. Imagine 100,000 or so race fans streaming into town and looking for a place to stay. As you can guess, space is tight.

Before taking off for a race with your spouse and children, call beforehand to make hotel reservations. The simplest way to find out what hotels have vacancies is to call the chamber of commerce in the town where the racetrack is located. They usually have a list of hotels with available rooms and can also suggest hotels in your price range. (Turn to Chapter 13 for phone numbers of the chamber of commerce in each town with a NASCAR NEXTEL Cup race.)

Because the demand for lodging is so high, hotel rooms during race weekends generally aren't cheap. Expect to pay up to $150 to $250 for a hotel room close to the track. But don't expect to stay in luxury, even at those prices. Even the smallest hotels increase prices when so many race fans are looking for so few rooms.

Be aware that most hotels ask for three- or four-night minimums for race weekends and many ask for a one-night deposit when you make the reservation. Of course, the farther away the hotel, the cheaper the room, so if you can't bear to part with all that cash, just get in your car and drive an hour or so away from the track.

Leaving Early to Make the Race

To avoid the bumper-to-bumper traffic that clogs up roadways two hours or so before the race, prepare to leave early for the race: I'm talking about at the crack of dawn if the race is at noon. After you get to the track, you can sleep in your car or walk around the grounds to check out what the vendors are selling as souvenirs. You can also grab breakfast and then head to your seat early to watch the pre-race activities. NASCAR hands out awards before each race and introduces each driver to the crowd. Be in your seat at least 45 minutes before the race if you don't want to miss all the action.

Buying a program

If you're a novice NASCAR fan, buying a race program helps guide you through your afternoon or evening. Programs usually contain stories about the top drivers or teams. They also have a list of drivers, which may contain biographical information, car number, team affiliation, and paint scheme (the design on a car). While some paint schemes, such as the one on Jeff Gordon's multi-color No. 24 Chevy, stay virtually the same from year to year, some teams have ever-changing paint schemes. Keep that in mind when you're looking for a car on the speedway. Sometimes looking for the car number, not the car color, is a better move.

Programs also may have race records, NASCAR records, and charts that translate lap times into miles per hour. As a beginner fan, all that information, for the price of about $10, can help you become a savvy NASCAR devotee.

Another way to avoid race-day traffic jams is to show up at the track a few minutes before the event begins because most fans have already arrived and taken their seats. You're taking a chance if you do this, though, because leaving just in time for a race may leave you in traffic if there's an unexpected tie-up on the road.

Dos and Don'ts of Being at a Race

If you haven't been to a race before, here's a handy list of dos and don'ts for you to follow:

- ✔ Do bring binoculars to a race, no matter where you're sitting. Even if you have the best seats in the house, it's difficult to see the teams, cars, and drivers up close, especially at a big track.

- ✔ Do bring a camera with a telephoto lens (which brings the action closer to you) if you want a good picture of the cars on the track.

- ✔ Do bring earplugs, especially for children. NASCAR races are loud, with decibel levels that can rival the roar of an airplane engine. The best kinds of noise deterrents are headsets that actually muffle the sound. If you're the macho type who doesn't want to wear earplugs, your ears may ring and your head may hurt the next day.

- ✔ Do bring a raincoat. Umbrellas aren't allowed in the grandstands because they get in the way of other fans' views of the track.

- ✔ Do dress for the weather. It can be steamy and sweltering at races held in the summer, but cold, damp, and windy at races in the spring or fall. Be prepared and check the weather forecast before you leave for a race.

- ✔ Do wear sunscreen. You're a perfect candidate for sunburn when you watch a race. You sit in aluminum grandstands for four hours in the middle of the day. Sunscreen can prevent an uncomfortable ride home.

- ✔ Do bring a seat cushion if you want a more comfortable perch in the stands.

- ✔ Do bring a radio or scanner (which I discuss in the "Riding Along with the Driver" section, later in this chapter) if you want to keep track of what's going on during a race. Wear headphones, though, so you can hear the conversations without the huge distraction of the engine noise.

- ✔ Do stay hydrated on hot days. Just like drivers and crews, fans need to drink plenty of liquids to keep themselves from dehydrating. You wouldn't believe the number of fans who are taken to the hospital with heat stroke or exhaustion on a hot Sunday race day.

- ✔ Do pack food if you don't want to spend money on concessions.

- ✔ Don't bring any glass containers into the grandstands.

✔ Don't bring any coolers that are bigger than 14x14x14 inches.

✔ Don't throw anything onto the racetrack or in the grandstands. If you do, security guards will kick you out of the speedway with no refund.

✔ Don't drink too much and do crazy things. If you do, you'll be kicked out before you know it — which will most likely sober you up.

✔ Don't curse and carry on. The people around you paid good money for their seats and don't want to hear you ranting about how much you dislike a particular driver. Also, remember that kids are in the stands.

Fitting In with a NASCAR Crowd

If you're sitting at your first NASCAR race with a bunch of veteran fans, what do you do to fit in? Well, if you don't know much, the best plan is to keep quiet, watch the race, and learn. If you want to join in on the fun, though, you can cheer for your favorite driver and take part in some of the conversations around you.

One sure-fire way of sounding like a longtime NASCAR fan is to refer to teams by their car numbers. So, when talking about Dale Earnhardt Jr.'s team, you can say, "The 8 car is really kicking it today." Or, if someone asks which team you like, you can say, "Oh, I like the 88." An educated fan would immediately know that you're a Dale Jarrett supporter. If you really want to dazzle the fans around you, you can use a multi-numeric scheme such as, "Wow, did you see the 33 pass the 25 on the inside? I thought he was going to spin out the 22 or at least smack into the 8 when he did that."

First aid at the track

Every track has first aid centers set up throughout the grounds, as well as a medical care center in the infield. Experienced medical personnel are on hand to help you if you fall and scrape your leg, hurt your back, break your wrist, or even have a serious medical emergency such as a heart attack. If you're too hurt to walk to a first aid center, send a friend to get help or contact one of the ushers in the grandstands. Everyone is connected via two-way radio, so help will arrive shortly.

The same goes for fans in the infield. At many tracks with motor homes parked inside them, emergency workers rove through the grounds on four-wheelers. The infield care center also is available for fans who need medical assistance.

Dressing the part also helps you fit into the crowd at NASCAR races. That means you should at least have a T-shirt or hat with a driver's or team's logo on it. You rarely see fans at a NASCAR race with plain, button-down shirts and khakis on. If you wear an outfit like this, you'll stick out like — like a prepster at a Metallica concert. NASCAR fans are loyal and love to support their drivers — and are proud to show it.

Going behind the Scenes

While grandstand tickets and infield passes give fans a great view of NASCAR races, *garage passes* let you go into the pits and the garages before the race starts and get a behind-the-scenes look at the sport. Unfortunately, fans can't buy garage passes at most tracks, particularly for NASCAR NEXTEL Cup races. Those passes are reserved for sponsors, friends, and family of race teams, or people who are affiliated with the sport in some way. Call a track ahead of time, though, to see whether passes are for sale for other races, especially for NASCAR Busch races or NASCAR Craftsman Truck races, which may be less restrictive than NASCAR NEXTEL Cup races. You may get lucky.

Following the rules

If you're lucky enough to get a garage pass, you get a unique view of the drivers and the crews preparing for a NASCAR race. You can walk through the garage area and look at crews working on their cars. You can hang out around the team haulers (see Chapter 6 for a description) to get a glimpse of drivers as they walk to their cars. You can take all the photos you want to remember your day. But remember the following no-nos before heading into the garage:

✔ You need to stay on your toes in the NASCAR garage because you really are in the middle of the action. Practice time is precious for NASCAR teams, so the cars often zoom in and out of their garages to get as much track time as possible. The drivers are focused on making their cars just right, which means they aren't necessarily watching out for people strolling through the garage like tourists at Walt Disney World.

Because of driver lobbying, fewer (non-necessary) people are allowed in the garage area. Their complaint: There were so many people watching the action that drivers and teams didn't have enough room do their work. To help solve the problem, NASCAR came up with "cold" and "hot" passes. While some tracks sell a minimal amount of cold passes (which can be used at times when engines are not turned on), hot passes are not for sale. A certain amount of television, print, and radio reporters are allowed in the garage area and along pit road when a "red light" designates a hot period, as are drivers' families, some sponsor representatives, and, of course, team members.

✔ When in the garage, revert to the wise words of advice your mom gave you when the two of you took a trip to the china store when you were six: *Look, but don't touch.* You are fortunate to get a peek at NASCAR teams at work, so don't get uppity when someone tells you to stop touching a piece of equipment or stand back from a car. The drivers and crew members are at work and don't want to be disturbed — and they don't want their equipment to be disturbed either. So walk through the garage with respect.

✔ You must adhere to the following dress code if you want to step foot in the garage area — no ifs, ands, or buts about it:

• You have to wear long pants. No shorts, culottes, clam diggers, Bermuda shorts, or capris are allowed — your legs have to be completely covered.

• Your shirt must cover your shoulders. No tank tops, tube tops, or sleeveless shirts allowed.

• You can't wear open-toed shoes such as sandals, flip-flops, or strappy stiletto high heels.

✔ Stay clear of the garage during Happy Hour, which is the final hour of practice before the race. It's dangerous to linger in the garage because cars are rushing in and out of the garage while teams make last-minute changes.

✔ Don't bring any alcoholic beverages into the garage. They aren't allowed.

✔ You must keep your garage pass visible at all times and a form of identification in your possession; otherwise, you will be asked to leave.

Getting autographs in the garage

Usually, you can find autograph cards outside each team hauler, where drivers and crews congregate when not working on their cars. An *autograph card* is a sheet of heavy-duty paper with a driver's picture on the front and his vital statistics on the reverse side. It's for — you guessed it — getting autographs. Some people take them for souvenirs, though, because they're free. (It's not good form to take more than one.)

If you want to use the autograph card to get an autograph, you can try to corner a driver in the garage area to get him to sign it. This can be tricky business because drivers are so focused while they're in the garage — they're at work. But if you insist on getting autographs or getting your picture taken with a driver, try to use a little courtesy. Don't approach them as they prepare for practice runs, prior to qualifying or immediately before the race. You will likely fail, which builds up hard feelings between drivers and fans. Remember, the garage is their office, and they are much more concerned with how their car is performing then signing an autograph card. Another tip: When they do have a few minutes of free time, most drivers will sign cards or hats fans hand them through the fence between the garage area and the infield.

Here are some hints:

- **Wait outside a team hauler to catch a driver.** He isn't around his car, so he isn't going to be as distracted. But don't dare go *into* the hauler. It's off-limits to fans because that's where drivers and teams have meetings.

- **Don't bother drivers just before qualifying.** They may be nervous about their fast lap and scowl in your photo.

- **Pay attention to whether a driver is running well during practice.** If he isn't, he probably won't be in the mood to sign autographs. If you do approach him for an autograph or photo, at least have something positive to say.

- **Keep sponsor loyalty in mind.** Think twice before asking Jeff Gordon (a Chevy driver) to sign a Ford hat, or before asking Tony Stewart (who drives for The Home Depot) to sign a Lowe's Home Improvement Warehouse T-shirt. Remember that loyalty runs deep in NASCAR. You don't want to put a driver in an awkward position.

- **Bring your own pen.** A black felt-tipped marker, such as an indelible Sharpie, is best.

- **Be prepared to walk with a driver as he signs your item.** Most drivers know that if they stop, they'll soon be mobbed. They use the walk-and-sign technique, so be prepared to stride alongside them.

- **Don't expect to have a full-blown conversation with a driver.** They're on the job and trying to concentrate. If you want to chat with your favorite driver, go to a pre-scheduled appearance he's making in the area (see Chapter 7 for more on drivers making appearances). For example, Matt Kenseth may sit down and sign autographs at a local Dewalt Power Tools outlet. No doubt he'll be more relaxed in that atmosphere than he is at the track.

- **Even if you've been waiting all day in the sun, don't chastise a driver if he walks out to his car without stopping to give you his autograph.** Maybe he's in a rush to get somewhere. Maybe his car isn't running well. Maybe he doesn't feel well. Maybe he has personal things on his mind. Remember: A garage pass doesn't guarantee you autographs, but it does guarantee you a rare look at drivers and teams at work — a look that most people aren't fortunate enough to get.

- **Saying "thank you" always helps.**

Riding Along with the Driver

Whether you're watching a race from the grandstands or the infield, you can be even closer to the action if you bring a radio with a headset. The Motor Racing Network and the Performance Racing Network radio announcers offer analysis, race statistics, and play-by-play commentary of what's going on during a race. They tell you what's going on in turn 2, when all you can see is the cars coming out of turn 4. They also let you know what kinds of problems different cars are experiencing. You may see Jeff Gordon slow down on the track, but unless you're tuned into the broadcast, you won't know why. Local frequencies are listed inside the packages in which the radios are purchased and can also be found on the Internet.

A good number of fans have hand-held *radio frequency scanners* — Walkman-sized instruments that pick up pre-selected two-way radio channels in the immediate area. They allow you to listen in on conversations between drivers and their crews during practice, qualifying, and races. You also can hear NASCAR officials talk among themselves and with the teams. It's sort of like a legal way to eavesdrop — and it's fun.

You can rent a scanner with headphones at the racetrack (at booths set up on the grounds) for between $25 and $50 a day.

If you attend NASCAR races often, you may want to invest in your own scanner. You can buy one at your local electronics store such as Radio Shack or at radio companies that have booths at the racetrack. The scanners cost from $100 to $350, depending on their features. Look for a scanner that scans at least 100 channels per second, and one that scans VHF and UHF high and low bands. Really, you don't need a scanner much fancier than that when you're at a NASCAR race — you just need the correct frequencies of the drivers, teams, officials, and radio broadcast to get your money's worth. You can buy updated scanner lists outside the racetrack where souvenirs are sold.

Here are some companies you can call to buy scanners or get information on obtaining frequency lists:

- ✔ **Race-Scan:** 1-800-441-2841 or www.racescan.com on the Web.
- ✔ **Racing Electronics:** 1-800-272-7111 or www.racingelectronics.com on the Web.
- ✔ **Racing Radios:** 1-800-669-1522.

If you buy or rent a scanner, be sure to get a frequency list at the track, which has a bunch of numbers on it, each coinciding with a team, a NASCAR official, or a radio broadcast. Usually each frequency consists of three numbers, followed by a decimal point and then more numbers — such as 484.340. If you're programming your scanner on your own, you have to input all those numbers into the scanner and assign them another number. For example, you can program my frequency under the number 6 on your scanner because I drive the No. 6 Ford. So, when you tune to Channel 6 on your scanner, my frequency pops up and you can listen to me chat with my crew. Some teams keep the same radio channel for years and years, but others change their frequencies from time to time, so you want to get the latest frequency lists to stay on top of all the action.

After you get your scanner and input the frequencies, you're ready to listen in. There are a few different techniques to listening to a race on a scanner. You can listen to the radio broadcast, then tune into teams' frequencies from time to time. Or you can put your scanner on scan mode, so it stops at a frequency only when there is communication going on. Or you can listen to one team only, keeping your scanner tuned to the same frequency all day. Whatever way you choose to use your scanner, it's bound to make things more interesting for you. You can hear a crew chief tell a driver when to make a pit stop. You can hear a driver complain about his car. You even can hear a driver's reaction just after he gets into an accident.

When using a scanner, keep in mind that conversations between a team and a driver may not be appropriate for children.

Leaving with Souvenirs

It's hard to miss all the souvenir trailers lined up at the track. The trailers are colorful and are always in a conspicuous area, such as just outside the main entrance. If you have time before or after a race, you can mill around the souvenir area and pick up a bumper sticker, T-shirt, or cap. (For more on souvenirs, turn to Chapter 2.) But if you really want a unique souvenir, you have to look a bit harder.

Sometimes you'll stumble upon someone selling racing tires that were used in an actual NASCAR race. They go for anywhere from $10 to $60. Why would you want a racing tire? Well, it certainly would be a conversation piece sitting smack in the middle of your living room. Many fans lay the tires on their sides and put a sheet of glass on top of them, which makes good coffee or end tables. Some fans put them in their yards, fill them with dirt, and plant flowers in them. Whatever their use, they are unusual souvenirs from a race.

Fans with infield passes or garage passes always comb the infield for trinkets after an event is over: used tires, pieces of mangled sheet metal from a car that wrecked, or even lug nuts that flew off of a car during a pit stop. If you plan to do this, make sure the item you take is something that a team is leaving behind — otherwise, you can be arrested for stealing. Ask a team whether you can take it before you go walking off with an entire hood or a used tire. Otherwise, you may be embarrassed when a security guard grabs you and makes you take the piece of equipment back to its owner. Sometimes, though, teams leave their used tires behind (without wheels) — near their pit stall or in the garage. Those are free for your taking because they're not going to use them again.

Chapter 15

Tracking NASCAR Events from the Comfort of Home

Most NASCAR fans are lucky to attend one or two races a year. The rest of the time, they rely on TV, radio, newspapers, and Web sites to keep up on what's going on. Luckily, plenty of media outlets cover NASCAR races, NASCAR drivers, and the goings-on in the sport. In fact, NASCAR's growth has attracted much attention in the news, so it's difficult to get away from it even if you wanted to.

You can also join fan clubs or log onto a team's Web site to catch up on the latest news about drivers. In this chapter, I give you all the details you need to immerse yourself in the sport — even if you can't make it to many races.

Grab That Remote: Watching Races on Television

When you can't go to races, watching them on television is a great alternative. You may miss the roar of the engines and the smell of rubber on the track, but in general you actually get to see more than the fans at the track. This section gives you the advantages of watching from home (or your favorite bar), as well as where to find NASCAR TV coverage.

Catching all the angles

During every race, TV cameras mounted around the track catch the action at every point on the speedway. The cameras usually cover the following angles:

- ✔ **Cars racing down the frontstretch, backstretch, and through all the turns.**

- ✔ **Cars zooming by the grandstands:** Sometimes in a blur of color; other times so you can recognize which car is which, all captured by cameras placed near the outer edge of the track.

- ✔ **Fans cheering in the grandstands up close** and also a view of the fans in the grandstands taken by cameras in a blimp or helicopter above the speedway.

- ✔ **Ground shots of groups of cars coming through the turns:** Those cameras are positioned at ground level in the infield.

- ✔ **Interior shots from cars:** Several cars have in-car cameras set up during each race. This gives viewers at home a close look at drivers while they're in their race cars, including what a driver sees when he swerves to miss an accident or when he gets into an accident himself. It shows you how violent a crash can be for a driver, too. You see the whole car shake and hear the loud thud of the impact. You know a driver is involved in a bad accident when the in-car camera goes dead and all you see is static.

- ✔ **Views of what's behind and in front of cars:** Small cameras mounted to the front and back bumpers of several cars are especially helpful when there's an accident on the track because they give you an up-close view of how the wreck started or who started it.

- ✔ **The pit road action:** You see pit crew members crouched on the pit wall, waiting for their car to come down pit road. You also see, from all different angles, the pit crew servicing the car.

TV cameras don't capture only the action on the track — they bring you all the action off the track, too. When drivers take their cars into the garage during a race — after blowing an engine or having a wreck — the TV cameras follow. That's when you, as a home viewer, can see more than the people in the grandstands do. You see the driver get out of his car, sometimes red-faced after falling out of a race, and you hear his explanation of why he's in the garage and not on the track. You also get to see the car, banged up and all.

Getting a running commentary

During every televised race, commentators describe what's happening on the track, which is especially helpful if you're a NASCAR NEXTEL Cup Series novice. Commentators sit above the track in a booth where they can usually see the entire speedway. Monitors keep them updated on the action and who is running where. The commentators give you all the information you could want, including who is where on each lap, team statistics, driver status, and crew chief interviews. If a car stalls on the track, they tell you why. If a tire rolls off a car and down pit road, they tell you how it happened. The commentators don't do all the work, though — reporters are running from pit to pit asking crew chiefs and team members for information. If a tire on a car goes flat, for example, the pit reporter reports live from that driver's pit, shows the flat tire, and describes what has happened.

NASCAR races are covered differently from football or basketball games because commentators can talk to the pit crews while the event is going on. Sometimes the commentators even have negotiated with a driver to talk to him via a radio during caution periods. You don't see sideline reporters in football interviewing the coach in the middle of the fourth quarter. And you certainly don't hear reporters chatting with the quarterback between plays.

Finding TV racing broadcasts

You can find NASCAR NEXTEL Cup Series and NASCAR Busch Series races on NBC and FOX networks and their respective cable affiliates, TNT and FX. The NASCAR Craftsman Truck Series and other NASCAR news and talk shows and events such as qualifyings are shown on the Speed Channel. (Check your local TV listings to track down a specific event.) The networks have different commentators and pit reporters, but the overall coverage is informative and interesting.

All races are scheduled for live broadcast. Occasionally, a weekend rainout, with the race rescheduled for Monday, will then be shown on tape. Most NASCAR NEXTEL Cup Series races are on Sunday afternoon, but a handful are run on Saturdays or Saturday nights. It's not like the old days in the early 1960s, when you could count on one hand the number of stock car races telecast in a year and those races were broadcast on ABC's Wide World of Sports a week or more after the event!

The NBC and FOX networks took over NASCAR broadcasts from several other networks starting in 2001. FOX or FX broadcasts the first half of the season, while NBC or TNT broadcast the second half. FOX and NBC alternate coverage of the Daytona 500.

Taking in the daily and weekly shows

If you can't get enough NASCAR on weekends, plenty of networks have daily and weekly NASCAR shows — so you can inundate yourself with information. These shows give you breaking news, driver interviews, race reviews, technical information, and almost everything you'd ever want to know in a 30- to 60-minute segment.

Here are some of the TV shows that feature NASCAR:

- ✔ *NASCAR Performance* **on SPEED Channel:** *NASCAR Performance* will take on a new look in 2005 as it broadcasts from the track Saturday nights. Crew chiefs (see Figure 15-1) are the centerpiece of this show, giving their perspective on technical and automotive-related topics.

- ✔ *NASCAR TV* **on SPEED Channel:** The SPEED Channel offers a complete slate of pre- and post-race shows, mid-week specials, and nightly programming. SPEED's NASCAR block also includes *Trackside, NASCAR Victory Lane,* and *Inside NEXTEL Cup,* along with shows that feature the history of the sport and day-to-day happenings on the track. SPEED also airs a reality series *(NBS 24-7)* built around the NASCAR Busch Series. SPEED Channel also airs event qualifying.

- ✔ *Inside NASCAR NEXTEL Cup Series Racing* **on Fox Sports:** A commentator and group of drivers talk about NASCAR racing every week, delving into the previous race and news from the circuit.

Figure 15-1:
NASCAR crew chiefs Chad Knaus, Doug Richert, Bootie Barker, and show host Ray Dunlap talk it up on *NASCAR Performance.*

Tuning In to Radio Broadcasts

Radio provides great play-by-play descriptions of races. In fact, they're so good that some people watch races on TV, but turn down the sound so that they can listen to the radio broadcast instead. Radio reporters are everywhere on race day: above the track, in the pits, talking to crew chiefs and crew members during the race, in the garage, and interviewing drivers that have fallen out of the race, giving play-by-play commentary without missing a beat. Radio reporters also work after the race, doing driver interviews after television gets done with them.

When you're listening to a race broadcast, you may have several network options. To find out which radio station in your area carries the race, call one of the following networks for a list of their affiliate stations:

- ✔ **Motor Racing Network (MRN),** a division of International Speedway Corporation (ISC), is based in Daytona Beach. In addition to NASCAR NEXTEL Cup Series races, MRN also carries the majority of NASCAR Busch events and all NASCAR Craftsman Truck Series races. MRN, which has hundreds of affiliates in 48 states and Canada, reaches 150 countries worldwide and many ships at sea on Armed Forces Radio. In addition, MRN carries the NASCAR-related programs "NASCAR Today" and "NASCAR Live." For a complete schedule, write MRN, 1801 W. International Speedway Blvd., Daytona Beach, FL 32114 or call 904-947-6400.

- ✔ **Performance Racing Network (PRN)** is based in Concord, North Carolina, and is owned by Speedway Motorsports, Inc. (SMI), the company that also owns Lowe's Motor Speedway, among other tracks hosting NASCAR races. PRN broadcasts approximately a third of the season's races, including the Coca-Cola 600 at Lowe's Motor Speedway, the Goody's 500 at Bristol Motor Speedway, and the Bass Pro Shops MBNA 500 at Atlanta Motor Speedway, among others. For information, write PRN, P.O. Box 600, Concord, NC 28026-0600 or call 704-455-3228.

- ✔ **The Indianapolis Motor Speedway (IMS)** Radio Network broadcasts all races from Indianapolis Motor Speedway, including the Brickyard 400. For information write 500 Brickyard Plaza, Indianapolis, IN 46222 or call 317-481-0060.

- ✔ **NASCAR on XM Satellite Radio** is the first and only 24-hour radio channel dedicated to a single sport. In 2005, NASCAR XM Radio added another NASCAR channel. They both carry live coverage of NASCAR's three national series through MRN, PRN, and IMS. NASCAR XM Radio also provides in-depth news coverage, interviews, talk shows, and other original programming.

- ✔ *NASCAR Performance LIVE* **Radio Show** on XM Satellite Radio and MRN. Originating from a special radio studio at the NASCAR Technical Institute in Mooresville, North Carolina, *NASCAR Performance Live* delves into the lives of the men and women who turn the wrenches and prepare the greatest race cars in the world — NASCAR crews and crew chiefs. Hosted by MRN pit road reporter Steve Post alongside former crew chief and current color analyst for NASCAR on FOX, Larry McReynolds, the program includes a rotating active crew chief in-studio to cover all the day's hot topics.

Following NASCAR in Print

Many newspapers and magazines cover NASCAR racing, but the depth of the coverage varies. Some newspapers run stories on races and who won them. Others run features throughout the week leading up to a race and report on breaking news. Some magazines run a NASCAR story only once every three weeks, while other magazines are entirely devoted to the sport.

If you want to purchase a newspaper or magazine that covers NASCAR regularly, here are some you can choose from:

- *Chase for the NASCAR NEXTEL Cup Magazine* is a yearly publication highlighting the last ten races of the season. It provides driver bios on the top ten drivers as well as race highlights for all races leading up to the Chase.

- *NASCAR Superstars* is a magazine full of insight into the top personalities in NASCAR NEXTEL Cup racing. This annual publication brings you face-to-face with photos and stories on your favorite drivers.

- *NASCAR Preview and Press Guide* is a magazine that comes out once a year, profiling drivers and providing statistics of drivers in every NASCAR division. It also has a section devoted to NASCAR's tracks.

- *NASCAR Illustrated* is a monthly magazine with features, commentary, and profiles of people in NASCAR racing.

- *NASCAR Scene* is a weekly newspaper published in tabloid form, which covers the NASCAR NEXTEL Cup Series, the NASCAR Busch Series, and the NASCAR Craftsman Truck Series and gives you features, race statistics, and the NASCAR lowdown.

- *NASCAR NEXTEL Cup Series Preview* is an annual magazine published at the beginning of the year. This publication highlights drivers as well as races for the upcoming season.

- *The NASCAR Review* is also an annual publication. This magazine hits shelves just in time for Christmas and features a run-down on the previous season. It highlights drivers, races, and the NASCAR NEXTEL Cup Series champion.

Staying in Touch with Your Favorite Driver

You can also keep tabs on your favorite driver through the Internet and fan clubs. You can find everything from a driver's schedule to his statistics to where to purchase souvenirs. Many drivers also will autograph pictures or hats sent to him at his race shop. It's all part of how fans stay close to NASCAR drivers and how NASCAR drivers stay linked to their fans, even though drivers travel to different racetracks — and sometimes different parts of the country — every weekend.

Surfing over to your favorite driver Web sites

It's easy to keep up with your favorite driver if you have access to the Internet. Most drivers have their own Web sites that are chock full of information, so, if you hop onto a search engine such as Yahoo! (www.yahoo.com) or Google (www.google.com) and type in the driver's name, you can easily find the driver's Web site if he has one. The sites have biographical information, statistics, photographs, race schedules, and personal appearance schedules (meaning you can find out where a driver will sign autographs and be there to meet him).

Joining a driver fan club

If you can't get enough of your favorite driver just by watching him race, then you may want to join his fan club. *Fan clubs* are groups of people who ardently support a driver and want to show that support by banding together. Membership fees ranges from $8 to $25, depending on the driver and the perks you get for being in the club. Most clubs provide you with an ID card, a signed postcard, and a discount card to buy your driver's souvenirs at the racetrack. Some even send you a personalized card, signed by the driver, on your birthday and during the holidays. Many clubs have meetings where fans can get together and discuss their driver or just talk shop.

If you're doing an Internet search for a driver fan club, remember many of the sites are unofficial. While those are fine to look up, keep in mind a driver's official site is the only one that will guarantee that the posted information is correct. When you go to the Web site, it will say "official" somewhere on it, meaning it's the real one set up by a driver or his company. Your best option is to contact a driver's shop for information on his fan clubs and Internet sites.

Writing to the race shops

If you'd like to get a souvenir autographed by a driver or a crew member, send it to his race shop with return postage. Usually, the race shop has a room just for souvenirs, where a driver goes to sign all types of T-shirts, die-cast cars, posters, and other trinkets. It may take them awhile to send your souvenir back to you, maybe six months to a year if it's Jeff Gordon or Dale Earnhardt Jr., so don't get impatient. They're signing as fast as they can!

Here are addresses for some of the bigger race shops. Just address your package to the driver, care of the race shop:

- Greg Biffle, 4202 Roush Place, Concord, NC 28027; telephone 704-720-4200.
- Brett Bodine, 304 Performance Rd., Mooresville, NC 28115; telephone 704-664-1111.
- Ward Burton, 6780 Hudspeth Road, Harrisburg, NC 28075; telephone 704-454-5381.
- Kurt Busch, 4101 Roush Place, Concord, NC 28027; telephone 704-720-4100.
- Ricky Craven, 3051 Firsts Avenue Ct. S.E., Hickory, NC 28602; telephone 828-267-0250.
- Dale Earnhardt Jr., 1675 Dale Earnhardt Highway 3, Mooresville, NC 28115; telephone 704-662-8000.
- Bill Elliott, 320 Aviation Dr., Statesville, NC 28677; telephone 704-924-9404.
- Brendan Gaughan, 110 Knob Hill Rd., Mooresville, NC 28117; telephone 704-662-6222.
- Jeff Gordon, 4443 Papa Joe Hendrick Blvd., Harrisburg, NC 28075; telephone 704-455-0324.
- Robby Gordon, 425 Industrial Dr., Welcome, NC 27374; telephone 704-731-3334.
- Jeff Green, 311 Branson Mill Rd., Randleman, NC 27317; telephone 336-498-1443.
- Kevin Harvick, 425 Industrial Dr., Welcome, NC 27374; telephone 336-731-3334.
- Dale Jarrett, 112 Byers Creek Rd., Mooresville, NC 28117; telephone 704-662-9625.
- Jimmie Johnson, 4443 Papa Joe Hendrick Blvd., P.O. Box 9, Harrisburg, NC 28075; telephone 704-455-0324.

✔ Kasey Kahne, 320 Aviation Dr., Statesville, NC 28677; telephone 704-924-9404.

✔ Matt Kenseth, 4101 Roush Place, Concord, NC 28027; telephone 704-720-4100.

✔ Bobby Labonte, 13415 Reese Blvd., Huntersville, NC 28078; telephone 704-944-5000.

✔ Terry Labonte, 4441 Papa Joe Hendrick Blvd., Harrisburg, NC 28075; telephone 704-455-3400.

✔ Kevin Lepage, 26502 Newbanks Rd., Abingdon, VA 24210; telephone 276-628-3683.

✔ Sterling Marlin, 114 Meadow Hill Cr., Mooresville, NC 28117; telephone 704-662-9642.

✔ Mark Martin, 4202 Roush Place, Concord, NC 28027; telephone 704-720-4200.

✔ Jeremy Mayfield, 320 Aviation Dr., Statesville, NC 28677; telephone 704-924-9404.

✔ Jamie McMurray, 114 Meadow Hill Circle, Mooresville, NC 28177; telephone 704-662-9642

✔ Casey Mears, 114 Meadow Hill Circle, Mooresville, NC 28117; telephone 704-662-9642

✔ Jerry Nadeau, MB2 Motorsports, 7065 Zephyr Place NW, Concord, NC 28027; telephone 704-720-0733.

✔ Joe Nemechek, 7065 Zephyr Place NW, Concord, NC 28027; telephone 704-720-0733.

✔ Ryan Newman, 136 Knob Hill Rd., Mooresville, NC 28115; telephone 704-664-2300.

✔ Kyle Petty, 311 Branson Mill Rd, Randleman, NC 27317; telephone 336-498-1443.

✔ Scott Riggs, 7065 Zephyr Place NW, Concord, NC 28027; telephone 704-720-0733.

✔ Ricky Rudd, 292 Rolling Hills Rd., Mooresville, NC 28117; telephone 704-799-2133.

✔ Elliott Sadler, 112 Byers Creek Rd, Mooresville, NC 28117; telephone 704-662-9625.

✔ Ken Schrader, 11881 Vance Davis Dr., Charlotte, NC 28269; telephone 704-947-9696.

- ✔ Jimmy Spencer, 222 Raceway Dr., Mooresville, NC 28115; telephone 704-662-8655.

- ✔ Tony Stewart, 13415 Reese Blvd. W, Huntersville, NC 28078; telephone 704-944-5000.

- ✔ Brian Vickers, 4423 Papa Joe Hendrick Blvd. Charlotte, NC 28262; telephone 704-455-0362.

- ✔ Kenny Wallace, 300 Old Thomasville Rd., High Point NC 27260; telephone 336-887-2222.

- ✔ Rusty Wallace, 136 Knob Hill Rd., Mooresville, NC 28115; telephone 704-664-2300.

- ✔ Michael Waltrip, 1675 Dale Earnhardt Hwy 3, Mooresville, NC 28115; telephone 704-662-8000.

- ✔ Scott Wimmer, 300 Old Thomasville Rd., High Point NC 27260; telephone 336-887-2222.

Part V
The Part of Tens

In this part . . .

This part gives you tidbits of information about some of the greatest racers and the greatest races in NASCAR — my unsolicited opinion on a few important subjects. You find out who I think are NASCAR's greatest drivers and future stars, and which NASCAR races I think are the best — from a fan's standpoint of course. (This is why I list superspeedway races, which most drivers dread.) If you're in a rush to digest as much NASCAR information in the least amount of time, this part is the perfect place to turn.

Chapter 16

The Greatest NASCAR Drivers of All Time

In This Chapter

▶ Reviewing my pick of NASCAR's legendary drivers

▶ Looking at the stellar statistics of great drivers

Many drivers win races, but only a few — those with special talent, charisma, and personalities you just can't forget — become legends. These drivers have left an indelible mark on the sport of stock-car racing, and while they may not be the drivers you cheer for, they are the ones who garner your respect.

The list of greatest NASCAR drivers of all time can be argued until the end of the next millennium, but here are the ones — in alphabetical order — that I think are the best. Some have won championships. Some have won a lot of races. Some have shown unparalleled determination. I've raced against a lot of them, so I've gotten to know their driving styles and personalities firsthand. Because of that, I'm convinced that they're some of the best drivers ever.

Bobby Allison

In his 25 years of NASCAR Cup Series racing, Bobby Allison was fearless. And, from time to time, he was reckless. But that in-your-face driving style and unmistakable talent was the reason he was one of the most successful drivers in NASCAR history. He won the 1983 NASCAR Cup Series championship and 84 races in his career, tying him with Darrell Waltrip for third on the all-time wins list.

The most memorable moment of his career came when he won the 1988 Daytona 500 — his third Daytona 500 victory — and his son, the late Davey Allison, finished second. The two celebrated together in Victory Lane, with son proud of dad, and dad proud of son. Bobby retired in 1988, but still attends many races.

Dale Earnhardt

Ask any NASCAR driver, and they'll tell you that Dale Earnhardt was the one person they didn't want to see in their rear-view mirrors, especially during the final laps of a race. There's a reason he was called the Intimidator, and it's not just that he didn't always exude warmth. Earnhardt was the quintessential bully on the racetrack, driving rough enough and fast enough to win 76 NASCAR Cup races from 1975 through his final 2001 season (he died following an accident that year). That ranks the driver from rural North Carolina sixth on the all-time victories list. But the number of championships Earnhardt won overshadows his race victories: He won seven titles, tying him with Richard Petty for the most NASCAR Cup championships in history. He also won more than $41 million in his career, second only to Jeff Gordon's $68 million on NASCAR's money list. While Earnhardt won on nearly every NASCAR track, his forte was on superspeedways where, as legend has it, he could "see" air coming off the cars around him and thus navigate through it better than anyone (see Chapter 9 for more on this phenomenon). No matter on what type of track he raced, Earnhardt's sixth sense allowed him to make smart moves that helped him thread through the field and stay up front once he got there.

Jeff Gordon

When Jeff Gordon came into NASCAR Cup Series racing in 1992, everybody thought he was going to make it big and become the next greatest NASCAR driver of the century. Everybody was right.

In 1995, Gordon clinched the first of his four NASCAR Cup Series championships, winning it when he was just 24 to become the youngest champion in NASCAR's modern era, dating from 1972. After his immediate success, Gordon was quickly dubbed "Wonder Boy" and booed at nearly every track in the series. Why? Perhaps because he won too much, too early. Perhaps because he grew up in California and then moved to Indiana to race, so he wasn't a Southerner or a good ol' boy like Earnhardt or Bill Elliott. Perhaps because he seemed too goody-goody. Perhaps because he becomes more and more unstoppable as the years go by.

Gordon won back-to-back NASCAR Cup Series titles in 1997 and 1998, and in 1998 he won 13 races to tie Richard Petty's modern-era record for victories in a single season. In 2001, he won a personal-best $10.8 million in prize money en route to the title. The scary part is, he's not retiring any time soon and has many more years to win races, break records, and clinch championships. That's good for his fans — bad for his competition. For all his success, Gordon remains the target of boo-birds in the stands, which he says he has learned to largely ignore. The one exception? Gordon is the overwhelming fan favorite in the Brickyard 400, run at Indianapolis Motor Speedway, where he is considered a home-town racer.

Dale Jarrett

The son of two-time NASCAR Cup Series champion Ned Jarrett, it didn't take Dale long to step out from behind his father's shadow and begin making a name for himself. Signing on with (then) new team owner Joe Gibbs in 1993, he and his team started the season with a bang, winning the Daytona 500. Three years later, he captured his second Daytona 500 crown with team owner Robert Yates, a feat they pulled off for the third time in 2000. Highly thought of with both his race team and fans, Jarrett was a popular series champion, winning the NASCAR Cup title in 1999. A gentleman on and off the track, Jarrett and his wife, Kelley, are heavily involved in the sports endeavors of his four children. He is also sought after as a golf partner in tournaments sponsored by sponsors and tracks, as he is as talented on the links as he is behind the wheel of a race car.

Alan Kulwicki

Even though Alan Kulwicki won only five NASCAR Cup Series races in his career, he was good enough to win the 1992 NASCAR Cup championship. And he made an impact on the sport that no statistics can measure. He was one of the first competitors to treat the sport as a science. Kulwicki grew up in Wisconsin, driving in the American Speed Association in the midwestern United States before moving south to try his hand at NASCAR racing. But Kulwicki was different than most drivers. He had a college degree in engineering and used the physics and math that he learned to set up his race car. At first, people laughed when he showed up at races with a briefcase filled with calculators — but now briefcases have become part of the mandatory gear for crew chiefs and those who work on a car's setup. Kulwicki was also determined to field his own car and make it to the top the hard way without sponsorship. He did just that, clinching the 1992 championship after winning only two races. Kulwicki wasn't able to defend his title, however, because he died in 1993 in a plane crash.

David Pearson

No one wanted to mess with David Pearson when he was driving on the circuit. He was just the kind of quiet, cool, confident guy you didn't want to make angry. People called him the "Silver Fox" because of his sly, cunning style. Perhaps that's why Pearson, who is retired from the sport, won 105 races in his NASCAR Cup Series career. He ranks second on the all-time wins list.

Pearson was a versatile driver who did well on superspeedways, intermediate tracks, short tracks, and road courses. He won nearly everywhere, so much so that Richard Petty still insists Pearson is the best driver in NASCAR history. Pearson won three NASCAR Cup Series championships — in 1966, 1968, and 1969, but continued to drive until 1986, when he retired. Even during his final years as a racer, though, he was a daunting sight on the track for his opponents. Not that he tried to be — that's just the way he was. He made racing and winning look easy.

Richard Petty

Richard Petty isn't called stock-car racing's king for nothing. He won a record 200 races in his 35-year career, nearly twice as many as anyone else. He also won a record seven NASCAR Cup Series championships, tying him with Dale Earnhardt for the series lead. He won a record seven Daytona 500s and a shocking 27 of 49 races in 1967, including ten in a row. Petty retired from driving in 1992 and is now a NASCAR car owner.

Petty wasn't just a successful driver. He was adored by the public and became the sport's unofficial public relations director, signing autographs and posing for pictures for hours, selling stock-car racing — which started out as a Southern sport — to mainstream America. When he won the 200th race of his career, President Ronald Reagan just happened to be at the track to congratulate him; their meeting made all the papers. With his trademark cowboy hat, dark sunglasses, wide smile, and winning ways, it's no wonder Petty became a fan favorite and sports icon. He's part of racing's most famous family — which began with his father, Lee Petty, who won three championships and the inaugural Daytona 500, and has continued with his son, Kyle. It will be nearly impossible for anyone to top what Petty did in the sport, what he did *for* the sport, and what he continues to do. In an effort to give fans a first-hand experience with the excitement that comes from driving a race car, he opened the Richard Petty Driving Experience, a race school. (For more information on driving schools, see Chapter 3.)

Rusty Wallace

In an age when most drivers just hop into their cars and head for the race-track, Rusty Wallace is old-school. He still gets under the car to check things out himself. He tells his crew chief exactly what to do with the car, going far beyond just saying, "it's loose" or "it's tight." This hands-on involvement is what's made him so good over the years. Wallace learned the ins and outs of a race car growing up racing on short tracks in the Midwest, where he built his own cars, raced his own cars, and repaired his own cars.

When he began his NASCAR Cup Series career in 1980, he took that knowledge of cars with him — and translated it into stardom right away. In his first race in the series that year in Atlanta, the bushy-headed redhead finished second to Dale Earnhardt and immediately earned the respect of his competitors. Now Wallace is one of the most successful and popular drivers in NASCAR history. In addition to the 1989 NASCAR Cup Series championship, he has won 55 races (through the 2004 season).

Darrell Waltrip

Darrell Waltrip energized NASCAR Cup Series racing from the moment he started in 1972. Back then Waltrip was a fast-talker with a quick wit and not a pinch of humility. His personality grew even more outrageous every time he won a race. In fact, he earned the nickname "Jaws" for talking so much and boasting about his accomplishments. Fans either loved or loathed him because of his brashness. The thing is, Waltrip wasn't totally out of line when he bragged about himself — because he backed up his words with success on the track. He won 84 races in his NASCAR Cup career, which ties him for third all-time. He also won three series championships.

Waltrip has mellowed over the years, but he still loves to gab and trash-talk, good qualities for a driver-turned-television commentator. Behind the microphone since retiring from driving in 2000, Waltrip has become as successful and entertaining a commentator as he was a driver.

Cale Yarborough

A three-time NASCAR Cup Series champion, Cale Yarborough never thought twice about pushing himself or his cars to the limit, especially when he was teamed with legendary car owner Junior Johnson — who didn't have any limits himself. Yarborough, who retired as a driver in 1988, was a spitfire even before getting into a race car, claiming to have wrestled snakes and alligators — and even insisting he got hit by lightning when he was young. Yarborough won 83 races to put himself fifth on NASCAR's all-time wins list. That includes four Daytona 500s, which he won in 1968, 1977, 1983, and 1984. For a while, though, Yarborough defected from the stock-car ranks to go Indy-car racing. He raced Indy cars in 1971 and 1972, and then headed back to what he knew best. And that was winning NASCAR races.

Chapter 17

Ten Can't-Miss Races of the Year

In This Chapter

▶ Listing the NASCAR NEXTEL Cup Series races that you can't miss

▶ Finding out why certain races are so special

*E*ven though you may want to see every NASCAR race, it's okay to admit you don't have the time or the means to watch 36 NASCAR NEXTEL Cup Series races each year. Because you probably can't catch them all, however, this chapter outlines some of the most exciting, hair-raising, or historically important races that every self-respecting NASCAR fan should see at least once.

Fans and drivers all have their own favorite races, but these are some of the ones on everybody's list. Sure, it's all subjective, but these races consistently provide action. Check out Chapter 13 for a full description of each track.

Daytona 500

The Daytona 500, held in February at the Daytona International Speedway, is NASCAR's Super Bowl — the most revered and most heralded race of the year. Some of the most famous drivers have won it, including Richard Petty (seven times!), Bobby Allison, Cale Yarborough, and even Indy car legends Mario Andretti and A. J. Foyt. Unlike the Super Bowl, though, the Daytona 500 is the season-opener, which is what makes it so special. Teams spend almost the entire off-season preparing for this one race and come to Daytona in February hoping to win that year's championship. If you have a good finish in the Daytona 500, it sets the tone for your entire season; so emotions — and speeds — run high throughout the afternoon.

Watching the Daytona 500 not only gives you high speeds and plenty of thrills, but it also gives you a preview of who may race strong during the upcoming season.

Coca-Cola 600

The Coca-Cola 600, formerly known as the World 600, is held the Sunday before Memorial Day at Lowe's Motor Speedway north of Charlotte, North Carolina, and is NASCAR's longest event. With 600 miles of racing, it's NASCAR's version of a marathon, so fans have to be tenacious to watch the entire race. The race starts in late afternoon and isn't finished until well after dark, so drivers and teams have to face constantly changing track conditions. The extra 100 miles also puts extraordinary strain on the engines. Drivers, crews, and cars are tested in this endurance race where only the competitors with the most stamina and the cars with the sturdiest parts finish up front.

Pepsi 400 at Daytona

Races at superspeedways are naturally fun to watch because the cars run so fast and so close together. What makes them even more fun is when a race is held at night under the lights at Daytona International Speedway. The Pepsi 400, formerly called the Firecracker 400, is held the Saturday of the Fourth of July weekend. It was moved from daytime to night in 1998 after track officials spent $5 million to install lights around the 2.5-mile superspeedway. Not only is the race cooler to watch for spectators because it's no longer held in the sweltering midday heat of Central Florida in July — but it's also one of the year's most heart-pounding and spectacular events. To top that, the post-race fireworks show is awesome.

Brickyard 400

Indy car purists said hell would freeze over before stock cars raced at Indianapolis Motor Speedway, the legendary home of the Indianapolis 500. Well, it froze over for good reason. The Brickyard 400, held in the beginning of August, is one of the year's most interesting NASCAR races. With a hefty paycheck at stake for the winner, drivers take chances to get to the front.

NASCAR only goes to the 2.5-mile Brickyard once a year, which makes the event all that more special. But every time a stock-car driver goes to Victory Lane at the storied track, he makes history. Stock cars made their debut there in 1994, when Jeff Gordon won the inaugural event. Since then, the Brickyard 400 has been one of the best tickets in racing.

Sharpie 500

If you want to guarantee yourself a good time, watch the night race at Bristol Motor Speedway, held every August. What could be better than 43 cars circling a tiny, high-banked, half-mile track and bumping into each other the whole way? See all that at night — when sparks fly and tempers flare at the track tucked into the mountains of eastern Tennessee.

Actually, both races at Bristol, even the one held during the day in April, are must-sees, but the night race is absolutely electric — as well as action-packed.

EA Sports 500

NASCAR has two superspeedways where cars run in packs only inches apart — the 2.66-mile Talladega Superspeedway in Alabama and the 2.5-mile Daytona International Speedway in Florida. Of those two, Talladega is bigger and faster. Both races at Talladega are sensational to watch: the Aaron's 499 is held in April and the EA Sports 500 in the fall. By the fall race, the race for the championship may be hot — and the title chase may close up at the super-big, super-daunting track. As a fan, you can't see the entire racetrack no matter where you sit in the grandstands, but seeing the swarm of cars coming off one of the turns is jaw-dropping. They race two-, three-, four-, and even five-wide at times, and you may wonder how they do it.

Chevy Monte Carlo 400

Races at Richmond International Raceway have long been fan-favorites featuring drivers racing side by side, door handle to door handle, all the way around the track, lap after lap. But the Chevy Monte Carlo 400 at the .75-mile Virginia track is now a must-attend race because it's now the last chance for drivers to make the final cut for the Chase for the NASCAR NEXTEL Cup. Following that race, only drivers in the top-10 in the points standings, or those within 400 points of the leader, remain (with 10 races to go) as championship contenders.

The NASCAR NEXTEL All-Star Challenge

Even though the All-Star Challenge doesn't count toward the NASCAR NEXTEL Cup Series championship, it still should be one of the races you see — even if it's just for the novelty. It's held a week before the Coca-Cola 600 at Lowe's Motor Speedway in May, but it's not at all like a normal NASCAR race. In fact, few of the real rules count. The race is primarily for winners from the previous and current NASCAR Cup seasons. It also invites any past NASCAR Cup Champions who haven't qualified via a race victory, plus the winner of the NEXTEL Open, a preliminary event for teams that have not qualified for the showcase event. Two other past champions — who are also still active drivers — are eligible; previously, there was a five-year retroactive cut-off for past champions. While the 90-lap/135-mile overall distance is divided into 40-, 30-, and 20-lap segments, drivers are no longer eliminated after each segment, ensuring that a full field of cars is racing for the winner's purse of approximately $1 million.

Mountain Dew Southern 500

Darlington Raceway is NASCAR's first superspeedway — it opened in 1950 — and the Mountain Dew Southern 500 is one of NASCAR's most prized races. But winning the classic and becoming a part of Darlington history isn't an easy task. Darlington is arguably the most unique and challenging track in NASCAR racing. Its walls seem to jump out and attack cars as the vehicles zoom through the corners. The rough racing surface chews up tires in a blink. So you can see why only the bravest, most skillful drivers make it to Victory Lane at the South Carolina track.

Cale Yarborough and Jeff Gordon have the record for most Southern 500 wins with five — but Bobby Allison isn't far behind with four. That alone puts these drivers a notch above other drivers in the history book. Watching drivers as talented as those navigating this tricky track is worth the price of admission.

Ford 400

What makes the Ford 400 at Homestead-Miami Speedway a don't-miss race is that it's the NASCAR NEXTEL Cup Series season finale. If it's a close race for the championship, the race may be a nail-biter for drivers and teams who are in the running for the title — as well as for their fans. At least the Florida sunshine helps. With the new Chase for the NASCAR NEXTEL Cup Championship, fans have a better chance than ever to see the actual crowning of the series champion.

Dodge Save Mart 350

Having made hard left turns the first half of the season, the majority of NASCAR's drivers look forward to the season's first road-course test, which comes in June at Infineon Raceway in Sonoma, California. Half of the 11 turns spread over the winding 1.95-mile course just outside San Francisco are to the right — a direction drivers generally avoid on ovals as they usually mean a trip into the wall. While some drivers struggle on road courses (Infineon Raceway and Watkins Glen in northern New York are the series' only two tracks with twists and turns), others enjoy non-oval racing, including four-time event champion Jeff Gordon. Other drivers with victories at Infineon Raceway include two-time winner Rusty Wallace, Ricky Rudd, Tony Stewart, and Mark Martin. For fans interested in making a "road trip," the Dodge Save Mart 350 race at Infineon Raceway is the place to be.

Chapter 18

NASCAR's Young Stars

· ·

· ·

*E*ven though some of NASCAR's most famous drivers — including NASCAR NEXTEL Cup Series champion Rusty Wallace — are nearing the end of their careers, NASCAR won't lack superstars in the new millennium. Look for a new crop of talented racers to inject youth, energy, and pizzazz into NASCAR in the coming years.

Greg Biffle

Washington State isn't exactly a hotbed of NASCAR racing, but Greg Biffle has proven the Northwest can produce talented and determined drivers. Just like many other NASCAR Cup drivers, Biffle started out racing on short tracks, but unlike others, he captured the 1996 Pacific Coast Region championship by winning a whopping 27 times in 47 starts — 57 percent of the time! After dominating like that, Biffle was hired by team owner Jack Roush (who has an impeccable eye for talent) to drive in the NASCAR Craftsman Truck Series; he was that series' top rookie in 1998. He went on to win nine races and compete for the Craftsman Truck series championship the following year, eventually finishing third in the point standings. Biffle made his first trip to NASCAR Cup's victory lane in the 2003 Pepsi 400 at Daytona International Speedway. Not bad for a guy who runs a fabricating business in his hometown of Vancouver, Washington, in his spare time.

Kurt Busch

Every sport needs its bad boy, and NASCAR has Kurt Busch. That's not to say he isn't a nice fellow. He's just more concerned with driving his race car than setting himself up as the sport's paragon of etiquette, especially at the short tracks. A native of Las Vegas, Busch ended the 2003 season on a tear and proved to be a driver to watch in 2004. Busch makes no apologies for the fact he comes to the track to race; he's there for the dance, not the buffet. Fans get their money's worth every time the No. 97 Ford driver straps himself in.

Dale Earnhardt Jr.

On the track, there's no doubt Dale Earnhardt Jr. is similar to his father and namesake, seven-time NASCAR Cup champion Dale Earnhardt. The two are winners — both confident, aggressive drivers who know how to get to the front. Earnhardt Jr.'s grandfather, Ralph, was a NASCAR Late Model Sportsman (now the NASCAR Busch Series) champion in 1956. Still, no one expected Earnhardt Jr. to wow the racing world when he ran his first full season in the NASCAR Busch Series in 1998 when he was 24.

But he proved everyone wrong by winning the Busch Series championship — and seven races — that season and winning the title again in 1999. Earnhardt Jr. described his 2003 season as the foundation for a NASCAR NEXTEL Cup Series championship and by all accounts is perfectly poised to make that dream a reality.

Jimmie Johnson

The runner-up to Matt Kenseth in the 2003 NASCAR Cup Series championship, Johnson was the only driver to stay in the top 10 in the points through all 36 races of the season. Think this Jeff Gordon teammate has the goods to eventually reach the top? Absolutely. He is a threat to win everywhere the Rick Hendrick Motorsports No. 48 team unloads. Hendrick is a strong believer in what he calls the "fit factor," the compatibility among the people in his organization. Johnson has a strong supporting cast behind him; most notably crew chief Chad Knaus. And who could ask for a better mentor than teammate and co-owner Gordon?

Kasey Kahne

As if driving the No. 9 Dodge isn't enough, this Washington State native even looks a bit like his cockpit predecessor, NASCAR Cup Series champion Bill Elliott. Hooking up with Dodge team owner Ray Evernham has been a dream come true for Kahne, who out of the box in 2004 won pole positions and racked up an impressive string of runner-up finishes. Making things even better, Kahne has become the retired Elliott's star pupil and can also rely on teammate Jeremy Mayfield for advice. Kahne is just one of the latest new talents to benefit from the trend among car owners to gravitate toward young drivers in an effort to get a leg up on future competition.

Jeremy Mayfield

When rumors ran rampant in the new millennium that his job was in jeopardy, Jeremy Mayfield knew how to respond to his critics: with his heavy right foot. Like a sleeping giant stirred, the Owensboro, Kentucky, native put the hammer down, driving Ray Evernham's Dodge into the wonderful world of job security. A middle of the road driver for 18 months, Mayfield literally raced the last five months of 2003 as if his career were on the line — which it was. He didn't make it to victory lane, but he placed among the top-10 in 11 of the final 21 races on the schedule, highlighted by two runner-up and two third-place finishes in the final 11.

Mayfield's turnaround was so dramatic that several other car owners came courting, but he felt they had finally turned the corner. Teamed with NASCAR Cup rookie Kasey Kahne in 2004, Mayfield took a back seat in racing headlines, as Kahne quickly registered four pole positions and four runner-up finishes. But when the 2004 championship field was reduced to 10 drivers with 10 races remaining, it was Mayfield, not Kahne, who had made the cut.

Jamie McMurray

Who is the only driver in NASCAR Cup Series history to win a race the season before he was named series rookie of the year? Jamie McMurray, who rocked the racing world in 2002 when he won a race in only his second NASCAR Cup career start while substituting for injured teammate Sterling Marlin. In 2003, McMurray earned top rookie honors on the strength of being the highest-finishing freshman driver 21 times, 12 more than runner-up Greg Biffle.

McMurray's season was the most productive for team owner Chip Ganassi's three-car operation; he led the organization with 5 top-five finishes and 13 top-10 finishes. The young speedster threatened to win the Brickyard 400 and scored his first pole position at Homestead, Florida. McMurray, a notable cutup when goofing with Marlin, exhibits poise and confidence on the track and is notable for not tangling with his fellow drivers at speeds in excess of 170 miles per hour.

Ryan Newman

This Roger Penske pilot has been on everyone's list to win a NASCAR Cup championship since being crowned the 2002 Raybestos Rookie of the Year as the sport's top-performing first-year driver. What's held him back? He hasn't finished a lot of his races because of mechanical failure or accidents. A championship contender in 2004, the Indiana native is brutally quick and gets arguably the best fuel mileage on the circuit with his Dodge. The Newman-Penske pairing could be the one that matches the feat of teammate Rusty Wallace, NASCAR's Cup champion in 1989. Newman was a man on fire in 2003, leading the series with 8 victories, 11 pole wins, and the most miles led with 1,509, but his inability to finish races left him sixth in the NASCAR NEXTEL Cup Series standings.

Elliott Sadler

You won't find a more likeable guy in the NASCAR garage than Elliott Sadler. But just because Sadler walks around with a smile while humming his favorite country tunes doesn't mean he's not serious about racing. While Tony Stewart overshadowed him in their quests for a rookie of the year title in 1999, Sadler had a solid first year in the NASCAR Cup Series. He wasn't at all discouraged by Stewart's unusually stellar rookie performance — and it's that positive attitude that will help him in racing, where seasons can be as unpredictable as a derailed roller coaster.

He developed that upbeat demeanor while growing up in Emporia, Virginia, a rural town not far from South Boston Speedway (the same speedway where NASCAR Cup racers Ward and Jeff Burton first made their names in the sport). Sadler won the 1995 Late Model Stock championship at that track before making his NASCAR Busch Series debut there that same year. He was only 21. Just two years later, he found himself in the NASCAR Cup Series racing for the legendary Wood Brothers before jumping to Robert Yates Racing in 2003.

Tony Stewart

Winner of the 2002 NASCAR Cup Series championship, Tony Stewart doesn't exactly fit the mold of an up-and-coming star: He already is one. Unlike some other drivers, however, Stewart is considered a good bet to win a second, third, and even fourth Cup title, which puts him in the category of superstar of the future. By all accounts, Stewart made the right decision when he moved from open-wheel Indy Cars to stock cars. Crowned the 1997 (open-wheel) Indy Racing League champion, Stewart had always wanted to race in NASCAR, so he packed up and headed for NASCAR Cup Series racing full-time in 1999. That's when he made history, becoming the first rookie to win a NASCAR Cup race since the late Davey Allison did so in 1987.

Stewart also finished the season as one of only three rookies in NASCAR history to finish in the top five in points (finishing fourth) and the first rookie to do so since 1996. Although a humble NASCAR Cup Series rookie, Stewart didn't hide his fiery personality on or off the track — which has made him one of the sport's most popular drivers. He has repeatedly shown his passion for racing in any form by driving in both the Indianapolis 500 (Indy Car race) and NASCAR's Coca-Cola 600 on the same day each May. His competitiveness and dedication ensure Stewart is a force to be reckoned with, no matter in which series he chooses to race.

Part VI
Appendixes

In this part . . .

*P*art of the fun of getting into a new sport and the fun of being an old hand is knowing all those statistics that make you seem so smart. In this part, I give you all the best NASCAR jargon, statistics, and key milestones that you need.

Appendix A

NASCAR Jargon

Aerodynamics

Race car aerodynamics refers to how the air flows over the surfaces and under the body of a car. It also includes the wake of turbulent air left behind a car as it travels.

A-Frame

Either the upper or lower connecting suspension piece (shaped like an A) that locks the frame to the spindle.

Air dam

An air dam is an extension below the front bumper that blocks air as it hits the front of a car, keeping too much air from flowing under the vehicle and reducing the car's speed and stability. It plays a big role in the aerodynamics of a car by keeping the front end stable.

Appearance

When a driver makes an appearance, he shows up to sign posters, programs, and trading cards for fans or employees at supermarket grand openings, auto shows, conventions, car dealerships, fairgrounds, and auto stores.

Apron

The paved portion of a racetrack that separates the racing surface from the infield.

Associate sponsor

Associate sponsors are companies that sponsor racing teams. They pay less money and, in turn, get less exposure on the car or the uniform than the primary sponsors do.

Autograph card

An autograph card is a sheet of heavy-duty paper with a driver's picture on the front and his vital statistics on the back. They are free for fans and used for souvenirs and for autographs.

Backstretch

The straight section of the track located on the side of the track opposite the start/finish line. On an oval track, it's between the second and third turns.

Banking

The sloping of a racetrack, particularly at a curve or corner, from the apron to the outside wall. Degree of banking refers to the angle or steepness of a track's slope at its outside edge.

Battling for position

When two cars are racing each other for the same spot in the field — whether 1st place or 20th.

Being on the lead lap

When a driver has completed the same number of laps as the leader.

Bite

See *wedge.*

Blocking

When a driver positions his car to keep the driver behind him from passing him.

Blowing an engine

When a driver suffers engine failure beyond immediate repair and can't finish the race. Engines blow when their connecting rods or pistons break or when the engine block cracks, among other reasons.

Camber

The amount that a tire is tilted from vertical so that more of the tire surface can touch more of the racing surface in a banked turn.

Car chief

Team mechanic who works most closely with the crew chief in figuring out setups for the car. He directs the rest of the car crew, who physically make the changes (although car chiefs also often do hands-on work, too).

Carburetor

The device above the engine where air and fuel mix on their way into an internal combustion engine.

Carburetor restrictor plate

A thin metal plate with four holes that restrict the flow of air into an engine's carburetor, thus reducing horsepower and speed. Used only at Daytona and Talladega — NASCAR's two superspeedways — to keep speeds below 200 mph.

Catch can man

During pit stops, the catch can man stands behind the car on the left side and holds a special container at the end of the car to collect gas that overflows from the gas tank after it's filled.

Caution flag

A yellow flag waved by the flagman in the starter's stand to indicate trouble on the racetrack, including oil or debris on the racing surface. It signals drivers to slow down and follow the pace car around the track.

Champion's provisional

The champion's provisional is the last or 43rd starting spot given out for a race. Former series champions are eligible to use this if they don't make the race based on their qualifying speed. See also *provisional entry*.

Chassis

The steel frame or undercarriage of a car.

Chassis dynamometer

A machine that measures the amount of power translated from the wheels to the ground.

Competition Performance Index (CPI)

A formula that evaluates driver performance in the NASCAR Dodge Weekly Series, including average finish, number of wins, driver attendance, and the average number of cars in the field.

Compression ratio

The volume of a cylinder compared to the its compressed volume when the piston is fully extended. The higher the compression ratio, the more horsepower.

Contingency programs

Bonus money given by companies whose products a driver uses or whose decals a driver runs on his car.

C-Post

The post extending from the roofline of a race car to the base of the rear window to the top of the deck lid.

Crew chief

A crew chief is the leader of the race team who oversees employees and handles the building and fine-tuning of a race car. He's responsible for deciding which changes to make to the race car throughout race weekend and what race strategies to use on race day.

Deck lid

The rear trunk lid of a race car. It opens like the trunk lid of a passenger car and allows access to the fuel cell.

Displacement

The size of an engine measured in cubic inches. A NASCAR NEXTEL Cup Series car's engine can't be larger than 358 cubic inches.

Donuts

Slang term for the black, circular, dent-like marks on the side panels of stock cars, usually caused after rubbing against other cars at high speed.

Downforce

The air pressure and downward force that pushes a car onto the track, causing it to stick to the racing surface. It keeps cars from losing traction at high speeds, especially going through the turns.

Drafting

When drivers race in single file on large speedways and share air flow among their cars. Cars cut through the air much faster together than they do separately — the first car creates a vacuum effect that actually pulls the car behind it.

Drag

Drag is the aerodynamic force of resistance that hinders a race car as it moves through air. It's caused by air flowing beneath the car and lifting it higher in the air, as well as air flowing through the cooling system, ducts in the body, and open windows. Air travels into these openings instead of smoothly sliding over the car. With less drag, a car can accelerate faster, especially at higher speeds, because the car needs less horsepower to move forward through the air.

Engine builder

Team member in charge of building engines and coaching people to build engines nearly from scratch. His goal is to make each engine as lightweight — but still as durable — as possible. The engine builder is in charge of the engine assemblers, who actually put the engine together.

Engine specialist

Team member in charge of preparing the engines at the race shop and then taking care of and tuning them after they get to the racetrack. Also called *engine tuner.*

Esses

Slang term used for a series of acute left- and right-hand turns on a road course, one turn immediately following another.

Fabricator

Team member who puts sheet metal on the car's frame and molds it to the shape of the car, creating the body or outside shell of the car.

Five-point seat belts

Five belts that come together at the center of a driver's chest. Each of the belts passes through a steel guide that is welded onto the car's frame: one belt goes over a driver's left shoulder, one goes over his right shoulder, another comes from the left side of the seat, one comes from the right side of the seat, and still another goes between a driver's legs. They're all latched together at a single point with a quick-release buckle.

Flagman

The NASCAR official perched over the racetrack, just above the start/finish line. The flagman signals to the drivers by waving different-colored flags that mean different things.

Flags

- **Green:** The race is started.

- **Yellow:** Caution — all drivers must slow down.

- **Red:** All drivers must stop.

- **Black:** The driver at whom the black flag is waved must get off the track.

- **White:** The lead car has one lap to go.

- **Blue with diagonal yellow stripe:** Signals a slow driver to move over.

- **Green-white-checkered sequence:** Used near the end of the race in an attempt to keep it from finishing under caution. Can add as many as two laps to the length of the race.

- **Checkered:** The winning car has crossed the finish line.

Frontstretch

The straight section of racetrack between the first and last turns.

Fuel cell

A rectangular rubber holding tank for a race car's supply of gasoline. A NASCAR fuel cell holds 22 gallons.

Garage pass

A permit that lets someone into the garage area during a race weekend, obtained through the racetrack or through NASCAR and reserved for people who know someone who works in the sport (at the racetrack, as a sponsor, on a team, and so on). Also called a *pit pass*.

Gas-and-go

A quick pit stop where a car gets only gas — but no new tires.

Gas man

Pit crew member who steps over the pit wall carrying a 90-pound, 11-gallon can of gas and fills the gas tank. When the first can empties, he usually gets a second can from the second gas man (who doesn't go over the wall) and finishes filling the tank.

General mechanics

Crew members who help the car chief set up the car, build shocks back in the trailer, rework the body of a car after a driver crashes it into the wall, and so on. They're not specialized.

Getting hung out to dry

Racing slang that means a driver has lost the draft and is losing positions by the split second. To remedy the situation, the driver must get back in line with other cars where the aerodynamics are much more conducive to going fast.

Going behind the wall

When a car is too damaged to be repaired on pit road, the team brings it to the garage behind the pit wall.

Handling

How a car responds on the track. A car's handling is determined by how it was built (including its suspension, tires, aerodynamics, and body style) and how it's prepared for the race.

Hanging a body

Sizing sheet metal, cutting sheet metal, and then molding it onto a car's frame to form the shell of a car.

Happy Hour

The final hour of practice before an event, usually held in the late afternoon the day before the race.

Hat dance

When a race winner puts on dozens of baseball caps with sponsors logos in Victory Lane. Each time a driver puts the cap on, the photographers snap photos to send or sell to the sponsor involved.

Head protectors

Protection built into a driver's seat to keep his head from moving to the left or right during an accident.

Hitting points

When a driver talks about "hitting his points" or "hitting his marks" on the racetrack, he's referring to being able to drive the fastest route around the track that he has mapped out in his head. Usually, a driver will record in his mind various small marks or other points of reference around the track, especially entering and exiting the turns, and then will try to visually hit those spots each time around the track.

Horsepower

A unit of measurement representing how much power an engine generates.

Hospitality

Pre-race gathering that drivers hold with a group of employees or guests from one of their sponsors.

Inspections

The process NASCAR officials go through to approve cars to race, qualify, and practice.

Intermediate track

Tracks more than one mile long but less than two miles. See also *short track, superspeedway.*

Jackman

Pit crew member who positions the jack under a specific spot on each side of the car, pumps the handle of the jack one or two times so that it lifts the car off the ground enough for the tire changers to change the tires, and then drops the jack and lowers the car.

Lapped traffic

Cars that aren't on the lead lap. These cars are usually considerably slower than the leaders.

Licensee

The licensee is the person or entity who sells NASCAR goods and must pay royalty payments to the licensor (who gives the rights to sell the goods) at pre-arranged times.

Licensor

The licensor is the person or entity who gives the rights to sell NASCAR or race team goods, receiving royalty payments from the licensee (who sells the goods) in return.

Loose

A car is termed *loose* when a driver goes through a turn and the rear of his car starts to fishtail, making the driver feel as if he's losing control of the car and about to spin out. The rear tires aren't sticking well to the track and providing enough traction. This is also called *oversteer*. See also *tight*.

Lug nuts

Large nuts that secure tires in place. All NASCAR cars use five lug nuts on each wheel, and penalties are assessed if a team fails to put on all five during a pit stop.

Modern era

Period in NASCAR history that began in 1972, when a new points system and a radically streamlined schedule were introduced.

MPH

Miles per hour.

Motor home lot

Where drivers and owners parks their motor homes during race weekend.

Motor mounts

Where the motor is mounted to the frame of the car.

Motor Racing Outreach (MRO)

Organization that provides religious services, a daycare for team members' children, and events for drivers and their families at the track.

NASCAR

NASCAR stands for the National Association for Stock Car Auto Racing, the organization that governs and makes rules for NASCAR racing.

NASCAR Busch Series

A different series from the NASCAR NEXTEL Cup Series, where many drivers begin their professional racing careers. Drivers train themselves and hone their driving skills before moving up to NASCAR NEXTEL Cup Series.

NASCAR Craftsman Truck Series

The NASCAR Craftsman Truck Series is the newest of the three national NASCAR touring series, in its 11th season of existence featuring four different manufactured field trucks, all based upon the popular, half-ton short bed models.

NASCAR NEXTEL Cup Series

The top series of NASCAR.

One-groove racetrack

A racetrack that has just one route around it where cars can stick to the track and handle well. If a driver gets out of that path, he may not get enough grip to keep his car stable — and that means he could end up in the wall. Some tracks have more than one groove — a high groove and a low groove — meaning cars can run side-by-side around the track. Some tracks have no particular groove because cars race easily on any part of the track.

Over-the-wall guys

See *pit crew*.

Owner

The owner of the entire racing team. He or she has a financial stake in the race team and therefore has final say in hiring everyone who works on the team, from the driver to the crew chief to everyone who prepares the cars for racing. The owner must also secure a sponsor to help pay the bills.

Paint scheme

The way a car is painted and decorated.

Panhard bar

See *track bar*.

Pit boxes

Pit areas, delineated with yellow lines, for the 43 cars in the race to use during pit stops.

Pit crew

The seven people allowed to go over the pit wall and service a car during a pit stop. See also *over-the-wall guys*.

Pit pass

See *garage pass*.

Pit road

A separate road inside a racetrack that usually runs parallel to a track's frontstretch. It's where cars go when they need gas, tires, or repairs.

Pit stall

Where teams watch the race and keep their equipment — separated from the pit box by the pit wall.

Pit stop

When a car pulls off the racetrack and travels down pit road where his crew services his car.

Pit wall

The cement wall separating the pit box from the pit stalls.

Pit window

An estimate of the range of laps the crew thinks the driver can go before needing to make a pit stop to refuel.

Pole winner (pole sitter)

Driver who records the fastest lap during qualifying and is rewarded by starting the race from the inside (closest to the grass) of the two-car front row. The outside pole winner is the driver who had the second-fastest lap during qualifying. He starts the race from the outside of the front row.

Primary sponsor

A company or entity that pays the most money to a team. Primary sponsors get their decals on the car hoods, which is the best place to advertise because fans see them so well.

Provisional entry

Guaranteed spot in a race given to regular series drivers who qualify poorly during the weekend but who are high enough in points. See also *champion's provisional.*

Quad ovals

A modified oval racetrack with two extra slight turns entering both the frontstretch and backstretch.

Radio frequency scanner

See *scanner.*

Real money

The money that a team actually gets after winning a race. Most teams aren't eligible for all the award money because they aren't affiliated with all the companies that provide financial awards to the race winner.

Rear spoiler

Metal blade that runs the width of the car atop the back of its trunk. It regulates air as it flows over a car and helps push the back end of the car into the track, which gives the car more traction and better handling.

Relief driver

A driver who replaces the original driver because of an injury or illness.

Restart

The waving of the green flag following a caution period.

Right off the truck

A driver usually says his car was great "right off the truck" when his car runs well in the first practice without any tweaking.

Road courses

Racetracks with complex configurations of left and right turns at varying angles. The track may have elevation changes as well. Infineon Raceway and Watkins Glen International are the only two NASCAR NEXTEL Cup Series road courses.

Roll bars

The part of the car's frame that protects the driver because it's made of strong steel tubing with a standardized thickness.

Roll cage

The protective frame of steel surrounding a driver. It keeps the driver safe during an accident because it protects him from the impact of another car or of a wall if the car flips over. The roll cage consists of roll bars made from steel tubing.

Roof flaps

Rectangular pieces of metal attached to the roof of a car that lie flat when the car is moving forward, but pop into the air when a car spins backwards or sideways, helping to keep a car from becoming airborne.

Rookie of the year

NASCAR awards rookie of the year honors to the first-year driver whose best 15 finishes are higher than any other first-year driver.

Rounds of wedge

Putting rounds of wedge into a car means a crew member is adjusting the handling by changing the pressure on the rear springs.

RPM

Short for revolutions per minute, a measurement of how fast an engine is turning and how hard it's working. See also *tachometer*.

Rubber

A piece of rubber placed between the coils of a spring to increase tension and taken out to decrease tension. This changes how a car handles.

Running wide open

When drivers depress the accelerator all the way to the ground.

Saving tires

A driver takes it easy through the turns and doesn't run the car too hard in order to keep his tires from wearing out too early.

Scanners

Small instruments that pick up radio waves in the immediate area. They allow you to listen in on conversations between drivers and their crews during practice, qualifying, and races.

Scuffs

Tires that have been on the car during practice, used only for one or two laps. See also *sticker tires*.

Setup

The way a car is prepared for qualifying and a race, including the suspension package, weight distribution, and engine tuning.

Shock absorbers

Hydraulic cylinders attached to the car's wheels that make the car ride more smoothly over bumps.

Shock dynamometer

Machine that pumps the shock absorber up and down, feeding information to the team's computer.

Short track

Racetracks shorter than one mile in length, where aerodynamics and horsepower aren't particularly important in winning the race. Bristol Motor Speedway, Martinsville Speedway, and Richmond International Raceway are the three NASCAR short tracks. See also *intermediate track, superspeedway*.

Show car

Former real race car that was taken out of the rotation for being too old, suffering irreparable damage, or just not being suited to the driver.

Show-car driver

A driver whose job is to drive a show car all over the country, bringing the car to stores, fairs, and driver appearances.

Silly season

Slang for a rumor-filled period that begins during the latter part of the current season, wherein some teams contemplate or announce driver, crew, and/or sponsor changes for the following year.

Slick

A track condition where, for a number of reasons, it's hard for a car's tires to adhere to the surface. A slick racetrack is not necessarily wet or slippery because of oil or water.

Slingshot

A maneuver in which a car following the leader in a draft suddenly steers around it, breaking the vacuum and providing an extra burst of speed that allows the second car to take the lead.

Spoiler

See *rear spoiler*.

Sponsors

The companies that pay for the right to have their names on cars and team uniforms. See also *primary sponsors* and *associate sponsors*.

Spotter

Team member who watches a race from on top of the grandstands or press box. His job is to be the driver's second set of eyes, telling the driver where to go on the racetrack to avoid an accident or when to pass another car.

Sticker tires

New tires that still have the manufacturer's sticker on them. See also *scuffs*.

Stop-and-go penalty

When a driver must come down pit road, stop in his pit box for a moment, and then drive down pit road to the racetrack.

Superspeedway

A racetrack of a mile or more in distance.

Suspension

The system of springs, shock absorbers, sway bars, and so on, directly connected to the wheels or the axles, which affects the handling of a race car.

Sway bars

Alter the amount a car rolls to one side or the other through the turns.

Tachometer

The instrument used to measure the number of revolutions per minute. Drivers use it to determine how fast they are going. See also *rpm*.

Taking air off a spoiler

Instead of the air flowing onto the lead car's spoiler and pressing the car's rear-end into the track, it flows off the spoiler and onto the second car's front end. That leaves the lead car with little rear-end downforce and causes it to become unstable and wiggle out of control, especially going through turns. See also *rear spoiler*.

Taping a car off

A crew places tape over the radiator grille of the car in order to keep air from entering the radiator and slowing the car down. Done to improve aerodynamics, but only during qualifying because the engine would overheat and fail if taped off during a race.

Team hauler

A large semi truck where the team hangs out when they're not working on their car. It's a place to eat and hold meetings at the racetrack — some even take naps in the forward lounge.

Team manager

Team member who serves as the owner's representative in the shop, overseeing everything including ordering equipment, hiring personnel, and organizing test sessions.

Tearing down

When cars are torn down, teams take apart the engines and whatever else NASCAR officials want them to. The winning team goes through a thorough tear down, meaning it takes apart the engine, the suspension, the power train, or whatever else officials want to check out.

Tech

NASCAR lingo for technical inspection. See also *inspection*.

Telemetry

Telemetry is a series of sensors attached to various parts of the car that transmit information such as miles per hour, engine revolutions per minute, and braking and transmission gear selection to a remote computer. Telemetry is used by broadcasters to help explain a car's performance and can also be used by teams during *testing*. Telemetry cannot be used during an official NASCAR event.

Templates

Individual pieces of metal that conform to the body of a car. They are blueprints of each car's shape, used to ensure that cars conform to NASCAR specifications.

Tight

When the front tires don't turn well through the turns because they're losing traction before the rear tires are. When a car is tight, it also means it's pushing — and if a driver isn't careful, he'll end up zooming right into the wall. See also *loose*.

Tire carrier

Pit crew member who hands the tires to the tire changers and takes the used tires away.

Tire changer

Pit crew member who changes tires — one changes the front tires, another changes the rear tires.

Tire management

A driver keeps from pushing his car too hard so that his tires last longer.

Tire specialist

Team member who changes the air pressure, measures the wear, and monitors the temperature of the tires during practice, qualifying, and races.

Track bar

The part of the rear suspension that's attached to the frame on one side and to the rear axle on the other. It keeps the car's rear tires centered within the car's body. Also called the *Panhard bar*.

Transponder

A transponder is a transmitter that teams attach to the right side of the car's fuel cell container. It is used for timing and scoring.

Tri-oval

A modified oval racetrack with an extra turn to it, albeit a slight turn, instead of just four turns. Usually that turn is located mid-way down the frontstretch.

Trunk lid

See *deck lid*.

Victory Lane

A roped-off or fenced-in area located in the infield where drivers, crews, owners, sponsors, and their families celebrate a victory.

Wedge

Putting in wedge means putting more weight onto a wheel by compressing the spring. Teams can put wedge into the rear tires only during a race by inserting a wrench into a hole above the tires. A round of wedge is also called a round *of bite*.

Wheelbase

The distance between the axles on the same side of the car.

Wind tunnel

A tunnel that shoots wind at a car. It's used to research how a car cuts through air as it moves forward. The car can be rotated so the tunnel shoots wind at the car from all different angles.

Window nets

Screens made of a nylon mesh material that cover the driver's side window. They keep the driver's arms and head in the car in the event of an accident.

Appendix B
NASCAR Statistics

The NASCAR Cup Series champions from 1949 to 2003 are as follows:

Year	Driver	No.	Car Owner	Car Type	Wins	Poles
1949	Red Byron	22	Raymond Parks	Oldsmobile	2	1
1950	Bill Rexford	60	Julian Buesink	Oldsmobile	1	0
1951	Herb Thomas	92	Herb Thomas	Hudson	7	4
1952	Tim Flock	91	Ted Chester	Hudson	8	4
1953	Herb Thomas	92	Herb Thomas	Hudson	11	10
1954	Lee Petty	42	Petty Enterprises	Chrysler	7	3
1955	Tim Flock	300	Carl Kiekhaefer	Chrysler	18	19
1956	Buck Baker	300B	Carl Kiekhaefer	Chrysler	14	12
1957	Buck Baker	87	Buck Baker	Chevrolet	10	5
1958	Lee Petty	42	Petty Enterprises	Oldsmobile	7	4
1959	Lee Petty	42	Petty Enterprises	Plymouth	10	2
1960	Rex White	4	White-Clements	Chevrolet	6	3
1961	Ned Jarrett	11	W.G. Holloway Jr.	Chevrolet	1	4
1962	Joe Weatherly	8	Bud Moore	Pontiac	9	6
1963	Joe Weatherly	8	Bud Moore	Mercury	3	6
1964	Richard Petty	43	Petty Enterprises	Plymouth	9	8
1965	Ned Jarrett	11	Bondy Long	Ford	13	9
1966	David Pearson	6	Cotton Owens	Dodge	14	7
1967	Richard Petty	43	Petty Enterprises	Plymouth	27	18
1968	David Pearson	17	Holman-Moody	Ford	16	12
1969	David Pearson	17	Holman-Moody	Ford	11	14

(continued)

Year	Driver	No.	Car Owner	Car Type	Wins	Poles
1970	Bobby Isaac	71	Nord Krauskopf	Dodge	11	13
1971	Richard Petty	43	Petty Enterprises	Plymouth	21	9
1972	Richard Petty	43	Petty Enterprises	Plymouth	8	3
1973	Benny Parsons	72	L.G. DeWitt	Chevrolet	1	0
1974	Richard Petty	43	Petty Enterprises	Dodge	10	7
1975	Richard Petty	43	Petty Enterprises	Dodge	13	3
1976	Cale Yarborough	11	Junior Johnson	Chevrolet	9	2
1977	Cale Yarborough	11	Junior Johnson	Chevrolet	9	3
1978	Cale Yarborough	11	Junior Johnson	Oldsmobile	10	8
1979	Richard Petty	43	Petty Enterprises	Chevrolet	5	1
1980	Dale Earnhardt	2	Rod Osterlund	Chevrolet	5	0
1981	Darrell Waltrip	11	Junior Johnson	Buick	12	11
1982	Darrell Waltrip	11	Junior Johnson	Buick	12	7
1983	Bobby Allison	22	Bill Gardner	Buick	6	0
1984	Terry Labonte	44	Billy Hagan	Chevrolet	2	2
1985	Darrell Waltrip	11	Junior Johnson	Chevrolet	3	4
1986	Dale Earnhardt	3	Richard Childress	Chevrolet	5	1
1987	Dale Earnhardt	3	Richard Childress	Chevrolet	11	1
1988	Bill Elliott	9	Harry Melling	Ford	6	6
1989	Rusty Wallace	27	Raymond Beadle	Pontiac	6	4
1990	Dale Earnhardt	3	Richard Childress	Chevrolet	9	4
1991	Dale Earnhardt	3	Richard Childress	Chevrolet	4	0
1992	Alan Kulwicki	7	Alan Kulwicki	Ford	2	6
1993	Dale Earnhardt	3	Richard Childress	Chevrolet	6	2
1994	Dale Earnhardt	3	Richard Childress	Chevrolet	4	2
1995	Jeff Gordon	24	Rick Hendrick	Chevrolet	7	8
1996	Terry Labonte	5	Rick Hendrick	Chevrolet	2	4
1997	Jeff Gordon	24	Rick Hendrick	Chevrolet	10	1
1998	Jeff Gordon	24	Rick Hendrick	Chevrolet	13	7

Year	Driver	No.	Car Owner	Car Type	Wins	Poles
1999	Dale Jarrett	88	Robert Yates	Ford	4	0
2000	Bobby Labonte	18	Joe Gibbs	Chevrolet	4	2
2001	Jeff Gordon	24	Rick Hendrick	Chevrolet	6	6
2002	Tony Stewart	20	Joe Gibbs	Chevrolet	3	2
2003	Matt Kenseth	17	Jack Roush	Ford	1	0

The top NASCAR Cup race winners from 1949 to 2003 are as follows:

Rank	Driver	Number of Wins
1.	Richard Petty*	200
2.	David Pearson*	105
3. (tie)	Bobby Allison*	84
	Darrell Waltrip	84
4.	Cale Yarborough*	83
5.	Dale Earnhardt*	76
6.	Jeff Gordon	64
7. (tie)	Rusty Wallace	54
	Lee Petty*	54
8. (tie)	Junior Johnson*	50
	Ned Jarrett*	50
9.	Herb Thomas*	48
10.	Buck Baker*	46
11.	Bill Elliott	44
12.	Tim Flock*	39
13.	Bobby Isaac*	37
14. (tie)	Fireball Roberts*	33
	Mark Martin	33
15.	Dale Jarrett	31
16.	Rex White*	28

(continued)

Rank	Driver	Number of Wins
17.	Fred Lorenzen*	27
18. (tie)	Jim Paschal*	25
	Joe Weatherly*	25
19.	Ricky Rudd	23
20.	Terry Labonte	22
21. (tie)	Benny Parsons*	21
	Jack Smith*	21
	Bobby Labonte	21
22. (tie)	Ricky Rudd	20
	Speedy Thompson*	20
23. (tie)	Buddy Baker*	19
	Davey Allison*	19
	Fonty Flock*	19
24. (tie)	Geoffrey Bodine	18
	Harry Gant*	18
	Neil Bonnett*	18
25. (tie)	Marvin Panch*	17
	Curtis Turner*	17
	Jeff Burton	17
	Tony Stewart	17
26.	Ernie Irvan*	15
27. (tie)	Dick Hutcherson*	14
	Lee Roy Yarborough*	14
28. (tie)	Tim Richmond*	13
	Dick Rathmann*	13
29. (tie)	Donnie Allison*	10
	Sterling Marlin	10
30. (tie)	Cotton Owens*	9
	Paul Goldsmith*	9

Rank	Driver	Number of Wins
	Ryan Newman	9
	Dale Earnhardt Jr.	9
31. (tie)	Kyle Petty	8
	Kurt Busch	8
32. (tie)	Jim Reed*	7
	A. J. Foyt*	7
	Bob Welborn	7
	Darel Dieringer	7
	Marshall Teague	7
	Matt Kenseth	7
	Darel Dieringer	7
33.	Jimmie Johnson	6
34. (tie)	Dave Marcis	5
	Ward Burton	5
	Ralph Moody*	5
	Dan Gurney*	5
	Alan Kulwicki	5
	Tiny Lund	5
35. (tie)	Ken Schrader	4
	Morgan Shepherd	4
	Hershel McGriff*	4
	Glen Wood*	4
	Lloyd Dane*	4
	Charlie Glotzbach*	4
	Pete Hamilton*	4
	Nelson Stacy	4
	Bob Flock	4
	Eddie Gray	4

(continued)

Rank	Driver	Number of Wins
	Billy Wade	4
	Eddie Pagan	4
	Bobby Hamilton	4
	Parnelli Jones*	4
36. (tie)	Tiny Lund	3
	Bill Blair	3
	Dick Linder	3
	Jeremy Mayfield	3
	Joe Nemechek	3
	Gwyn Staley	3
37. (tie)	Tiny Lund	2
	John Andretti	2
	Derrike Cope	2
	Jimmy Spencer	2
	Bobby Johns*	2
	Al Keller	2
	Elmo Langley	2
	Danny Letner*	2
	Billy Myers	2
	Jimmy Pardue	2
	Tom Pistone*	2
	Marvin Porter*	2
	Gober Sosebee	2
	Gwyn Staley	2
	Emanuel Zervakis*	2
	Red Byron	2
	Johnny Beauchamp	2
	Ray Elder*	2
	James Hylton*	2

Rank	Driver	Number of Wins
	Joe Lee Johnson	2
	Ricky Craven	2
	Steve Park	2
38.	Richard Brickhouse*	1
	Brett Bodine	1
	Bobby Hillin Jr.	1
	Phil Parsons	1
	Greg Sacks	1
	Lake Speed	1
	Dick Brooks*	1
	Bob Burdick*	1
	Marvin Burke*	1
	June Cleveland*	1
	Jim Cook*	1
	Mark Donohue	1
	Joe Eubanks	1
	Lou Figaro	1
	Jimmy Florian*	1
	Larry Frank*	1
	Danny Graves*	1
	Royce Hagerty	1
	Jim Hurtubise	1
	John Kieper*	1
	Harold Kite	1
	Paul Lewis*	1
	Johnny Mantz	1
	Sam McQuagg*	1
	Lloyd Moore*	1

(continued)

Rank	Driver	Number of Wins
	Norm Nelson*	1
	Bill Norton*	1
	Dick Passwater*	1
	Lennie Pond*	1
	Bill Rexford	1
	Jody Ridley*	1
	Shorty Rollins*	1
	Jim Roper*	1
	Earl Ross*	1
	John Rostek*	1
	Johnny Rutherford*	1
	Leon Sales*	1
	Frankie Schneider*	1
	Wendell Scott	1
	Buddy Shuman	1
	John Soares Jr.*	1
	Chuck Stevenson*	1
	Donald Thomas	1
	Tommy Thompson*	1
	Art Watts*	1
	Danny Weinberg*	1
	Jack White*	1
	Mario Andretti*	1
	Earl Balmer*	1
	Bill Amick	1
	Ron Bouchard*	1
	Johnny Allen*	1
	Neil Cole*	1
	Johnny Benson	1

Rank	Driver	Number of Wins
	Greg Biffle	1
	Jamie McMurray	1
	Elliot Sadler	1
	Leon Sales	1

*Retired

Appendix C

Race Car Numbers

*I*n NASCAR racing, each car has its own *car number,* just as each pro basketball player has a number on his or her jersey. It's an easy way to identify a car on the track, especially when you can't see the driver's face as he zooms by or read his name on the car. If you want to be a knowledgeable race fan and fit in with the race crowd, car numbers are vital to know. A lot of times, people refer to a car number only, not the team name or driver, when they're talking about a car. A person might say, "The 17 was the strongest car out there, don't you think?" What he just said was that he thought Matt Kenseth's Ford Taurus was great that day.

Teams have to apply for their car number at the beginning of each season, however, a few of the racers have become linked to their car numbers for eternity, such as Dale Earnhardt and his No. 3 Chevy (which was actually retired at the end of his career) or Richard Petty and his No. 43 car. Jeff Gordon will always be known as the driver of the No. 24 Chevy — particularly since he plans to drive that car until he retires.

Look for the following race car numbers to locate your favorite drivers during a race:

Car Number (2004)	Driver
0	Ward Burton
00	Kenny Wallace
01	Joe Nemechek
2	Rusty Wallace
4	Jimmy Spencer
5	Terry Labonte
6	Mark Martin
8	Dale Earnhardt Jr.
9	Kasey Kahne
10	Scott Riggs
12	Ryan Newman

15	Michael Waltrip
16	Greg Biffle
17	Matt Kenseth
18	Bobby Labonte
19	Jeremy Mayfield
20	Tony Stewart
21	Ricky Rudd
22	Scott Wimmer
24	Jeff Gordon
25	Brian Vickers
29	Kevin Harvick
30	Jeff Burton
31	Robby Gordon
32	Ricky Craven
37	Kevin Lepage
38	Elliott Sadler
40	Sterling Marlin
41	Casey Mears
42	Jamie McMurray
43	Jeff Green
45	Kyle Petty
48	Jimmie Johnson
49	Ken Schrader
50	Todd Bodine
51	Tony Raines
77	Brendan Gaughan
88	Dale Jarrett
89	Morgan Shepherd
97	Kurt Busch
98	Bill Elliott
99	Carl Edwards

Appendix D

NASCAR Milestones

• •

*A*ll major sports undergo change, and NASCAR is no exception. In the beginning, the strictly stock division cars were driven off the street and onto the track. But as safety technology advanced, alterations were made to the cars; the racing machines of today are more complicated than ever. NASCAR itself also has grown with the series from a small organization formed on the beaches of Daytona to one of the premier sports in America. This appendix gives you a rundown of important NASCAR milestones:

December 14, 1947: Bill France, Sr., organizes a meeting at the Streamline Hotel in Daytona Beach, Florida, to discuss the future of stock car racing. The National Association for Stock Car Auto Racing (NASCAR) is conceived.

February 15, 1948: NASCAR runs its first race in Daytona at the beach road course, which is won by Red Byron with a Ford.

February 21, 1948: NASCAR is incorporated.

June 19, 1949: The first NASCAR "Strictly Stock" (the current NASCAR NEXTEL Cup Series) race is held at Charlotte Fairgrounds Speedway in North Carolina, with Bob Flock winning the pole and Jim Roper the race. Sara Christian was the first woman to start a race in NASCAR's premier division; she finished 14th.

October 16, 1949: Red Byron becomes the first NASCAR Strictly Stock champion, earning $5,800 for two wins in six starts.

1950: Bill France, Sr., changes the name of NASCAR's premier series from Strictly Stock to Grand National.

September 4, 1950: Darlington Raceway, NASCAR's first superspeedway, hosts the Southern 500. Johnny Mantz with a Plymouth won the series' first 500-mile race, which started a field of 75 drivers and took more than six hours.

April 8, 1951: The first Grand National race west of the Mississippi River is held at Carrell Speedway, a half-mile dirt track in Gardena, California.

June 13, 1954: The International 100 is held at Linden Airport in New Jersey, becoming the series' first road race.

1955: Car owner Carl Kiekhaefer enters 40 Grand National events, winning 22 and becoming the first owner to introduce major sponsorships for teams

1958: Florida's sportswriters vote Fireball Roberts as Professional Athlete of the Year, the first time the honor went to a race car driver.

February 23, 1958: Paul Goldsmith captures the final race on Daytona's beach course.

February 22, 1959: The high-banked, 2.5-mile Daytona International Speedway hosts the first Daytona 500, drawing more than 41,000 fans. Lee Petty wins in a photo finish over Johnny Beauchamp 61 hours after the checkered flag flew. The NASCAR superspeedway era begins.

January 31, 1960: CBS Sports broadcasts portions of its first live Grand National event.

June 19, 1960: Atlanta International Raceway and Charlotte Motor Speedway host their first NASCAR event. NASCAR's superspeedway era shifts into high gear with these additions to the Series.

July 16, 1961: ABC Sports televises two hours of the Firecracker 250 from Daytona as part of its Wide World of Sports.

September 13, 1962: Mamie Reynolds becomes the first winning female car owner, with Fred Lorenzen taking the checkered at Augusta Speedway in Georgia.

December 1, 1963: Wendell Scott is the first African-American to win a premier division race, beating Buck Baker at Jacksonville Speedway.

1964: Goodyear Tire & Rubber begins use of an inner liner for all race car tires.

1964: Richard Petty, the series' all-time victory leader, wins the first of seven driving championships.

1967: Richard Petty sets three records, including most victories in one season (27), most consecutive wins (10), and most victories from the pole (15).

September 14, 1969: Alabama International Speedway, the series' largest oval (2.66 miles) opens in Talladega.

March 24, 1970: Buddy Baker is the first driver to post a test-speed run faster than 200 mph, doing so at Talladega.

September 30, 1970: The final Grand National race is run on dirt at State Fairgrounds Speedway in Raleigh, North Carolina, ending the era of NASCAR under the Grand National title.

1971: R.J. Reynolds becomes the series' first major sponsor.

February 14, 1971: Motor Racing Network (MRN) broadcasts its first Daytona 500.

January 10, 1972: NASCAR founder Bill France, Sr., hands the leadership to his son Bill France, Jr.

February 15, 1976: David Pearson and Richard Petty battle on national TV in the Daytona 500; their cars tangle near the finish and Pearson wins. This broadcast helped in bringing the sport national attention.

February 20, 1977: Janet Guthrie, the first woman to qualify for the Daytona 500, finishes 12th.

1978: President Jimmy Carter invites NASCAR drivers to the White House, the same year Cale Yarborough wins his third consecutive series title.

February 18, 1979: CBS Sports carries the first flag-to-flag coverage of a NASCAR event, the Daytona 500, which becomes a classic as Richard Petty avoids an incident between Cale Yarborough and Donnie Allison on the last lap to win.

November 18, 1979: Richard Petty wins his record seventh series championship.

April 29, 1982: Benny Parsons is the first driver to post an official qualifying lap over 200 mph, at Talladega.

May 6, 1984: The series' most competitive race, in which 75 lead changes were spread among 13 drivers, takes place at Talladega.

July 4, 1984: Richard Petty earns his record 200th victory in the Firecracker 400 at Daytona.

September 1, 1985: Bill Elliott claims a $1 million bonus for winning three of four crown jewel races: the Daytona 500, the Winston 500 at Talladega, and the Southern 500 at Darlington.

1986: NASCAR drops Grand National from its top division, renaming it the NASCAR Winston Cup Series.

April 30, 1987: Bill Elliott sets the fastest time in series history, 212.809 mph at Talladega.

February 14, 1988: Bobby Allison and his son, Davey, finish one-two in the Daytona 500.

1989: Every race in the NASCAR Cup Series is televised.

February 18, 1990: Dale Earnhardt leads 155 of 200 laps of the Daytona 500, losing with a blown tire on the last mile.

September 1991: Harry Gant, at age 51, is tabbed "Mr. September" after winning four consecutive races in a month.

May 16, 1992: Charlotte Motor Speedway holds the all-star race under the lights for the first time, with Davey Allison winning and then losing control of his car just past the finish line.

November 15, 1992: Richard Petty retires after 35 years of racing, ending with 200 victories and 549 top-five finishes in 1,177 starts. Alan Kulwicki, who leads by one more lap than Bill Elliott, wins the championship.

August 6, 1994: Jeff Gordon wins the first NASCAR race at Indianapolis Motor Speedway.

1994: Dale Earnhardt joins Richard Petty as the series' only seven-time titlists.

November 24, 1996: The first demonstration event is run at Suzuka, Japan.

1997: Two new tracks, California Speedway and Texas Motor Speedway, are added to the schedule.

1998: NASCAR celebrates its 50th anniversary while adding Las Vegas Motor Speedway to the lineup. Mark Martin wins the inaugural event.

November 11, 1999: NASCAR inks multi-year partnerships with FOX, NBC, and Turner Sports; consolidated television package begins in 2001.

November 28, 2000: Mike Helton becomes the series' third president and its first leader who's not a France family member.

September 25, 2001: NASCAR Radio, the first 24-hour radio station dedicated to a single sport, debuts on XM Satellite Radio.

2001: The NASCAR Cup Series adds Chicagoland Speedway and Kansas Speedway.

2003: NASCAR's $10 million Research and Development Center is unveiled outside Charlotte, North Carolina.

June 13, 2003: California Speedway is given a second date in 2004, the Labor Day weekend race previously run at Darlington, South Carolina.

June 19, 2003: NASCAR announces a 10-year deal with primary sponsor NEXTEL beginning in 2004.

August 15, 2003: Sunoco, signing a 10-year contract, becomes the sport's official fuel.

October 2003: Brian Z. France becomes the Chairman of the Board and CEO of NASCAR, replacing his father, Bill France, Jr.

2004: The chase for the NASCAR NEXTEL Cup is introduced, with the top-10 drivers (and those within 400 points of the leader) given the green flag to race for the championship with 10 races remaining.

2004: NASCAR announces a new NASCAR Busch Series event in Mexico City for 2005.

Index

BUSINESS, CAREERS & PERSONAL FINANCE

Grant Writing FOR DUMMIES
A Reference for the Rest of Us!
0-7645-5307-0

Home Buying FOR DUMMIES
A Reference for the Rest of Us!
0-7645-5331-3 *†

Also available:

- Accounting For Dummies †
  0-7645-5314-3
- Business Plans Kit For Dummies †
  0-7645-5365-8
- Cover Letters For Dummies
  0-7645-5224-4
- Frugal Living For Dummies
  0-7645-5403-4
- Leadership For Dummies
  0-7645-5176-0
- Managing For Dummies
  0-7645-1771-6

- Marketing For Dummies
  0-7645-5600-2
- Personal Finance For Dummies *
  0-7645-2590-5
- Project Management For Dummies
  0-7645-5283-X
- Resumes For Dummies †
  0-7645-5471-9
- Selling For Dummies
  0-7645-5363-1
- Small Business Kit For Dummies *†
  0-7645-5093-4

HOME & BUSINESS COMPUTER BASICS

Windows XP FOR DUMMIES
A Reference for the Rest of Us!
0-7645-4074-2

Excel 2003 ALL-IN-ONE DESK REFERENCE FOR DUMMIES
9 BOOKS IN 1
0-7645-3758-X

Also available:

- ACT! 6 For Dummies
  0-7645-2645-6
- iLife '04 All-in-One Desk Reference
  For Dummies
  0-7645-7347-0
- iPAQ For Dummies
  0-7645-6769-1
- Mac OS X Panther Timesaving
  Techniques For Dummies
  0-7645-5812-9
- Macs For Dummies
  0-7645-5656-8

- Microsoft Money 2004 For Dummies
  0-7645-4195-1
- Office 2003 All-in-One Desk Reference
  For Dummies
  0-7645-3883-7
- Outlook 2003 For Dummies
  0-7645-3759-8
- PCs For Dummies
  0-7645-4074-2
- TiVo For Dummies
  0-7645-6923-6
- Upgrading and Fixing PCs For Dummies
  0-7645-1665-5
- Windows XP Timesaving Techniques
  For Dummies
  0-7645-3748-2

FOOD, HOME, GARDEN, HOBBIES, MUSIC & PETS

Feng Shui FOR DUMMIES
A Reference for the Rest of Us!
0-7645-5295-3

Poker FOR DUMMIES
A Reference for the Rest of Us!
0-7645-5232-5

Also available:

- Bass Guitar For Dummies
  0-7645-2487-9
- Diabetes Cookbook For Dummies
  0-7645-5230-9
- Gardening For Dummies *
  0-7645-5130-2
- Guitar For Dummies
  0-7645-5106-X
- Holiday Decorating For Dummies
  0-7645-2570-0
- Home Improvement All-in-One
  For Dummies
  0-7645-5680-0

- Knitting For Dummies
  0-7645-5395-X
- Piano For Dummies
  0-7645-5105-1
- Puppies For Dummies
  0-7645-5255-4
- Scrapbooking For Dummies
  0-7645-7208-3
- Senior Dogs For Dummies
  0-7645-5818-8
- Singing For Dummies
  0-7645-2475-5
- 30-Minute Meals For Dummies
  0-7645-2589-1

INTERNET & DIGITAL MEDIA

Digital Photography FOR DUMMIES
Photoshop Elements and other tryouts on CD-ROM
A Reference for the Rest of Us!
0-7645-1664-7

Starting an eBay Business FOR DUMMIES
A Reference for the Rest of Us!
0-7645-6924-4

Also available:

- 2005 Online Shopping Directory
  For Dummies
  0-7645-7495-7
- CD & DVD Recording For Dummies
  0-7645-5956-7
- eBay For Dummies
  0-7645-5654-1
- Fighting Spam For Dummies
  0-7645-5965-6
- Genealogy Online For Dummies
  0-7645-5964-8
- Google For Dummies
  0-7645-4420-9

- Home Recording For Musicians
  For Dummies
  0-7645-1634-5
- The Internet For Dummies
  0-7645-4173-0
- iPod & iTunes For Dummies
  0-7645-7772-7
- Preventing Identity Theft For Dummies
  0-7645-7336-5
- Pro Tools All-in-One Desk Reference
  For Dummies
  0-7645-5714-9
- Roxio Easy Media Creator For Dummies
  0-7645-7131-1

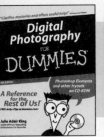

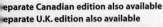
 WILEY

SPORTS, FITNESS, PARENTING, RELIGION & SPIRITUALITY

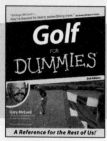

0-7645-5146-9

0-7645-5418-2

Also available:

- Adoption For Dummies
  0-7645-5488-3
- Basketball For Dummies
  0-7645-5248-1
- The Bible For Dummies
  0-7645-5296-1
- Buddhism For Dummies
  0-7645-5359-3
- Catholicism For Dummies
  0-7645-5391-7
- Hockey For Dummies
  0-7645-5228-7

- Judaism For Dummies
  0-7645-5299-6
- Martial Arts For Dummies
  0-7645-5358-5
- Pilates For Dummies
  0-7645-5397-6
- Religion For Dummies
  0-7645-5264-3
- Teaching Kids to Read For Dummies
  0-7645-4043-2
- Weight Training For Dummies
  0-7645-5168-X
- Yoga For Dummies
  0-7645-5117-5

TRAVEL

0-7645-5438-7

0-7645-5453-0

Also available:

- Alaska For Dummies
  0-7645-1761-9
- Arizona For Dummies
  0-7645-6938-4
- Cancún and the Yucatán For Dummies
  0-7645-2437-2
- Cruise Vacations For Dummies
  0-7645-6941-4
- Europe For Dummies
  0-7645-5456-5
- Ireland For Dummies
  0-7645-5455-7

- Las Vegas For Dummies
  0-7645-5448-4
- London For Dummies
  0-7645-4277-X
- New York City For Dummies
  0-7645-6945-7
- Paris For Dummies
  0-7645-5494-8
- RV Vacations For Dummies
  0-7645-5443-3
- Walt Disney World & Orlando For Dummies
  0-7645-6943-0

GRAPHICS, DESIGN & WEB DEVELOPMENT

0-7645-4345-8

0-7645-5589-8

Also available:

- Adobe Acrobat 6 PDF For Dummies
  0-7645-3760-1
- Building a Web Site For Dummies
  0-7645-7144-3
- Dreamweaver MX 2004 For Dummies
  0-7645-4342-3
- FrontPage 2003 For Dummies
  0-7645-3882-9
- HTML 4 For Dummies
  0-7645-1995-6
- Illustrator CS For Dummies
  0-7645-4084-X

- Macromedia Flash MX 2004 For Dummies
  0-7645-4358-X
- Photoshop 7 All-in-One Desk Reference For Dummies
  0-7645-1667-1
- Photoshop CS Timesaving Techniques For Dummies
  0-7645-6782-9
- PHP 5 For Dummies
  0-7645-4166-8
- PowerPoint 2003 For Dummies
  0-7645-3908-6
- QuarkXPress 6 For Dummies
  0-7645-2593-X

NETWORKING, SECURITY, PROGRAMMING & DATABASES

0-7645-6852-3

0-7645-5784-X

Also available:

- A+ Certification For Dummies
  0-7645-4187-0
- Access 2003 All-in-One Desk Reference For Dummies
  0-7645-3988-4
- Beginning Programming For Dummies
  0-7645-4997-9
- C For Dummies
  0-7645-7068-4
- Firewalls For Dummies
  0-7645-4048-3
- Home Networking For Dummies
  0-7645-42796

- Network Security For Dummies
  0-7645-1679-5
- Networking For Dummies
  0-7645-1677-9
- TCP/IP For Dummies
  0-7645-1760-0
- VBA For Dummies
  0-7645-3989-2
- Wireless All In-One Desk Reference For Dummies
  0-7645-7496-5
- Wireless Home Networking For Dummies
  0-7645-3910-8

0-7645-6820-5 *†

0-7645-2566-2

Also available:

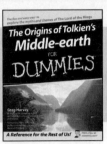

Also available:

- Alzheimer's For Dummies
  0-7645-3899-3
- Asthma For Dummies
  0-7645-4233-8
- Controlling Cholesterol For Dummies
  0-7645-5440-9
- Depression For Dummies
  0-7645-3900-0
- Dieting For Dummies
  0-7645-4149-8
- Fertility For Dummies
  0-7645-2549-2

- Fibromyalgia For Dummies
  0-7645-5441-7
- Improving Your Memory For Dummies
  0-7645-5435-2
- Pregnancy For Dummies †
  0-7645-4483-7
- Quitting Smoking For Dummies
  0-7645-2629-4
- Relationships For Dummies
  0-7645-5384-4
- Thyroid For Dummies
  0-7645-5385-2

UCATION, HISTORY, REFERENCE & TEST PREPARATION

0-7645-5194-9

0-7645-4186-2

Also available:

- Algebra For Dummies
  0-7645-5325-9
- British History For Dummies
  0-7645-7021-8
- Calculus For Dummies
  0-7645-2498-4
- English Grammar For Dummies
  0-7645-5322-4
- Forensics For Dummies
  0-7645-5580-4
- The GMAT For Dummies
  0-7645-5251-1
- Inglés Para Dummies
  0-7645-5427-1

- Italian For Dummies
  0-7645-5196-5
- Latin For Dummies
  0-7645-5431-X
- Lewis & Clark For Dummies
  0-7645-2545-X
- Research Papers For Dummies
  0-7645-5426-3
- The SAT I For Dummies
  0-7645-7193-1
- Science Fair Projects For Dummies
  0-7645-5460-3
- U.S. History For Dummies
  0-7645-5249-X

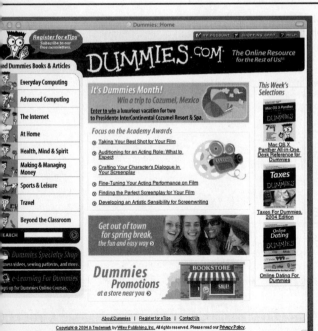

Get smart @ dummies.com®

- **Find a full list of Dummies titles**
- **Look into loads of FREE on-site articles**
- **Sign up for FREE eTips e-mailed to you weekly**
- **See what other products carry the Dummies name**
- **Shop directly from the Dummies bookstore**
- **Enter to win new prizes every month!**

eparate Canadian edition also available
eparate U.K. edition also available

ilable wherever books are sold. For more information or to order direct: U.S. customers visit www.dummies.com or call 1-877-762-2974.
. customers visit www.wileyeurope.com or call 0800 243407. Canadian customers visit www.wiley.ca or call 1-800-567-4797.